A Text Book Of

SOFTWARE ENGINEERING

For

BCA Semester - III

As per New Revised Syllabus of Pune University

Dr. D. D. BALSARAF
PRINCIPAL, INDRYANI MAHAVIDYALAYA,
TALEGOAN DABHADE, PUNE

UMAKANT S. SHIRSHETTI
SENIOR LECTURER IN IT DEPT.,
SOU. VENUTAI CHAVAN POLYTECHNIC,
VADGAON (BK.), PUNE

N2195

SOFTWARE ENGINEERING
ISBN 978-93-5164-078-3

Second Edition : July 2015
© : Authors

The text of this publication, or any part thereof, should not be reproduced or transmitted in any form or stored in any computer storage system or device for distribution including photocopy, recording, taping or information retrieval system or reproduced on any disc, tape, perforated media or other information storage device etc., without the written permission of Authors with whom the rights are reserved. Breach of this condition is liable for legal action.

Every effort has been made to avoid errors or omissions in this publication. In spite of this, errors may have crept in. Any mistake, error or discrepancy so noted and shall be brought to our notice shall be taken care of in the next edition. It is notified that neither the publisher nor the authors or seller shall be responsible for any damage or loss of action to any one, of any kind, in any manner, therefrom.

Published By :
NIRALI PRAKASHAN
Abhyudaya Pragati, 1312, Shivaji Nagar,
Off J.M. Road, PUNE – 411005
Tel - (020) 25512336/37/39, Fax - (020) 25511379
Email : niralipune@pragationline.com

Printed By :
Repro Knowledgecast Limited,
Thane

☞ DISTRIBUTION CENTRES

PUNE
Nirali Prakashan : 119, Budhwar Peth, Jogeshwari Mandir Lane, Pune 411002, Maharashtra
Tel : (020) 2445 2044, 66022708, Fax : (020) 2445 1538
Email : bookorder@pragationline.com, niralilocal@pragationline.com

Nirali Prakashan : S. No. 28/27, Dhyari, Near Pari Company, Pune 411041
Tel : (020) 24690204 Fax : (020) 24690316
Email : dhyari@pragationline.com, bookorder@pragationline.com

MUMBAI
Nirali Prakashan : 385, S.V.P. Road, Rasdhara Co-op. Hsg. Society Ltd.,
Girgaum, Mumbai 400004, Maharashtra
Tel : (022) 2385 6339 / 2386 9976, Fax : (022) 2386 9976
Email : niralimumbai@pragationline.com

☞ DISTRIBUTION BRANCHES

JALGAON
Nirali Prakashan : 34, V. V. Golani Market, Navi Peth, Jalgaon 425001,
Maharashtra, Tel : (0257) 222 0395, Mob : 94234 91860

KOLHAPUR
Nirali Prakashan : New Mahadvar Road, Kedar Plaza, 1st Floor Opp. IDBI Bank
Kolhapur 416 012, Maharashtra. Mob : 9850046155

NAGPUR
Pratibha Book Distributors : Above Maratha Mandir, Shop No. 3, First Floor,
Rani Jhanshi Square, Sitabuldi, Nagpur 440012, Maharashtra
Tel : (0712) 254 7129

DELHI
Nirali Prakashan : 4593/21, Basement, Aggarwal Lane 15, Ansari Road, Daryaganj
Near Times of India Building, New Delhi 110002
Mob : 08505972553

BENGALURU
Pragati Book House : House No. 1, Sanjeevappa Lane, Avenue Road Cross,
Opp. Rice Church, Bengaluru – 560002.
Tel : (080) 64513344, 64513355,Mob : 9880582331, 9845021552
Email:bharatsavla@yahoo.com

CHENNAI
Pragati Books : 9/1, Montieth Road, Behind Taas Mahal, Egmore,
Chennai 600008 Tamil Nadu, Tel : (044) 6518 3535,
Mob : 94440 01782 / 98450 21552 / 98805 82331,
Email : bharatsavla@yahoo.com

niralipune@pragationline.com | www.pragationline.com

Also find us on www.facebook.com/niralibooks

Contents ...

1. **Introduction to System Concepts** — 1.1 – 1.16

2. **Requirement Analysis** — 2.1 – 2.18

3. **Introduction to Software Engineering** — 3.1 – 3.14

4. **Software Development Methodologies** — 4.1 – 4.20

5. **Analysis and Design Tools** — 5.1 – 5.54

6. **Structured System Design** — 6.1 – 6.38

7. **Software Testing** — 7.1 – 7.28

* **Case Studies** — A.1 – A.46

* **University Question Paper** — P.1 – P.2

❖❖❖

Chapter 1...
Introduction to System Concepts

Contents ...

This chapter gives basic concepts of system such as:

1.1 INTRODUCTION

    1.1.1 What is a System ?

    1.1.2 Definition of System

    1.1.3 Elements of System

1.2 CHARACTERISTICS OF SYSTEM

1.3 TYPES OF SYSTEM

1.4 SYSTEM CONCEPTS

    1.4.1 Integrated System

    1.4.2 Subsystem

    1.4.3 Transaction Processing System (TPS)

1.1 INTRODUCTION

- We are surrounded by systems. There are many systems such as transportation system, the distribution of goods and services system, education, manufacturing and almost every other human economic activity systems. From conceptual point, we can view the economy and business as a set of interrelated systems.

- We can define System as **"A system is an orderly grouping of independent components linked together according to a plan to achieve a specific objective or goal"**.

- In the software engineering a system is often equated with software or perhaps with the combination of computer hardware and software. Here, we use the term system in its broader sense.

- Fig. 1.1 shows a *system* is the entire set of components, both computer related, and non-computer related, that provides a service to a user.

- For instance, an automobile is a system composed of many hundreds of components, some of which are likely to be computer subsystems running software.

- A system exists in an environment (For example, a space probe in deep space), and has operators and users (possibly the same).

- The system provides feedback to the operator and services to the user.
- Operators are shown inside the system because operator procedures are usually a part of the system design, and many system functions, including fault recovery, may involve operator action.
- Not shown in the Fig. 1.1, but of equal importance, are the system's designers and maintainers.

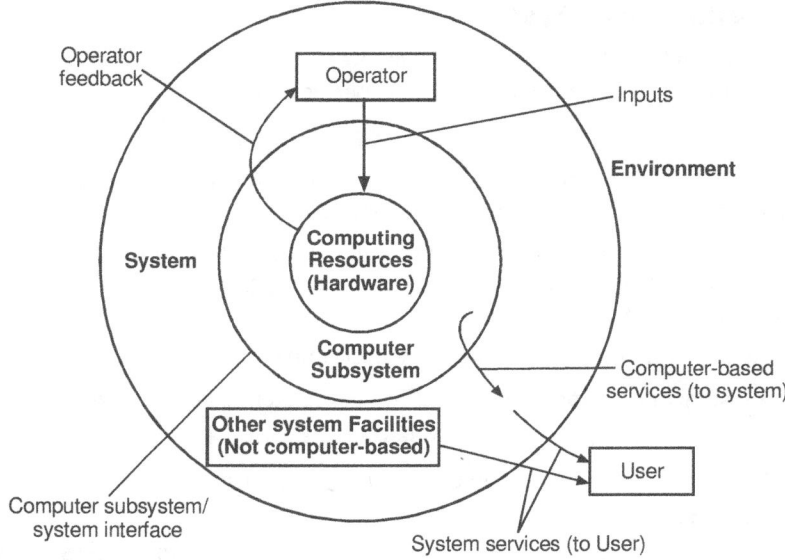

Fig. 1.1: System relationships

- Systems are developed to satisfy a set of requirements that meet a need. A requirement that is important in some systems is that they be highly dependable. Fault tolerance is a means of achieving dependability.

1.1.1 What is a System ?

- A system is a set or group of components that interact to accomplish some purpose.
- System around us. For example, complex nervous system which is made up of set of parts or components i.e. brain, spinal cord, nerves etc. Take another example of a publication firm that contains Authors, Proof readers, Typists, Editors are the set of components.
- Following are some points are related to the system.
    1. System interacts with their environment.
    2. The purpose of system is it's reason for existing.

3. All system has acceptable level of standards.
- The basic control model of the system consist of:
    1. **Standards:** Which acceptable performance.
    2. **Measurement:** Measuring actual performance.
    3. **Compare**: Comparing actual performance.
    4. **Feedback:** A method for feedback.

1.1.2 Definition of System (Oct. 11)

- A system can be defined as a network of interrelated procedures that are joined together to perform an activity or to accomplish a specific objective.

OR

- A system is an orderly grouping of interdependent components linked together according to a plan to achieve a specific objective.
- The word component may refer to physical parts (engines, wings of aircraft, and wheels of a car), managerial steps (planning, organizing, directing and controlling) or a subsystem in multi level structure.
- The study of system concepts, has three basic implications:
    1. A system must be designed to achieve a predetermined objective.
    2. Interrelationships and interdependence must exist among the components.
    3. A system must be user friendly and it should maintain security from unauthorized users as well as making selected data.

1.1.3 Elements of System (Oct. 09, 10, 11; April 12; 14)

- To reconstruct a system following are the elements of system to be considered:
    1. Outputs and Inputs,
    2. Processors,
    3. Control,
    4. Feedback,
    5. Environment, and
    6. Boundaries and Interfaces.

1. Outputs and Inputs:
- A major objective of a system is to produce the output as per the user's requirement.
- The output could be in the form of goods (finished products), information as services. It must be done with expectations of intended user.

- Inputs are elements that make the system to work in order to produce required output.
- Input could be material, human resources or information. Inputs are elements that enter the system for processing.
- Output is outcome of processing. It is important to point out that determining output is first step in specifying the nature, amount and regularity of input needed to operate a system.
- In system analysis, first concern is to determine user's requirement of a proposed system.

2. Processors:
- The processor is the element of a system that involves the actual transformation of Input into Output.
- The processor should be designed of such type that it can accept the input in the given form and can give output in desired format.
- It is the operational component of system. Processors may modify input totally or partially depending on specifications of output.

3. Control:
- The control elements guide the system. The control element controls the working of the system at all stages.
- It is necessary to control input, process and output, continuously, in order to get desired results.
- In a complete system operating system and accompanying software influence the behavior of system.
- Management support is required for screening control and supporting the objective of proposed change.

4. Feedback:
- Feedback measures output against a standard in some form of cybernetic procedure that includes communication and control.
- Feedback is a method that helps to compare output produced with output expected and make necessary changes in the process or input in order to reduce the difference between output produced and output expected.
- Input information is fed back to input for deliberation. After the output is compared against performance standards, changes can result in input or output processing and output.
- Feedback may be positive or negative. **Positive feedback** reinforces the performance of system. **Negative feedback** generally provides controller with information for action.
- During system change the user may be told the problems in given application verify the initial concerns and justify the need for change.

5. Environment:
- All the things which are outside the system are called environment of the system.
- The environment does affect working or progress of the system.
- The system should be sensitive to the changes in its environment. It determines how a system must function.
- The environment is the super system within which an organisation operates.

6. Boundaries and Interface: (April 10)
- The boundary indicates the extent or limit of the system.
- The boundary divides the things into the system and its environment.
- The things which are inside boundary are part of system otherwise which are outside boundary are its environment.
- It is very much essential to limit the system by its boundaries so that system's working can be controlled.
- **Interface** means interaction of different system parts with each other as interaction of the system with the system outside its boundaries.
- The system should be capable of dealing with the systems which are outside to it.
- **Boundaries** are the limits that identify its components, processes and interrelationships when it interfaces with another system.

1.2 CHARACTERISTICS OF A SYSTEM (April 10; Oct 12)

- Following are the some important characteristics of a system:
    1. Organisation,
    2. Interaction,
    3. Interdependence,
    4. Integration, and
    5. Central objective.

1. Organisation:
- Organisation implies structure and order of a system.
- Basically, Organisation means the arrangement of components that helps to achieve objectives.
- In the design of a college (polytechnic) system, the hierarchical relationship starting with the Chairman on top and leading downward to the blue-collar peon, represent the Organisation structure.

- Likewise, a computer system is designed around an input device, a central processing unit and an output device with one or more storage units, when linked together they work as a whole system for producing information.

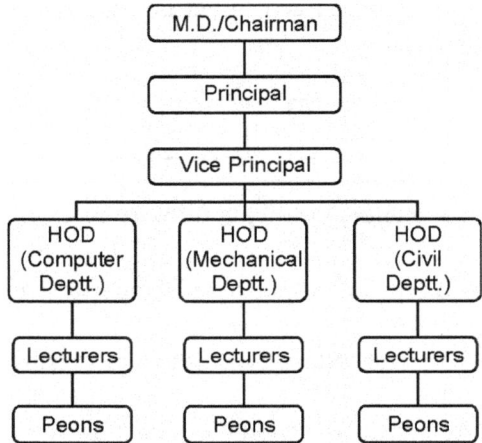

Fig. 1.2: Organisation structure for college system

2. **Interaction:**
- Interaction refers to the manner in which each component interacts with other components of the system.
- Thus, interaction means, it is the media, by means of which every component interact or communicate with other for proper functioning.
- In an Organisation, For example, purchasing must interact with production, advertising with sales and payrolls with personnel.
- In a computer system, the central processing must interact with input device to solve problem. In turn main memory holds programs and data that arithmetic unit uses for computation.
- The interrelationship between these components enables the computer to perform.

3. **Interdependence:**
- Interdependence means that parts of the Organisation depend on one another.
- They are co-ordinated and linked together according to plan. One subsystem depends on the input of another subsystem for proper functioning i.e. the output of one subsystem is the required input for another subsystem.
- In computer system, the three units Input, System unit, Output is interdependent for proper functioning.

- No subsystems can function in isolation because it is dependent on data (input) it receives from other subsystems to perform its required tasks.

  For example: A decision to computerize an application is initiated by user, analyzed and designed by analyst, programmed and tested by programmer and run by computer operator as shown in Fig. 1.3.

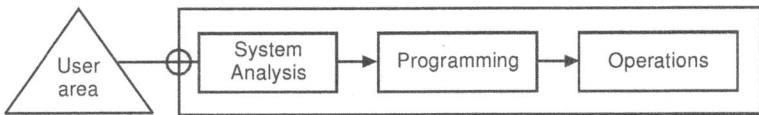

Fig. 1.3: Interdependency in software development

4. Integration:

- Integration is concerned with how a system is tied together in order to achieve common goal, thus forming integration.
- Integration refers to holism of system. Synthesis follows analysis to achieve the central objective of Organisation.
- It means that parts of system work together within system even though each part performs unique function.

5. Central Objective:

- Objectives may be stated or real.
- The stated objective and real objective of the system could differ based on the policy of the company.
- The user should develop a central objective by taking into consideration real objective and stated objective.
- The important point is that the users must know the central objective of computer application in analysis for successful design and conversion.
- This means that the analyst must work around the obstacles to identify real objective of proposed change.

1.3 TYPES OF SYSTEMS (Oct. 12; April 13, 14)

Several types of systems are listed below:

1. Physical system:

- The physical system could be static or dynamic in nature.
- Static means which do not change as far as working or life of the system is concerned. On the other hand, dynamic system may change due to processing of the system.

  For example: In computer system the hardware parts are static, but the data which changes due to processing is dynamic. These both together form physical system along with programs controlling the data.

2. Abstract System:

- The systems which are represented conceptually (i.e. nonexisting) non physical systems are called abstract system.
- The abstract systems are prepared for studying the physical system. The computer itself is a physical system and its block diagram is called as abstract system. A model is representation of real or planned system.
- The use of model makes it easier for analyst to visualize relationship in system under study. There are following types of models:

(a) System model:

- The analyst begins by creating a model of reality i.e. facts, relationship, procedures etc. with which the system is concerned. Every computer system deals with real world.
- The analyst begins by modeling this reality before considering the function that system is to perform.
- Various business system models are used to show benefits of abstracting complete systems to model form. The major of this type models are:

    (i) **Schematic models:** It shows a two dimensional depicting system elements and their linkages.

    (ii) **Flow system models:** It shows the flow of material, energy and information that hold system together. A widely used example is Program Evaluation and Review Technique (PERT).

    (iii) **Static system models:** This type of model exhibits are pair of relationship such as activity time or cost quantity.

    The example is Gantt chart. It gives a static picture of an activity time relationship.

    (iv) **Dynamic system models:** Business Organisations are dynamic systems. It depicts constantly an ongoing constantly changing the system. It consists of:
    1. Inputs that enter the system.
    2. Processor through which transformation takes place.
    3. The programs required for processing.
    4. Output that results from processing.

3. Open and Closed System: (Oct. 09, 11)

(a) Open system:

- Another classification of systems is based on their degree of independence.

- An open system is a one which does not provide for its own control or modification. It does not supervise itself so it needs to be supervised by people.

  For example: If the high speed printer used with computer systems did not have a switch to sense whether paper is in the printer, then a person would have to notice when the paper runs out and signal the system (push a switch) to stop printing.

- It has many interfaces to its environment. It permits interaction across its boundary. Five important characteristics of open system are:

  (i) **Inputs from outside:** Open systems are self adjusting and self regulating. When functioning properly an open system reaches a steady state. The response gives the firm a steady state.

  (ii) **Entropy:** All dynamic system tends to run down over time resulting in entropy or loss of energy. Open system resist entropy by seeking new inputs or modifying the processes to return to a steady state.

  (iii) **Process, Output and Cycle:** Open systems produce useful output and operate in cycle following a continuous path.

  (iv) **Differentiation:** Open system have a tendency toward an increasing specialization of functions and greater differentiation of their components. This characteristic offers a completing reason for increasing value of concept of system in system analyst's thinking.

  (v) **Equifinality:** This term implies that the goals are achieved through differing courses of action and a variety of paths.

(b) Closed system: (Oct. 09, 11)

- A closed system in one which automatically controls or modifies its own operation by responding to data generated by the system itself.

  For example: High speed printers used with computer systems usually have a switch that senses whether there is paper in the printer. If the paper runs out, the switch signals to stop printing.

4. Manmade information system:

- With the help of information system, we can define some standards for the working of the system. This we can try to make the system to work according to the standards defined.
- We can define information system as a set of devices, procedures, rules but most of the work performs manually.
- It provides instructions, commands and feedback. It determines nature of relationship among decision makers.

5. **Formal information system:**
   - A formal information system is represented by Organisation chart. It gives a representation of the different parts of system and flow of information among them.
   - **Categories of information:** There are three categories of information related to management levels and decision managers make.
     (i) Strategic Information
     (ii) Managerial Information
     (iii) Operational Information.
   - The first level relates to long range planning policies that are of direct interest to upper management.
   - The second level is of direct use of middle management and department heads for implementation and control.
   - The third level is short term, daily information is used to operate department and enforce day-to-day rules and regulations of information.

6. **Informal information system:**
   - A formal information system is one which is shown on the chart, on the other hand, the informal information system is one which is working to meet requirements of employees.
   - Thus, informal information system is related with what is happening practically rather than what is shown on paper, it is an employee based system designed to meet personnel and vocational needs and help work related problem.

7. **Computer-based Information System:**
   - In manmade (manual) information system papers were used to hold the information. But toady entire world is of computer.
   - Computer based information systems are faster, more accurate, more neat and attractive. It is possible to perform different operations easily. Security of data is possible in this system.

8. **Management Information System (MIS):**
   - A MIS is a system that provides historical information, information on the current status. It is a communication process in which data are recorded and processed for further operational uses.
   - A MIS is a system that collects, processes, stores and distributes information to help in decision making for the managerial functions of planning, organizing, directing, controlling and staffing a business Organisation.
   - MIS are built using:
     (a) People, who are needed to operate the system.
     (b) Data processing, which provides the needed speed for information sorting and classifying.

(c) Data communications which is required in order to keep the information flowing between the different parts of the system and the people using the system.

(d) Information storage and retrieval, which is required in order to store information in its proper format and to make sure that the information can be retrieved when it is needed.

(e) System planning which is required in order to integrate the people, the data processing, the data communication, the information storage and retrieval and the uses of the system into an overall meaningful and well organized management information system.

- There are several advantages of database system:

    (i) Processing time and number of programs written are reduced.

    (ii) All applications share centralized files.

    (iii) Storage space duplication is eliminated.

    (iv) Data are stored once in database and are easily accessible when needed.

9. Decision Support Systems (DSS): (April 11)

- DSS systems make use of analytical planning modules (operation research model).
- DSS mostly used for assisting top-level management in decision making. Using DSS better decision are taken. DSS reduces clerical work and overtime.
- DSS also saves cost and time. It consists of decision making with support of other lower level systems (MIS).
- DSS systems used Organisational data as well as external data collected from environment of the Organisation. DSS uses two datas:
    1. Internal data,
    2. External data.
- Internal data mostly used for studying the trends while external data is mostly used for understanding the environment.
- **Benefits of DSS:**
    1. DSS improving personal efficiency.
    2. DSS improving problem solving.
    3. DSS increasing organisational control.

10. Expert Systems (ES): (April 11)

- ES operates with few rules. Effectiveness is a major goal of these types of systems. Human beings are experts in specific areas.

- ES are more flexible than other systems. ES increases output and productivity of the system.
- ES gives effective manipulation of large knowledge based system. The output is selected with the opinion of many experts.
- Expert system consist of following component:
    1. User interface.
    2. Explanation facility.
    3. Knowledge acquisition.
    4. Knowledge base, facts rules.
    5. Knowledge refining system.
- **Advantages of ES:** (April 11)
    1. ES improves quality by providing consistent advice and by making reduction in error rate.
    2. ES increase output as an ES works faster than human being.
    3. An ES can out perform a single human expert in many problem situations.
    4. ES helps to preserve and reproduce knowledge of experts.

11. Execution Information Systems (EIS):

- EIS systems operates continuously to keep management abreast of what is happening in all major areas.
- EIS is structured tracking system. It provides rapid access to timely information and direct access to management reports.
- EIS contains extensive graphics capabilities. It serves the information needs of top executives. EIS gives quick and easy access to detailed information.
- **Advantages of EIS:**
    1. EIS is easy for upper-level executives.
    2. EIS provides timely delivery of company summary information.
    3. EIS improves to tracking information.
    4. EIS filters data for management.
    5. EIS offers efficiency to decision making.

1.4 SYSTEM CONCEPTS (April 12, 14)

- System is related to the answer of the following questions:
    1. What is to be done ?
    2. Who will do it ?
    3. When it will be done ?
    4. How it will be done ?
- General system theory is concerned with developing a systematic, theoretical framework upon which to make decisions.
- Organisations can be viewed as total systems. The idea of system becomes most practical and necessary in conceptualizing the interrelationship and integration of operations, especially when using components.
- Thus, a system is a way of thinking about Organisations and their problems. It also involves a set of techniques that help in solving the problems.

1.4.1 Integrated System

- Integrated system consists of individual computers may be workstations or multiple systems. Each of them runs a set of standard software and deals initially with it's own applications.
- It is a different approach, sometimes called the integrated model and provides truly distributed system by designing it from scratch. In this integrated model, distributed of resources and services is fully transparent to the application program.
- When user request a program to be executed, the integrated system chooses a computer on to run it. In general integrated distributed systems may also expect and claim most of the advantage.

1.4.2 Subsystem

- Subsystems is a unit that is a part of a larger system that means a larger system divided into subparts the subpart is known as subsystem.
- For example: Microprocessor of a motherboard.
- Where Motherboard is system and microprocessor is subsystem.

1.4.3 Transaction Processing System (TPS) (April 11)

- A Transaction Processing System (TPS) is a type of information system. TPSs collect, store, modify and retrieve the transactions of an Organisation. A transaction is an event that generates or modifies data that is eventually stored in an information system.

- A transaction processing system is a set of information which processes the data transaction in database system that monitors transaction programs. The system is useful when something is sold over the internet. It allows for a time delay between when an item is being sold to when it is actually sold.
- An example is that of a sporting event ticket. While the customer is filling out their information to purchase the seat ticket; the transaction processing system is holding the ticket so that another customer cannot also buy it. It allows for a ticket not to be sold to two different customers.

Practice Questions

1. What is a system ?
2. Define system.
3. Give characteristics of a system.
4. List out elements of a system with their brief description.
5. Explain different types of system.
6. What is meant by system ? Explain briefly.
7. Explain system concept with definition.
8. Write short notes on:
    (a) Computer based system,
    (b) Management Information System (MIS).

University Questions & Answers

October 2009

1. Define open and closed system. [2 M]
Ans. Please refer to Section 1.3 (Point 3).

2. Write short note on: Element of system. [4 M]
Ans. Please refer to Section 1.1.3.

April 2010

1. Define Interface concept of system with example. [2 M]
Ans. Please refer to Section 1.1.3 (Point 6).

2. Write short note on: (i) System characteristics. [4 M]
Ans. Please refer to Section 1.2.

October 2010

1. What are elements of system ? Explain one in short. [2 M]

Ans. Please refer to Section 1.1.3.

April 2011

1. Distinguish between TPS and DSS. [4 M]

Ans. Please refer to Sections 1.4.3 and 1.3 (Point 9).

2. Write short note on: Expert system. [4 M]

Ans. Please refer to Section 1.3 (point 10).

3. What are the benefits of expert system. [2 M]

Ans. Please refer to Section 1.3 (Point 10)

October 2011

1. Define system and its elements. [2 M]

Ans. Please refer to Sections 1.1.2 and 1.1.3.

2. Define open and closed system. [2 M]

Ans. Please refer to Section 1.3 (Point 3).

April 2012

1. What are the elements of a system. [2 M]

Ans. Please refer to Section 1.1.3.

2. Write short note on: System concepts. [4 M]

Ans. Please refer to Section 1.4.

October 2012

1. Explain open and closed system, deterministic and probabilistic. [2 M]

Ans. Please refer to Section 1.3.

2. Write short note on: System characteristics. [4 M]

Ans. Please refer to Section 1.2.

April 2013

1. What is conceptual system and physical system. [2 M]

Ans. Please refer to Section 1.3.

2. Write short note on: System elements. [4 M]
Ans. Please refer to Section 1.1.3.

April 2014

1. Define system elements. [2 M]
Ans. Please refer to Section 1.1.3.

2. Write short note on: System Concept. [4 M]
Ans. Please refer to Section 1.4.

❖❖❖

Chapter 2...
Requirement Analysis

Contents ...

This chapter gives basic requirement analysis concepts such as:

2.1 INTRODUCTION
    2.1.1 Necessity

2.2 DEFINITION OF SYSTEM ANALYSIS

2.3 REQUIREMENT ANTICIPATION
    2.3.1 Requirement Investigation
    2.3.2 Requirement Specification

2.4 KNOWLEDGE AND QUALITIES OF SYSTEM ANALYST
    2.4.1 What Skills are Expected in a System Analyst

2.5 ROLE OF A SYSTEM ANALYST

2.6 FEASIBILITY STUDY AND IT'S TYPES

2.7 FACT GATHERING TECHNIQUES
    2.7.1 Interviews
    2.7.2 Questionnaires
    2.7.3 Record Inspection or View
    2.7.4 Observations

2.8 SYSTEM REQUIREMENT SPECIFICATION (SRS)

2.1 INTRODUCTION

- Requirement analysis is the first technical step in software process. At the start it is a general statement of software scope and then refined into the concrete specification that becomes the foundation for all software engineering activities that follow.
- It is a software engineering task that bridges the gap between the system level software allocation and software design.
- It mainly includes the following task.
    1. Enables the system engineering to specify software function and performance.
    2. Indicate software's interface with other system elements.
    3. Establish design constraints that the software must meet.
    4. Allow the analyst to refine the software allocation.

5. Provides the developer and the customer with the means to assess quality. Once, the software is built.
- Requirement analysis is a software engineering task that bridges the gap between the system level software allocation and software design, (See Fig. 2.1).

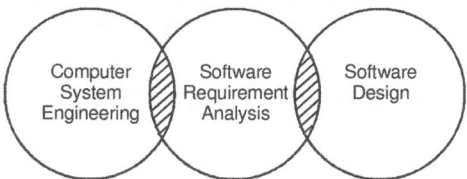

Fig. 2.1: Overlap of the analysis task

- Requirement analysis:
    o Enables the system engineering to specify software function and performance.
    o Indicate software's interface with other system elements.
    o Establish design constraints that the software must meet.
    o Allows the analyst to refine the software allocation.
    o Provides the developer and the customer with the means to assess quality once the software is built.
- System analysis means:
    1. Identification of system and its parts for achieving the goal.
    2. Understanding of system and its part for achieving the goal.
    3. Critically examining the system and its parts for achieving goal.
- System analysis also involves upgrading the system as a whole.

2.1.1 Necessity

- During system analysis some activities are carried out, such as problem definition, design implementation etc.
- Before designing the actual system/project, you should know,
    1. What is a problem?
    2. How to solve it?
    3. What are the technical factors required?
    4. What are the features, advantages and limitations?
- If a system is designed without considering above activities then the system will not work properly to the satisfaction of user's requirements.
- So system analysis is necessary to design perfect and accurate system which satisfies the user requirements.

2.2 DEFINITION OF SYSTEM ANALYSIS

- System analysis refers to the process of examining a business situation with the intent of improving it through better procedures and methods.
- It includes process of gathering and interpreting facts, diagnosing problems and using the information to recommend improvements to the system. This job is done by system analyst.
- Thus, analysis specifies what the system should do. The system analysis concern with:
  1. Investigation.
  2. Analysing.
  3. Implementing information system in Organisation.

2.3 REQUIREMENT ANTICIPATION

- Having hard experience in a particular business or having encounter system in an environment which is similar to the system which is currently under investigation will influence system analyst study.
- That is they may forces of certain problems or features and requirements for a new system. As a result, the feature they investigate for the current system, questions they raised or method they used may be based on this familiarity.
- Requirement anticipation has two approaches. On the one hand, experience from previous studies can lead to the investigation of areas that would otherwise to unnoticed by an inexperience analyst.
- Having the background to know what to ask or which aspect to investigate can be a substantial beneficial to the Organisation. On the other hand if a biased is introduced or shortcuts are taken in conducting the investigation then requirement anticipation is a problem.

2.3.1 Requirement Investigation

- This activity is as the heart of the system analysis. Using the varieties of tools and schemes, analyst studies the current system and documents its features for further analysis.
- Requirement investigation realise on the several fact finding technique which includes the methods for documenting and describing the system features, describes the structured analysis strategy, examine the prototyping strategy and explores computer assessed tools for documenting and specifying requirements.

2.3.2 Requirement Specification

- The data produced during fact finding investigation are analysed to determine requirement specification i.e. the description of features for new system.

- These activities have three inter related parts.
  1. **Analysis of factual data:** The data collected during the fact finding study and included in data flow and decision analysis documentation are examine to determine how well the system is performing and whether it will meet the Organisation demands.
  2. **Identification of essential requirement:** The features *that* must be included in the new system, ranging from operational details to performance criteria are specified.
  3. **Selection of requirements fulfilment strategies:** That will be used to achieve the stated requirement are selected. These formed the basis for system design which follows the requirement specification.
- All three activities are important and must be performed correctly.

2.4 KNOWLEDGE AND QUALITIES OF SYSTEM ANALYST (April 12)

- The individual who performs the system investigation and who may or may not be related to computer programming is called as system analyst.
- The programmer works with the frame work provided by system analyst. Thus a system analyst designs informations system which meet Organisation objective, promote integration of activity and provides facilities and controls which are flexible and robust.
- So, a system analyst job consists of:
  1. Gathering facts about existing information system.
  2. Analysing the basic methods and procedures of current information system.
  3. Determining information need.
  4. Modifying, redesigning and integrating the existing procedures in the new system to provide the needed information.
- The system analyst is more like a manager who:
  1. Determines the design of overall system.
  2. Obtain the necessary technical help from programmer, from specialist and equipment engineering.
  3. Follows the system through design, implementation, follow-up and revaluation.
- Main objective of the system analyst is to provide right type of information in right quantity in right time and at right cost to the management or end users.

Knowledge and Qualities of a System Design

1. **Business method:** The system analyst should have fairly good understanding of the Organisation structure, management and administration methods, system techniques, production planning and control, inventory control, accounting procedures, operation research and simulation techniques.

2. **Computing:** This includes the knowledge of data processing, programming languages and computer operations.

In addition the system analyst must have the knowledge of the new technologies in the market.

2.4.1 What Skills are Expected in a System Analyst (April 11)

- System analyst is a key person in system analysis and design. He/she should be a well knowledgeable person. He/she should have some skills.
- The skills required in a system analyst can be divided into two categories:
  1. Interpersonal skills.
  2. Technical skills.

1. **Interpersonal skills:** Interpersonal skills deal with relationship of the system analyst with the people in the business. They are useful in resolving conflicts, establishing trust and communication information. The interpersonal skills relevant to system work include the following:

   (i) **Communication:** The system analyst should be able to communicate with users in such a "Way that he/she can collect all the required information from them necessary for system design. He/She should be ready to interact from top level management to workers in industry.

   (ii) **Understanding:** The analyst should understand the problem for which system is to be designed. Once, he/she understands a problem, he/she must be able to produce different solutions to meet user requirement.

   (iii) **Teaching:** The analyst should train the different peoples such as programmers, technical writers and end users. He/she should be able to train programmer about how to code the system using programming language. Analyst should be able to train the technical writers about how to create different documents and analyst should give training to the end user about how to use the system.

   (iv) **Solving:** The analyst should introduce the people with the way of solving the problem by using computer by putting his ideas before them.

2. **Technical skills:** On the other hand, the analyst must have technical skills to technical activities.

   (i) **Creativity:** The system analyst must be creative and imaginative in producing new solutions to meet user requirements.

   (ii) **Problem solving:** The analyst must be able to solve problem and must be able to provide different solutions, to given problem.

   (iii) **Project management:** The analyst should prepare a plan/schedule for the design and development of the system. He/She should assign the jobs to the respective persons accordingly and keep co-ordination among them. He/She should also take care of costs and expenditures.

(iv) **Dynamic interface:** The analyst should properly co-ordinate technical and non-technical activities into functional specifications and general design.

(v) **Questioning attitude and Inquiring mind:** Knowing the what, when, why, where, who and how a system works.

In addition analyst must have knowledge of the basics of the computer and the business functions.

Academic Qualifications for System Analyst

- The system analyst is a person, no doubt, but he should have good academic qualifications which are important for system work.
    1. The system analyst may have knowledge in computer science, engineering, business administration, information systems or economics.
    2. The analyst should have background in systems theory and organisation behaviour.
    3. He/She should be familiar with the areas such as financial, accounting, personnel administration, marketing and sales, operation management, and model building and production control.
    4. He/She should be competent in system tools and methodologies and should have a practical knowledge of one or more programming and database languages.
    5. He/She should also have experience in hardware and software specifications.

Tasks of System Analyst

- System analyst consist of following tasks:
    1. Problem identification,
    2. Analysis problem,
    3. Problem understanding,
    4. Evaluation,
    5. Modeling,
    6. Synthesis,
    7. Specification, and
    8. Reviews.

Multifaceted Role of the Analyst

- The analyst plays his role in many characters. The various multifaced roles played by him are:
    1. Change agent,
    2. Monitor,
    3. Architect,
    4. Psychologist,
    5. Sales person,
    6. Motivator, and
    7. Politician.

1. **Change agent:** The analyst is called as change agent because sometimes he changes the entire policy of industry or organisation to improve overall working as well as profit of the organisation. This change is brought by implementing new software based computer system. In order to make this change successful the analyst should give user as much participation as possible while designing the system.

2. **Investigator and Monitor:** The analyst finds out why user is not satisfied with the not present system he is using. What are the drawbacks or pitfall in the present system, that user wants to remove by replacing it with new system.

   The analyst also monitors the activities going on while designing the new system. The activities to be monitored include successful completion of programs with respect to time, cost and quality.

3. **Architect:** System analyst is like architects. They must work with user to identify the goals and shapes of new system. Architect first prepares a plan and according to that plan he develops a building. System analyst also creates several plans and develops or builds system according to that plan.

4. **Psychologist:** Analyst plays the role of psychologist in the way he/she reaches people, interprets their behavior and draws conclusions from their interactions.

5. **Salesperson:** The analyst works as a salesperson by giving oral presentation of the system at each stage of development. The analyst should be very good in communication and in putting his ideas before the user. Also he should be able to clarify the issues raised by the user at the time of presentation.

6. **Motivator:** The analyst work as a motivator after the system is implemented. It is the responsibility of the analyst to motivate the users to use the new system. It is directly dependent how much user participation is given in the project design and how much efforts are taken to train the user that the user can be motivated to use the new system.

7. **Politician:** A politician should be a good diplomat, should have proper good control on his party members and should have a good influence on the people. Same is true for becoming a successful analyst. While designing a new system, the analyst should not only think about the technical side but also keeping good relations, good control and good influences on the people with and around him.

2.5 ROLE OF THE SYSTEM ANALYST (Oct. 09, 11, 12; April 12, 14)

Role of the system analyst are given below:

1. **System analyst has an agent of change:** A system analyst works towards the future. Future is uncertain and different. Change is the only thing which is permanent and the system analyst should be always ready to face the changing environment.

2. **System analyst as a motivator:** Proper identification of right personnel and exact feeding of right motivating factor can go a long way in making a system successful. A *good motivator* has to be a *good psychologist*.

3. **System analyst as an organizer:** The system analyst has to be clear about all *activities*. The sequence of activities, their purpose and their consequences must be clear to him. The system analyst is responsible for the execution of all activities and events of the system.

   The role of the organizer includes that of puzzle solver, whenever problem arrives. A system analyst is also an *evaluator* of its own system. So he diagnoses the problem in the system as well as opportunities in the system. The system analyst should have *professional loyalty*.

4. **System analyst as an architect:** A system analyst must have fairly good idea of its final system at the raw material stage itself. He prepares the blue print, modifies, improves and provides the proper values to his product. The system analyst may bring in a better change environment for the users. Therefore he is a simplifier, an artist and sculptor all role into one.

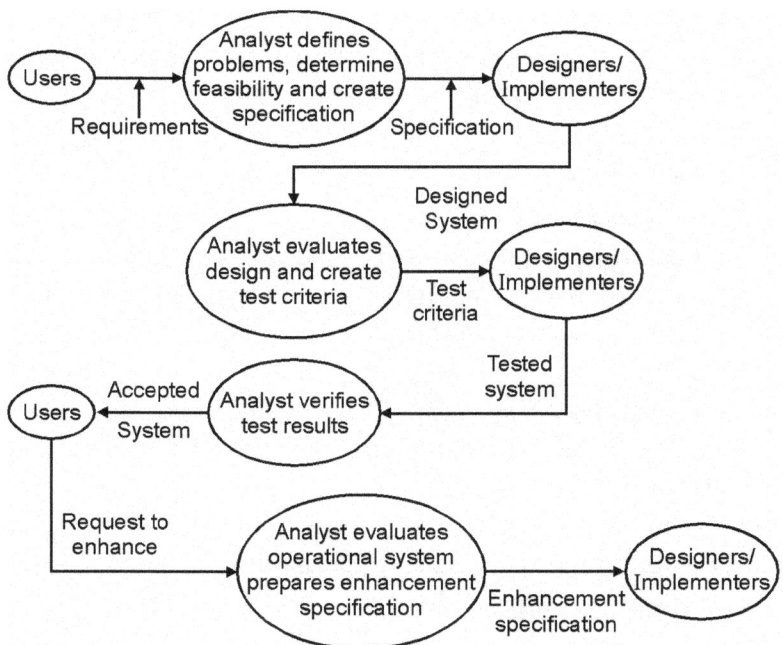

Fig. 2.2: Role of system analyst

5. **System analyst as an intelligent sales person:** A good system analyst is one who can sale a refrigerator to an Eskimo system. Sailing in harder than that because the system analyst has to sale it to the user who knows the existing system in and out. Therefore to sale his system he should be good communicator and should be interested in understanding the real needs of the user.

6. **System analyst as a politician:** In implementing a candidate system, the analyst tries to appear all parties involved. Diplomacy and fineness in dealing with people can improve acceptance of the system.

- In short, these multiple roles require analyst to be orderly, approach a problem in a logical, methodical way and put attention to details.

2.6 FEASIBILITY STUDY AND IT's TYPES (Oct. 09, 10; April 10, 12)

- Number of feasibility studies is disillusioning for system analyst and users.
    1. The study often presupposes that when the feasibility document is being prepared the analyst is in a position to evaluate solutions.
    2. Number of studies tends to over look the confusion inherent in system development.
- The preliminary investigation is carried out before the analysis in which request clarification, feasibility study and request approval is carried out.
- An important outcome of the preliminary investigation is the determination that the system requested is feasible.
- There are three aspects in feasibility study.
    1. **Technical feasibility:** It includes the study like can the work for the project is done with current equipment, existing software technology and with available manpower? If the new technology is required then what are the chances that it can be developed. (Oct. 10)
    2. **Economic feasibility:** Are there sufficient benefits in creating the system to make the cost acceptable or is the cost of not creating the system. So great that project must be undertaken? (Oct. 09)
    3. **Operational feasibility:** Will the system be used if it developed and implemented? Will there be a resistance from the user to the new system.
- The feasibility study is carried out by a small group of people who are familiar with information system technique, understand the part of the business and are skilled in the system analysis and designed process.

2.7 FACT GATHERING TECHNIQUES (Oct. 09, 10; April 11, 12, 14)

- The specific methods analyst used for collecting data about requirements are called as fact gathering techniques. These includes:
    1. Interviews.
    2. Questionnaires.
    3. Record inspection or View.
    4. Observations.

2.7.1 Interviews (April 10, 13, 14)

- Analyst used interviews to collect information from individual or from groups. The respondence is generally current users of the existing system or new users of the proposed system.
- The respondence may be manager or employee who provide data for the proposed system or who will be affected by it. Interviews are not always the best source for collecting the information because the time required for interviews.
- Respondance and Analyst converse during an interview. Interview provides opportunities for gathering information from respondence.
- The interview is the best method for producing the qualitative information like opinions, policies and subjective description of activities and problems.
- This method of fact finding is helpful for gathering information from individuals who do not communicate effectively in writing or who may not have time to complete questioning.
- Interviews allows analyst to discover areas of misunderstanding, unrealistic expectations and indication of resistance to the proposed system.
- Interviews can be of two types: (Oct. 09, 12, 14)
    1. Structured and, 2. Unstructured.
- Using a question and answer format analyst want to acquire general information about the system. This format encourages respondent to share their feeling, ideas etc.
- **Structured interviews** use standardised question, in either an open response or close response format.
- The **unstructured interviews** allows respondent to answer in their own words. Whereas, a structure interview uses the set of prescribe answers.
- The success of an interview depends on the skill of the interviewer and on the preparation for the interview.
- Analyst also needs to be sensitive to the kind of difficulties that some respondents create during interviews and know how to deal with the problems.

- **Advantages of Structured Interview:**
  1. Ensures uniform wording of questions for all respondent.
  2. Easy to administer and evaluate. Objective answer less interaction between respondent the interviewer.
  3. Limited interviewer training is needed.
  4. Results in shorter interviews.
- **Disadvantages of Structured Interview:**
  1. Cost of preparation is high.
  2. Respondent may not accept high level of structure and mechanical style of question.
  3. High level of structure may not be suitable for all situations.
  4. High level of structure reduces the respondence spontaneity and the ability of the interview to follow up on the comments of respondent.
  5. It is take less time.
- **Advantages of Unstructured Interview:**
  1. Interviewer has greater flexibility in wording question to suit the respondent.
  2. Interviewer can visit any area that arises spontaneously during paragraph format answers.
  3. May produce information about areas that were overlooked or not thought to be important.
- **Disadvantages of Unstructured Interview:**
  1. May be inefficient use of both respondent and interviewer time.
  2. Interviewers may introduce their basis in questions or reporting results.
  3. Extra or Unnecessary information may be gathered.
  4. Analysis and interpretation of results may be lengthy.
  5. Take extra time to collect essential facts.

2.7.2 Questionnaires (April 10; Oct. 11, 12)

- The use of this allows analyst to collect information about various aspects of a system from a large number of person.
- The use of the standardised question format can produce more reliable data than other fact finding technique.
- However this method does not allow analyst to observer the expressions or reactions of the respondents.
- In addition to this the answers may be limited since completing questionnaires may not have the high priority among the respondents.

- Analyst use **open ended questionnaires** to learn about feelings, opinions and general experiences or to explore a process or problems.
- **Close ended questionnaires** controlled the frame of reference by presenting respondent with specific responses from which to select. This format is appropriate for collecting factual information.
- Open ended questionnaire is written with space provided for the response.
- Close ended questionnaires are those in which the responses are presented as a set of alternatives.

2.7.3 Record Inspection or View

- Many kinds of records and reports can provide valuable information about Organisation and operation.
- In record reviews analyst examines information that has been recorded about the system and about the users.
- Record inspection can be performed at the beginning of the study as an introduction or it can be performed after the study as the basis for comparing actual operation with what the records indicate should be happening.
- Records includes writer policy manual, regulations and standard operating procedures used by most Organisation as a guide for managers and employee records do not show what activities are actually occurring, who takes the decisions, how the task is performed etc.
- However, they can help analyst in understanding the system with the actual operations which must be supported in the new system.

2.7.4 Observations

- Observation allows analyst to get information which they can not obtained by any other fact finding technique. Through the observation analyst can obtained the first hand information about how activities are carried out. This method is most useful when the analyst need to be actually observe how documents are handle, how processes are carried out and whether specified steps are actually followed or not.

2.8 SYSTEM REQUIREMENT SPECIFICATION (SRS)

(Oct. 09, 10, 11; April 12, 13, 14)

- The term specification means different things to different people.
- A specification can be in a form of a written document, a graphical model, a mathematical mode prototype or any combination of the above.
- Some people say that a standard should be developed for the system requirement specification.

- So the requirements presented will be consistent and therefore, it will be understood nicely.
- But sometimes it is necessary to remain flexible for the systems which are very large a combination of written document, natural language descriptions and graphical models is the best approach. For smaller systems usage scenarios are required.
- The system specification is the final output produced by the system and the requirements engineer. It serves the base line (foundation) for hardware engineering, software engineering, database engineering and human engineering.
- It describes the function and performance of a computer based system and also the constraints which will govern the development.
- The specification bounds each allocated system element. The system specification also describes the input and output from the system.
- The software requirement specification is produced at the culmination of the analysis task. The National Bureau of standards, IEEE (Standard No. - 830 - 1984) and the U.S. Department of Defence have all proposed candidate formats for software requirements specifications.
- However, the simplified outline presented in outline may be used as a framework for the specification. The "introduction" states the goals and objectives of the software, describing it in the content of the computer-based system. Actually, it is nothing but the software scope.
    1. The "**information description**" provides a detailed description of the problems that the software must solve. Information content and relationships, flow and structure are documented. Hardware, software, and human interfaces are described for external system elements and internal software functions. A description of each function required to solve the problem is presented in the "functional description." A processing narrative is provided for each function, design constraints are stated and justified; performance characteristics are stated, and one or more diagrams are included to graphically represent the overall structure of the software and interplay among software functions and other system elements.
    2. The "**behavioural description**" section of the specification examines the operation of the software as a consequence of external events and internally generated control characteristics. Probably the most important, and ironically, the most often neglected section of a software requirements specification are "validation criteria".
        - How do we recognize a successful implementation?
        - What classes of tests must be conducted to validate function, performance and constituents?
- The appendix contains information that supplements the specification. Tabular data, detailed description of algorithms, charts, graphs and other material are presented as appendices.

I.	Introduction	A. System reference		
		B. Overall description		
		C. Software project constraints		
II.	Information description	A. Information content representation		
		B. Information flow representation	1.	Data flow
			2.	Control flow
			1.	Processing narrative
		A. Functional partitioning	2.	Restrictions / limitations
III.	Functional description	B. Functional description	3.	Performance requirements
		C. Control description	4.	Design constraints
		↓	5.	Supporting diagrams
		1. Control specification 2. Design constraints		
IV.	Behavioural description	A. System states		
		B. Events and actions		
		A. Performance bounds		
		B. Classes of tests		
V.	Validation and criteria	C. Expected software response		
		D. Special consideration		
VI.	Bibliography			
VII.	Appendix			

Software Requirements Specification (SRS) outline

- Specification of validation criteria acts as an implicit review of all other requirements. It is essential that time and attention be given to this section.

- Finally, the software requirements specification includes a "bibliography" and "appendix". The bibliography contains references to all documents that relate to the software. These include:

    - Other software engineering documentation,
    - Technical references,
    - Vendor literature, and
    - Standards

Practice Questions

1. Give the definition of the system analysis.
2. Write short note on system analyst.
3. What is the role of the system analyst?
4. Why requirement analysis is required?
5. What is requirement determination?
6. What are the three activities in requirement determination?
7. Write short notes on:
   (a) Requirement anticipation
   (b) Requirement investigation.
   (c) Requirement specification.
   (d) User transaction requirement.
8. Explain the term feasibility study.
9. What is the fact gathering technique?
10. Compare structured interview and unstructured interview.
11. What are the skills expected in a system analyst?
12. Enlist various tasks of system analyst.
13. What do you mean by requirement investigation and specifications?
14. Describe various types of feasibility study.
15. Describe the following terms:
    (a) Observations
    (b) Questionnaires.
16. Compare transaction and decision making activities.

University Questions & Answers

October 2009

1. What are the different types of interviewing? [2 M]
Ans. Please refer to Section 2.7.1.

2. What is economical feasibility? [2 M]
Ans. Please refer to Section 2.6 (Point 2)

3. What is fact finding technique? Explain any one technique in detail. [4 M]
Ans. Please refer to Section 2.7.

	4.	Write short note on: Role of system analyst.	[4 M]
Ans.		Please refer to Section 2.5.	
	5.	Write short note on: SRS documentations.	[4 M]
Ans.		Please refer to Section 2.8.	

April 2010

	1.	Define open ended and close ended questionnaires.	[2 M]
Ans.		Please refer to Section 2.7.2.	
	2.	Write a note on feasibility study.	[4 M]
Ans.		Please refer to Section 2.6.	
	3.	Write a short note on: Interview	[4 M]
Ans.		Please refer to Section 2.7.1.	

October 2010

	1.	What is technical feasibility?	[2 M]
Ans.		Please refer to Section 2.6 (Point 2).	
	2.	Explain in detail SRS documentation.	[4 M]
Ans.		Please refer to Section 2.8.	
	3.	Write short note on: Fact finding techniques.	[4 M]
Ans.		Please refer to Section 2.7.	

April 2011

	1.	What are fact finding techniques? Explain any one.	[4 M]
Ans.		Please refer to Section 2.7.	
	2.	What skills are required in system analyst?	[4 M]
Ans.		Please refer to Section 2.4.1.	
	3.	Write short note on: SRS documentation.	[4 M]
Ans.		Please refer to Section 2.8.	

October 2011

	1.	Define open ended and close ended questionnaire.	[2 M]
Ans.		Please refer to Section 2.7.2.	
	2.	Explain role of system analyst.	[4 M]
Ans.		Please refer to Section 2.5.	
	3.	Explain in detail SRS documentation.	[4 M]
Ans.		Please refer to Section 2.8.	

April 2012

1. What is feasibility study? List out type of it. [2 M]
Ans. Please refer to Section 2.6.
2. What is system analysis? [2 M]
Ans. Please refer to Section 2.2.
3. Who is system analyst? Discuss the roles of system analyst. [4 M]
Ans. Please refer to Sections 2.4 and 2.5.
4. Discuss different fact finding techniques. [4 M]
Ans. Please refer to Section 2.7.

October 2012

1. Explain system analysis? [2 M]
Ans. Please refer to Section 2.5.
2. Write short note on: Structured and Unstructured Interview. [4 M]
Ans. Please refer to Section 2.7.1.

April 2013

1. What are rules of interview? [4 M]
Ans. Please refer to Section 2.7.1.
2. Differentiate structured interview and unstructured interview. [4 M]
Ans. Please refer to Section 2.6.1.
3. Write a note on SRS. [4 M]
Ans. Please refer to Section 2.8.
4. Write short note on System analysis. [4 M]
Ans. Please refer to Section 2.5.
5. Write short note on Fast gathering techniques. [4 M]
Ans. Please refer to Section 2.7.

October 2013

1. ?????????. [2 M]
Ans. Please refer to Section 2.
1. ?????????. [2 M]
Ans. Please refer to Section 2.
1. ?????????. [2 M]
Ans. Please refer to Section 2.

April 2014

1. Stare rules of interview. [2 M]
Ans. Please refer to Section 2.7.1.

2. Explain fact fining techniques. [2 M]
Ans. Please refer to Section 2.7.

3. Explain skills of system analyst. [4 M]
Ans. Please refer to Section 2.5.

4. Write short note on SRS Documentation. [4 M]
Ans. Please refer to Section 2.7.

❖❖❖

Chapter 3...
Introduction to Software Engineering

Contents ...

In this chapter we discuss various concepts of software engineering:

3.1 INTRODUCTION
    3.1.1 Software
    3.1.2 Software Product
    3.1.3 Software Components

3.2 DEFINITION NEED FOR SOFTWARE ENGINEERING
    3.2.1 Definition
    3.2.2 Need of Software Engineering
    3.2.3 Process, Methods and Tools

3.3 SOFTWARE CHARACTERISTICS

3.4 SOFTWARE QUALITIES
    3.4.1 Software Quality Assurance
    3.4.2 McCall's Quality Factors

3.1 INTRODUCTION

- Software engineering is the study and application of engineering to design development and maintenance of software.
- Software engineering is concerned with all aspects of software production from the early stages of system specification through to maintaining the system.

3.1.1 Software

- Software is set of instructions, (computer programs) that when executed provide desire function and performance.
- Software is a data structure that enables the programmer to adequately manipulate information.
- Software is documents that describe the operation and use of the programs.

3.1.2 Software Product

- The objective of software engineering is to produce software products.

- Software products are software systems delivered to a customer with the documentation which describes how to install and use the system.
- Software products fall into two broad categories:
    1. **Generic products:** These are stand alone systems which are produced by a development organisation and sold on the open market to any customer who is able to buy them.
    2. **Customized products:** These are systems which are commissioned by a particular customer. The software is developed specially for that customer by some contractor.

3.1.3 Software Components (April 13, 14)

- Computer software has information that exists in two basic forms:
    - non machine-executable components
    - Machine-executable components.
- Software components are created through a series of translations that map customer requirements to machine-executable code.
- 'Reusability' is an important characteristic of a high-quality software component. That is, the component should be designed and implemented so that it can be reused in many different programs.
- Software components are built using a programming language that has a limited vocabulary, an explicitly defined grammar and well-formed rules of syntax and semantics.

3.2 DEFINITION NEED FOR SOFTWARE ENGINEERING

- Computer software is a product that design and built by software engineers. They develop a product using software engineering approach.
- Software has become the key element in the evolution of computer based systems and products. Software is composed of programs, data and documents.
- Software engineering is concerned with development and maintenance of technological products, problem solving techniques which are followed in all engineering disciplines like project planning project management, system analysis, methodical design, proper fabrication, validation and ongoing maintenance activities within cost estimates.
- The intent of software engineering is to provide a framework for building software with higher quality. In this chapter we will discuss the software characteristics and how to gain the quality of a software engineering work product.
- These measures of the quality factor provide the software engineer with a real-time indication of the efficiency of the analysis, design and code models; the effectiveness of test cases; and the overall quality of the software to be built.

- A **primary goal of software engineering is to improve the quality of software products and to increase the productivity and job satisfaction of software engineers.**
- Software engineering is a new technological discipline distinct form, but based on the foundations of computer science, management science, economics, communication skills and the engineering approach to problem solving.
- Software engineering being a labour intensive activity requires both technical skill and managerial control. Management science provides the foundations for software project management.
- Software engineering activities occur within an organisational context and a high degree of communication is required among customers, managers, software engineers, hardware engineer and other technologies.
- **A fundamental principal of software engineering is to design software products that minimize the intellectual distance between problem and solution.**
- So we can say that "software engineering is the technological and managerial discipline concerned with systematic production and maintenance of software products that the developed and modified on time and within cost estimates".

3.2.1 Definition (Oct. 09, 10)

- An early definition of software engineering (by Fritz Bauer):

   The establishment and use of sound engineering principles in order to obtain economical software that is reliable and works efficiently on real machines.

   OR

   Software Engineering is the technological and managerial discipline concerned with systematic production and maintenance of software products which all developed and modified on time within the cost estimates.

   OR

- Software engineering is an outgrowth of hardware and system engineering. It encompasses a set of three key elements:
   1. Methods,
   2. Tools, and
   3. Procedures.
   1. **Software engineering 'methods'** encompass a broad array of tasks that include: project planning and estimation, system analysis, design of data structure, program architecture, coding, testing and maintenance.

2. **Software engineering 'tools'** provide automated or semi-automated support for methods.

3. **Software engineering procedures** are the glue that holds the methods and tools together and they enable rational and timely development of computer software.

3.2.2 Need of Software Engineering

- Following some points describes need of software engineering.

    1. Software engineering needed for building complex and critical software systems in a timely manner with high quality.

    2. Making a change within a complex program turned out to be very expensive. Often even to get the program to do something slightly different was so hard that it was easier to throw out the old program and start over. This, of course, was costly. Part of the evolution in the software engineering approach was learning to develop systems that are built well enough the first time so that simple changes can be made easily.

    3. As the cost of hardware plummeted, software continued to be written by humans, whose wages were rising. The savings from productivity improvements in software development from the use of assemblers, compilers, and data base management systems did not proceed as rapidly as the savings in hardware costs.

3.2.3 Process, Methods and Tools

- Software engineering is a layered technology (See, Fig. 3.1), any engineering approach must rest on an organisational commitment to quality.

- Total quality management and similar philosophies bring up a continuous process improvement culture and this culture ultimately leads to the development of increasingly more mature approaches to software engineering.

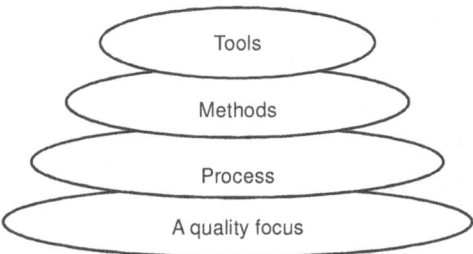

Fig. 3.1: Software engineering layers

- The foundation for software engineering is the process layer.

- Software engineering process is the glue that holds the technology layers together and enables rational and timely development of computer software.
- Process defines a framework for a set of **Key Process Areas** (KPAs) that must be established for effective delivery of SE technology.
- The KPAs from the basis for management control of software projects and establish the context in which technical methods are applied, work products (models, documents, data, reports, forms etc.) are produced, milestones are established, quality is ensured and change is properly managed.
- **Software engineering methods** provides the technical how-to's for building software.
- Methods encompass a broad array of tasks that include requirements analysis, design, program construction, testing and support.
- Software Engineering methods depends on a set of basic principles that govern each area of the technology and include modeling activities and other descriptive techniques.
- **Software engineering tools** provide automated or semi-automated support for the process and the methods.
- When tools are integrated so that information created by one tool can be used by another, a system for the support of software development, called Computer Aided Software Engineering (CASE), is established.
- CASE combines software, hardware and a software engineering database to create a software engineering environment analogous to CAD/CAE (Computer Aided Design/Engineering) for hardware.

3.3 SOFTWARE CHARACTERISTICS (Oct., 12; April 11, 13)

- Software is a logical rather than a physical system element. Therefore, software has characteristics that are considerably different than those of hardware.
- The main characteristics of software are:
    1. Software is developed or engineered; it is not manufactured in the classical sense.
    2. Software does not wear out.
    3. Software is not susceptible to the environmental melodies.
    4. Most software is custom-built, rather than being assembled from existing components.

1. Software is Developed or Engineered:

- In both software development and hardware manufacture, high quality is achieved through a good design, but the manufacturing phase for hardware can introduce quality problems that are non-existent (or easily created) for software.

- Software costs are concentrated in engineering. This means that software projects cannot be managed as if they were manufacturing projects.

2. Software does not Wear Out: (April 10, 12)

- Fig. 3.2 depicts failure rate as a function of time for hardware.

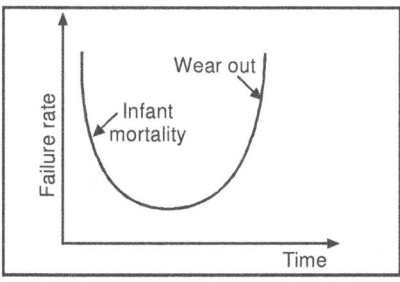

Fig. 3.2: Bath tub curve

- The relationship often called the 'bathtub-curve' indicates that hardware exhibits relatively high failure rates early in its life, defects are corrected and the failure-rate drops to a steady-state level for some period of time.

- As time passes, however, the failure rate rises again as hardware components from the cumulative effects of dust, vibration, abuse, temperature extremes and many other environmental melodies. Stated simply, the hardware begins to wear out.

- Software is not susceptible to the environmental melodies that cause hardware to wear out. Ideally, the failure rate curve for software should take the form of the curve shown in Fig. 3.3.

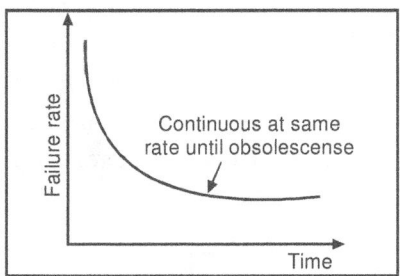

Fig. 3.3: Idealized software failure curve

- However, undiscovered defects will cause high failure rates in the life of a program. During its life, software will undergo change (or maintenance).

- As changes are made, it is likely that some new defects will be introduced, causing the failure rate curve to spike as shown in Fig. 3.4.

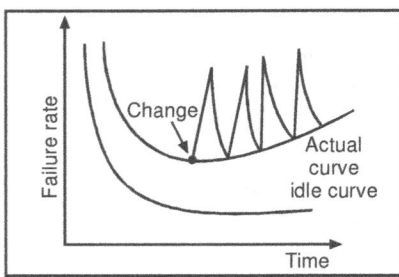

Fig. 3.4: Actual software

- Software is not susceptible to the environmental melodies that cause hardware to wear out.

3. **Most Software is Custom Built:**

- In case of building of hardware, the design engineer draws a software schematic of the digital circuitry, does some fundamental analysis to assure proper functioning, and goes through a catalog of a digital component.
- Each "IC" or a "chip" has a part-no, a well defined and validated function, a well defined interface and standard set of integration guidelines. On the other hand, software designers are not afforded luxury described above.

3.4 SOFTWARE QUALITY (Oct. 09; April 10, 11)

- In this section we discuss various software quality concepts.
- The American Heritage Dictionary defines "quality" as a "characteristic or attribute of something". As an attribute of an item, quality refers to measurable characteristics - things we are able to compare to known standards such as length, colour, electrical properties, and malleability and so on.
- "Quality of design" refers to the characteristics that designers specify for an item 1, whereas the "quality of conformance" is the degree to which the design specifications are followed during manufacturing. It is very difficult to define quality and more difficult to quantity it and measure it.

- The definition given by ISO-8402 of quality is "the totality of features and characteristics of a product, process or service that bears on its ability to satisfy stated or implied needs".

- All these definition serves to emphasize three important points.

  1. Software requirements are the foundation from which quality is measured.

  2. Specified standards define a set of development criteria that guide the manner in which software is engineered. If the criteria are not followed, lack of quality will almost surely result.

  3. There is a set of implicit requirements that often goes unmentioned. If software conforms to its explicit requirements but falls to meet implicit requirements, software quality is suspect.

- Software quality is a complex combination of factors that will vary across different applications and the customers who request them. In the next section, we will discuss software quality factors that are identified.

- The ultimate aim of the production process should be to produce a quality product or service.

3.4.1 Software Quality Assurance (Oct. 10)

- Software Quality Assurance (SQA) is defined as a planned and systematic approach to the evaluation of the quality of and adherence to software product standards, processes, and procedures.

- SQA is the process of ensuring that a software system and its associated documentation are in all respects of sufficient quality for their purpose.

- Software quality assurance consists of a means of monitoring the software engineering processes and methods used to ensure quality.

- The methods by which this is accomplished are many and varied, and may include ensuring conformance to one or more standards, such as ISO 9000 or a model such as CMMI.

- SQA encompasses the entire software development process, which includes processes such as requirements definition, software design, coding, source code control, code reviews, change management, configuration management, testing, release management and product integration.

- SQA is organized into goals, commitments, abilities, activities, measurements, and verifications.

3.4.2 McCall's Quality Factors (Oct. 09, 10, 11; April 10, 12, 14)

- The factors that affect software quality can be categorized in two broad groups:
    1. Factors that can be directly measured, and
    2. Factors that can be measured only indirectly.
       (For example, usability or maintainability).
- In each case measurement must occur.
- McCall, Richards and Walters propose a useful categorization of factors that affect software quality.
- These software quality factors, shown in Fig. 3.5, focus on three important aspects of a software product: its operational characteristics, its ability to undergo change and its adaptability to new environments. That is, product operation, product transition and product revision.

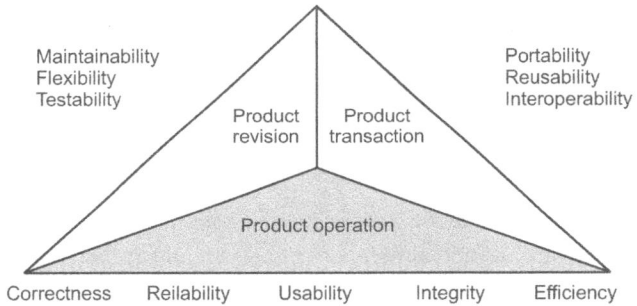

Fig. 3.5: McCall's software quality factors

- Individual factors in each of these groups are as follows:

    (a) Product operation:
    - Correctness
    - Reliability
    - Usability
    - Integrity
    - Efficiency

    (b) Product revision:
    - Maintainability
    - Flexibility
    - Testability

(c) Product transition:
- Portability
- Reusability
- Interoperabilty.

- In addition to these factors Bochm suggest that quality criteria include the following attributes:
  - Economy
  - Documentation
  - Understandability
  - Modularity
  - Validity
  - Fenerality
  - Resilience
  - Clarity
  - Performance

- Following is the description of the above factors:

1. **Correctness: "Does it do what I want?"**

   If the software performs its required functions according to the specification then it is functionally correct. The software should fulfill the customer's mission objectives.

2. **Reliability: "Does it do it accurately all the time?"**

   Reliability is the probability that the software will operate correctly over a specified time interval. Most of the errors are removed from the system (program) then more reliability is achieved. Hence, reliability is the extent to which a program can be expected to perform its intended function with required precision.

3. **Efficiency: "Will it run on my hardware as well as it can?"**

   It depends on the amount of computing resources, code required by a program to perform its function, execution speed and memory requirements. If the code is proper and algorithm is proper then less execution time is required. Good use of the available resources, both in space and time, is of course an essential requirement on any software product.

4. **Integrity: "It is secure?"**

   It is the ability of software system to product their various components (programs, data, documents) against unauthorised access and modification.

5. **Usability: "Is it designed for the user?"**

   If is the ease of learning how to use software systems, operating them, preparing input data, interpreting results, recovering form usage errors.

6. **Maintainability: "Can I fix it?"**

   This factor is nothing but the maintenance of the software product. It includes the steps of maintenance phase.

7. **Flexibility: "Can I change it ?"**

   It is the case with which software products may be adapted to changes of specifications.

8. **Testability: "Can I test it?"**

   It is the ease of preparing acceptance procedures particularly test data and procedures for detecting failures and tracing them to errors during the validation and operation phases.

9. **Portability: "Will I be able to use it on another machine ?"**

   It is the ease with which software products may be transferred to various hardware and software environments.

10. **Reusability: "Will I be able to reuse some of the software ?"**

    It is the ability of software products to be reused, in whole on in part, for new applications.

11. **Inter-operability: "Will I be able to interface it with another system ?"**

    It is the ease with which software products may be combined with others (i.e. compatibility or effort required to couple one system to another).

    It is difficult to direct measure of these quality factors, a set of matrices are defined and used to develop expressions for each of the factors according to the following relationship.

    $$F_q = c_1 \times m_1 + c_2 \times m_2 + ... + c_n \times m_n$$

where, F_q is a software quality factor, c_n are regression coefficients, m_n are the metrics that affect the quality factor McCall's proposed a grading system to measure the factors. The following metrics are used in the grading scheme:

- **Auditability:** The ease with which conformance to standards can be checked.
- **Accuracy:** The precision of computations and control.
- **Communication commonality:** The degree to which standard interfaces, protocols and bandwidth are used.
- **Completeness:** The degree to which full implementation of required function has been achieved.

- **Conciseness:** The compactness of the program in terms of lines of code.
- **Consistency:** The use of uniform design and documentation techniques throughout the software development project.
- **Data commonality:** The use of standard data structures and types throughout the program.
- **Error tolerance:** The damage that occurs when the program encounters an error.
- **Execution efficiency:** The run-time performance of a program.
- **Expandability:** The degree to which architectural, data or procedural design can be extended.
- **Generality:** The breadth of potential application of program components.
- **Modularity :** The functional independence of program components.
- **Security:** The ease of operation of a program.
- **Security:** The availability of mechanisms that control or protect programs and data.
- **Self-documentation:** The degree to which the source code provides meaningful documentation.
- **Simplicity:** The degree to which a program can be understood without difficulty.
- **Traceability:** The ability to trace a design representation or actual program component back to requirements.
- **Training:** The degree to which the software assists in enabling new users to apply the system.

Practice Questions

1. Define the following terms:
   (a) Software
   (b) Software Engineering.
2. What is meant by software engineering ?
3. What is software engineering ? Explain.
4. Explain components of softwares.
5. Why we required software engineering ?
6. Enlist various characteristics of software engineering.
7. What is Quality ?
8. Enlist various McCall's quality factors.

University Questions & Answers

October 2009

1. Define software engineering. [2 M]
Ans. Please refer to Section 3.2.1.
2. Explain different McCall's quality factors. [4 M]
Ans. Please refer to Section 3.4.2.

April 2010

1. Justify software does not ware out [2 M]
Ans. Please refer to Section 3.3 Point (2).
2. Write short note on: Software quality factors. [4 M]
Ans. Please refer to Section 3.4.

October 2010

1. Define software engineering. [2 M]
Ans. Please refer to Section 3.2.1.
2. What is software quality assurance ? Why quality assurance is important. [4 M]
Ans. Please refer to Section 3.4.1.
3. Write short note on: Software Qualities (McCall's Quality factors). [4 M]
Ans. Please refer to Section 3.4.2.

April 2011

1. State characteristics of software. [2 M]
Ans. Please refer to Section 3.3.

October 2011

1. Write short note on: Software qualities (McCall's Quality factors). [4 M]
Ans. Please refer to Section 3.4.2.

April 2012

1. Justify software does not wear out. [2 M]
Ans. Please refer to Section 3.3 Point (2).

2. Discuss software qualities (McCall's Quality factors). [4 M]
Ans. Please refer to Section 3.4.2.

October 2012

1. Justify software does not wear out. [4 M]
Ans. Please refer to Section 3.3.

2. Explain software characteristics. [4 M]
Ans. Please refer to Section 3.3.

April 2013

1. What is reusability of software. [2 M]
Ans. Please refer to Section 3.1.3.

2. What are characteristics of software.
Ans. Please refer to Section 3.3.

April 2014

1. Define software reusability. [2 M]
Ans. Please refer to Section 3.1.4.

2. Explain McCall's quality factors.
Ans. Please refer to Section 3.4.2.

❖❖❖

Chapter 4...
Software Development Methodologies

Contents ...

This chapter gives basic concepts of system such as:

4.1 Introduction

4.2 System Development Life Cycle (SDLC)

    4.2.1 What we do in System Development ?

4.3 Waterfall Model

4.4 Spiral Model

4.5 Prototyping Model

    4.5.1 Benefits

    4.5.2 Tools for Prototyping

4.6 RAD Model

4.1 INTRODUCTION

- Software development methodologies are used for computer information systems. The computer information systems serve different purposes, it provide the information needed to take decisions.
- The growth of an information system passes through variable identifiable stages and these stages put together are referred to as SDLC i.e. System Development Life Cycle.

4.2 SYSTEM DEVELOPMENT LIFE CYCLE (SDLC) (Oct. 10; April 11)

- Any story needs a plot, something to tie things together. In a programming job the plot is called a development cycle. Others have used the terms "**life cycle**", "**implementation cycle**" or "**linear cycle**", which mean essentially the same thing as "**system development life cycle**" (SDLC).
- The programming development cycle is simply a series of orderly, interrelated activities leading to the successful completion of set of programs. The periods of time during which these activities take place are called phases.
- "System Development Life Cycle (SDLC) is a set of steps, which are used for building a system".

- The SDLC has been widely used in the design of system that can be easily understood and which have well defined workflows.
- The analyst must progresses from one stage to another methodically, answering key questions and achieving the results in each stage.
- There are several ways to describe System Development Life Cycle. The most common way is given in this chapter.

4.2.1 What we do in System Development ? (Oct. 12; April 14)

- Before we describe system development cycle, let us look at what actually happens during system development.
- Many of the activities take place in system development such as:
    1. Understand the user requirement.
    2. Design and Decision making about system.
    3. Build a system.
    4. Form group memory.
    5. Development of software.
    6. System testing.
    7. Implementation and evaluation.
- Fig. 4.1 shows many of the activities in system development.
- First analyst have discussions with users to familiarize themselves with the system and to get better idea of user requirements and how they fit in with the environment.
- Previous knowledge is used to develop an understanding of the system and to become familiar with its problems. Ideas about new system are proposed and evaluated.
- There may be some experimentation to find out if some of the various proposed ideas can be put into practice and opinions are formed and often used in design.
- During this time we develop a group memory of what was discussed and what conclusions were reached about the system.

Table 4.1

Sr. No.	Stage	Key question	Result
1.	Recognition of need - Preliminary survey/Initial investigation.	What is the problem or opportunity ?	Statement of scope and objectives.
2.	Feasibility study Evaluation of existing system and analysis of alternative candidate system, cost, estimates.	What are the user's needs ? How can the problem be solved ?	Technical/behavioral feasibility, cost/benefit analysis.

Contd...

3.	Analysis - Detailed evaluation of present system.	What must be done to solve problem?	Logical model of system.
4.	Design - General design specifications, detailed design specifications - output/input, files, procedures.	In general how the problem should be solved?	Design of alternative solutions. Cost/Benefit analysis. Implementation of schedule.
5.	Program construction testing.	How will individual modules tested out?	Test plans, operating procedures.
6.	Implementation user training.	What is actual operation?	Training program user friendly documentation.
7.	Post implementation.	Where the key system running?	

- The steps involved in SDLC are shown below: **(April 11)**
  1. Recognition of need.
  2. Feasibility study.
  3. System analysis.
  4. System Design.
  5. Implementation.
  6. Post-implementation and Maintenance.

- **Phase 1 - Recognition of Need:** This is the first step in SDLC. In this step system analyst has to find out why a new system is required. In this stage he should understand what are the present methods of solving the problem for which we are designing the system and what new the user wants in the new system. In short system analysts describe user requirement, (system) project objectives, system and resource limits.

- **Phase 2 - Feasibility Study:** The feasibility study proposes one or more conceptual solutions to the problem set for the project. The conceptual solutions give an idea of what the new system will look like. They define what will be done on the computer and what will remain manual. They also indicate what input will be needed by the systems and what outputs will be produced i.e. in feasibility study the analyst has to do evaluation of existing systems and procedures. He has to present a number of alternative solutions to the user. After consulting with user, the analyst has to finalize one alternative which will be best for all the given solutions.

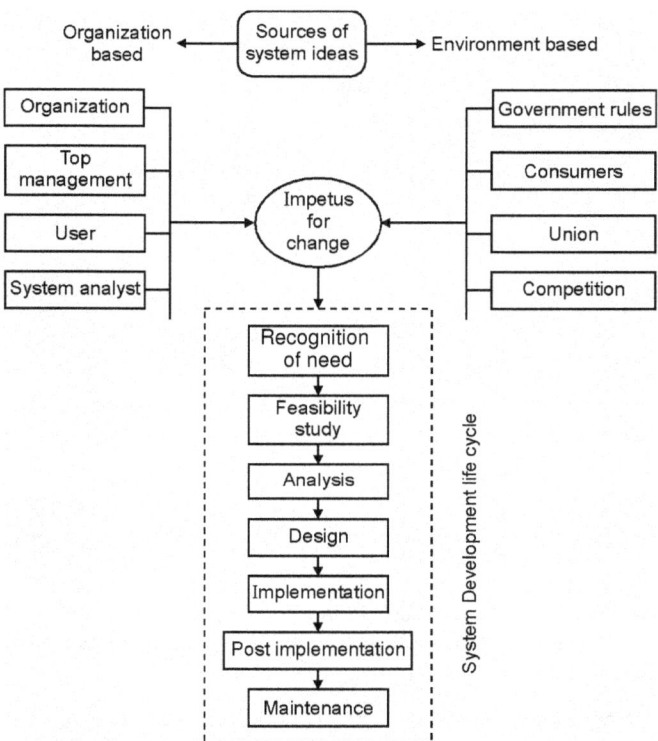

Fig. 4.1: Activities in software development

- **Phase 3 - System Analysis:** System analysis is a detailed study of the various operations performed by a system and their relationships within and outside of system i.e., it includes finding out in more detail what the system problems are and what the different new changes the user wants. During analysis, analysts use many of the commonly used system analysis techniques, such as data flow diagram, decision table and so on. Analyst must spend considerable time examining components, such as the various forms used in the system, as well as the operation of finishing computer systems.

- This phase results in a detailed model of the system. The model describe the system functions, system data and system information flows i.e. once analysis is completed, the analyst has a firm understanding what is to be done. The next step is to decide how the problem might be solved.

- **Phase 4 - System Design:** The system design is most important and challenging phase of the system development life cycle. Analysis phase is used to design the logical model of the system and system design phase is used to design the physical model of the system. The system design phase produces a design for the new system. There are many things to be done here. Designers must select the equipment needed to implement the system. They must specify new programs or changes to existing programs as well as a new database or changes to the existing database. Designers must also produce detailed documents that describe how users will use the system.

- Thus, in this phase, the designer/analyst designs:
    1. Output,
    2. Input,
    3. File, and
    4. Processing.
- Output design means that what should be the format for presenting the results obtained. It should be in most convenient, attractive format for the user.
- In input design phase, which is a part of system design phase the system analyst has to decide what inputs are required for the system and prepare input format to have input to system according to user requirement.
- File design deals with how the data has to be stored on physical devices. Finally process design includes the description of the procedure for carrying out operations on the given data.
- **Phase 5 - System Implementation:** During implementation, the components built during development are put into operational use. Following are the activities which takes place during system implementation phase.
    1. Writing, testing, debugging and documenting programs.
    2. Converting data from the old to the new system.
    3. Giving training to the users about how to operate the system.
    4. Ordering and Installing any new hardware.
    5. Developing operating procedures for the computer centre staff.
    6. Establishing a maintenance procedure to repair and enhance the system.
    7. Completing system documentation.
    8. Evaluating the final system to make sure that it is fulfilling original needs and that it began operation on time and within budget.
- **Phase 6 - Post Implementation and Maintenance:** The system is considered to be working when phase five has been completed. However, there are still a number of activities that take place after a system is completed. The two main activities are:

(April 10; Oct. 11, 12)

1. Post implementation
2. Maintenance.

The post-implementation activity take place after about a year to determine that whether the system is perfectly working or not, whether the system is satisfying the user needs or not, if not, changes are made to the system to make it perfect.

- Maintenance is a part of SDLC. It includes following tasks:
    1. Correcting errors.
    2. Resolving necessary changes.
    3. Enhances or Modifies the system.
    4. Assigns staff to perform maintenance activities.
    5. Provides for scheduled maintenance.
- **For example:** If Corporation changes octroi rate from one value to another, corresponding changes will have to be done in the programs which uses this octroi rate.

4.3 WATERFALL MODEL (Oct. 09, 11, 12; April 10, 12, 14)

- This is the first published model for the software development process. It is derived from other engineering process. Although the original waterfall model proposed by **Winston Royce**.
- He made the provision of feedback loops and this is linear model. This model cascade from one phase to another, where the output of one phase is the input to next phase. This model is also known as **software life cycle**.

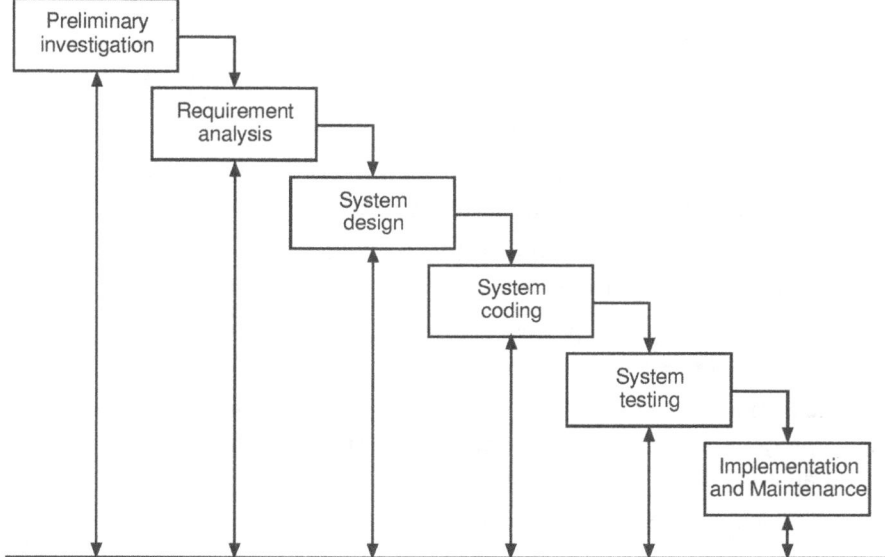

Fig. 4.2: Waterfall model

- Each phase is structured as a set of activity and may be executed by different people concurrently.
- Fig. 4.2 illustrates the waterfall model. This model provides a sequential, linear flow among different phases.
- The output of each phase must be produced using standards. If output of any phase is wrong it may affect the subsequent phases.
- Waterfall model is useful to measure the progress of the project as it is easy to check whether, a certain output is delivered exactly on the date when it was expected.
- The main activities are already discussed. Eventhough, we will have a overview of each point again.
    1. **Preliminary investigation or System engineering:** We decide the requirements of all system elements and then allocate some subset of these requirement to software.
    2. **Requirement analysis:** To understand the nature of the programs to be built, the system analyst must understand the information domain for the software as well as the required function, performance and interfacing.
    3. **System design:** It is actually a multistep process which focuses on four distinct attributes of the program:
        (i) Data structures.
        (ii) Software architecture.
        (iii) Procedural detail.
        (iv) Interface characterization.
        The design process translates requirement into a representation of the software that can be assessed for quality before coding begins.
    4. **System coding:** The design must be translated into a machine-readable form. The coding step performs this task.
    5. **System testing:** This process focuses on the logical internals of the software and functional externals.
    6. **System maintenance:** It reapplies each of the preceding if cycle step to an existing program rather than a new one. There are certain problems encountered while applying classic-life cycle paradigm.
        (i) 'Iteration' causes problem in the application.
        (ii) It is difficult to state all requirements explicitly by the customer.
        (iii) The customer must have patience.

- **Advantages of waterfall model:** (Oct. 09; April 11)
    1. Waterfall model is a linear model and of course, linear models are the most simple to be implemented.
    2. The amount of resources required to implement this model is very minimal.
    3. One great advantage of the waterfall model is that documentation is produced at every stage of the waterfall model development. This makes the understanding of the product designing procedure simpler.
    4. After every major stage of software coding, testing is done to check the correct running of the code.
    5. In waterfall model progress of system is measurable.
- **Disadvantages of waterfall model:**
    1. Basically, the biggest disadvantage of the waterfall model is one of its greatest advantages. You cannot go back, if the design phase has gone wrong, things can get very complicated in the implementation phase.
    2. Many a times, it happens that the client is not very clear of what he exactly wants from the software. Any changes that he mentions in between may cause a lot of confusion.
    3. Small changes or errors that arise in the completed software may cause a lot of problem.
    4. The lifecycle can take so long that the original requirements may no longer be valid by the time the system is implemented.
    5. Estimating time and costs is difficult for each stages.
    6. Time consuming as the testing process starts the last stage till the build is given for testing the testers will be idle hence man power is wasted.

4.4 SPIRAL MODEL (Oct. 09, 10; April 11)

- This is also called as process model. The spiral model of software process was originally proposed by **Boehm** in 1988.
- In place of representing the software process as a sequence of activities with some backtracking from one activity to another, the process is represented as a spiral.
- Each loop in the spiral represents a phase of the software process.
- The spiral model is useful in the following situations:
    1. When development of a project starts, it may be possible that work may be stopped due to any reason. If such situation arises what step must be taken to solve such problem should be known.
    2. Which path should be followed for a particular procedure must be known in advance to the development team. Because of this also, work will not be stopped in the middle.

- Spiral model helps us in this situations. This model guides the risks in the project. Risks are concerned with the future. The spiral model is useful for identifying and eliminating high risk problems by careful process design.
- The spiral model contains four stages and each stage is represented by one quadrant of a cartesian diagram.
- The radius of the spiral represents the cost incurred so far in the process. This is illustrated in Fig. 4.3.
- The major activities represented in above Fig. 4.3 are:
  1. **Planning:** It determines the objectives, alternatives and constraints of the portion of the product under consideration.
  2. **Risk analysis:** The alternatives are evaluated and potential risk areas are identified. The efforts are mode to resolve the risks.
  3. **Engineering:** By using the activities like simulation and prototyping, the development and verification of the next level product is done.
  4. **Customer evaluation:** The customer evaluates the engineering work and makes suggestions and modifications.

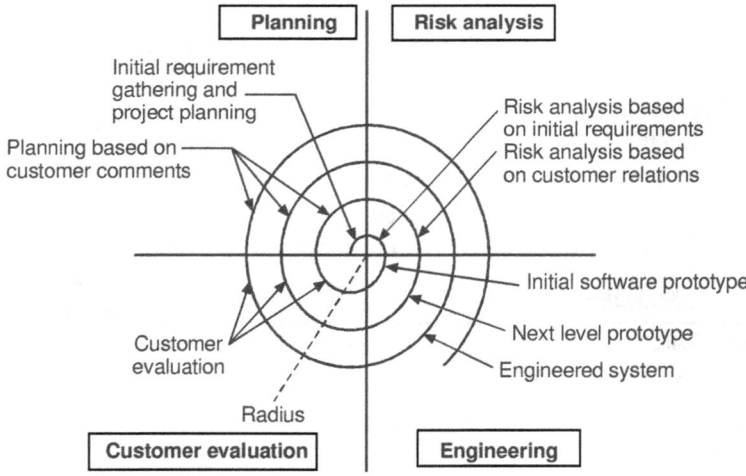

Fig. 4.3: Spiral model

- The spiral model has two concept:
  1. They provide guidance to software engineers on the order in which the various technical activities should be carried out within a project.
  2. They provide a framework for managing development and maintenance, in that they enable us to estimate resources, define intermediate milestones, monitor programs etc.

- The spiral or process model is an evolutionary model having most realistic approach to the development of the large systems.
- The model guides the developer to apply the prototyping approach and customer evaluation is done after that. So the final product made is as per the customer specification.
- It provides maximum customer satisfaction from the final product.
- **Advantages of the spiral model:**
    1. The spiral model is a realistic approach to the development of large-scale software products because the software evolves as the process progresses. In addition, the developer and the client better understand and react to risks at each evolutionary level.
    2. The spiral model uses prototyping as a risk reduction mechanism and allows for the development of prototypes at any stage of the evolutionary development.
    3. It maintains a systematic stepwise approach, like the classic life cycle model, but incorporates it into an iterative framework that more reflect the real world.
    4. If employed correctly, this model should reduce risks before they become problematic, as consideration of technical risks are considered at all stages.
- **Disadvantages of the spiral model:**
    1. Demands considerable risk-assessment expertise
    2. It has not been employed as much proven models (e.g. the WF model) and hence may prove difficult to 'sell' to the client that this model is controllable and efficient.

4.5 PROTOTYPING MODEL (Oct. 09, 12; April 11, 13)

- Prototyping is the process that enables the developer to create a working model of an information system application.
- It allows developer to create a model to the software that must be built.
- The model can take one of the three forms:
    1. A paper prototype or PC-based model.
    2. A working prototype.
    3. An existing program.
- Prototype just gives the idea about the system. It does not contain all features or perform all the necessary functions of the final system.
- Customer evaluates the prototype and then suggests what changes needed in the system. That's why prototyping is an interactive process as it is revised to satisfy the needs of the customer.

- It does not require lot of cost to build. It can be prepared by pen and pencil or computer software like green generators, report generators and application generators.
- The sequences of events for the prototyping are illustrated in Fig. 4.4.

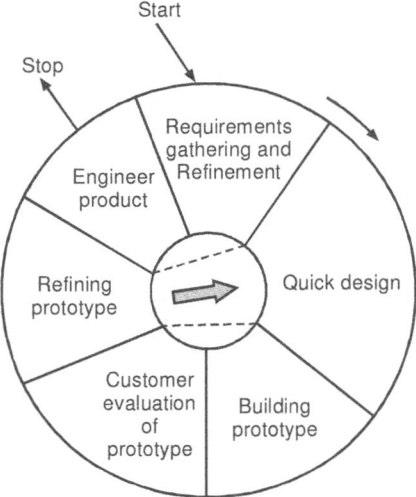

Fig. 4.4: Prototyping model

- Let us see all the steps in prototyping in detail.
    1. **Requirement gathering and Refinement:** Prototyping begins with the requirement gathering. In this step both developer i.e. system analyst and customer [user] work together and define the overall objectives for the software. They both together identify the requirement to be fulfilled.
    2. **Quick design:** This focuses on the representation of those aspects of the software that will be visible to the user. Analyst estimates a prototyping cost and gives this idea to management.
    3. **Building prototype:** The quick design leads to the construction of prototype. A prototype is constructed using several tools. Prototypes are prepared to represent input screen formats and output formats.
    4. **Customer evaluation of prototype:** The prototype is evaluated by the customer or user and is used to refine requirements for the software to be developed. User or customer works on the prototype to evaluate its features and operations.
    5. **Review prototype:** The prototype is refined, after getting information from user about what they want and what they do not want. Developer should understand the need of the customer properly for making modifications in the prototypes.

6. **Repeat as needed:** The process is repeated till both the users and developers find all the necessary features are fulfilled and there is no benefit of repeating the steps. At last user gets **engineer product** with his/her specifications.

- The prototyping is shown in the form of flowchart also. This is shown in Fig. 4.5.

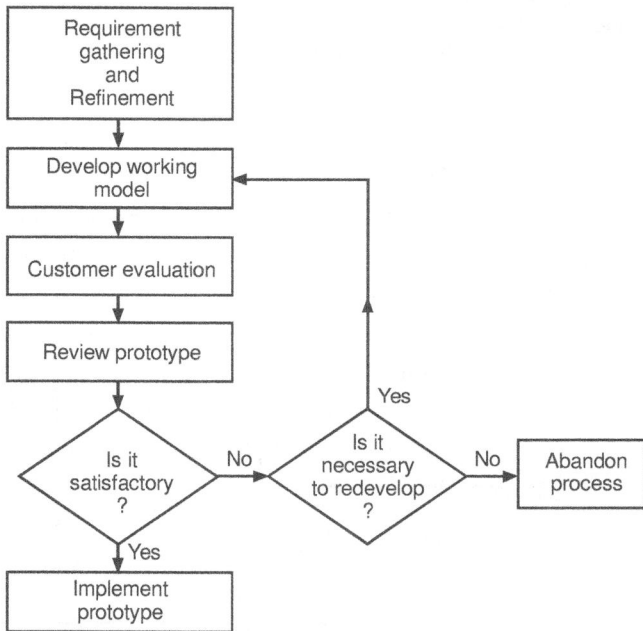

Fig. 4.5: Prototyping flowchart

- The prototype serves as a mechanism for identifying software requirements. The software prototyping and hardware prototyping have different objectives. When designing hardware system, a prototype is normally used to validate the system design.

  For example: Voice-mail. Here, the member subscribe to the system on a monthly basic by paying a fixed fee for services. They are assigned a voice "mailbox" in which incoming messages are stored. Each subscriber is given a 4-digit identification number. Subscriber has to dial 4-digit identification number whether he has to receive a message or send a message. She can send message anywhere in the world by knowing the telephone number of a person. The features of televoice system are shown in Fig. 4.6.

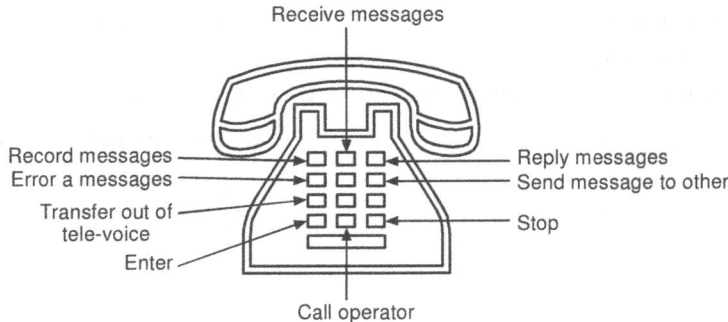

Fig. 4.6: Features of a Tele-voice system

- A software prototype is not normally intended for validation but to help, develop and check the real requirements for the system. The prototype design is quite different from that of the final system.

- If we compare the classic model with prototyping the following difference we can see where error detection is done in different ways. This is illustrated in Fig. 4.7 (a) and (b).

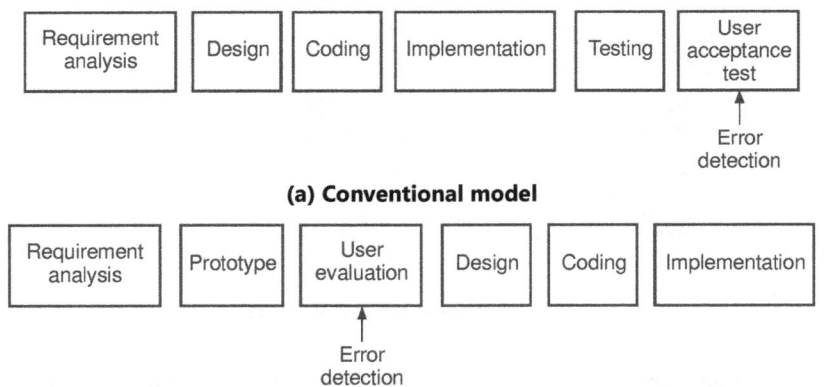

Fig. 4.7: Time for error detection

4.5.1 Benefits   (April 10; Oct. 11)

- The benefits of developing a prototyping early in the software process are:
    1. It saves time in system development.
    2. Encourages the communication between developer and user.
    3. Misunderstandings between software developers and users may be identified as the system functions are demonstrated.
    4. Missing user-services may be detected.

5. Prototyping helps to build the system with user's satisfaction and avoid wrong system delivery.
6. Difficult-to use or confusing user services may be identified and refined.
7. The prototype serves as a basis for writing the specification for a production quality system.
8. System can be delivered within proper time and therefore delays are minimized.
9. As prototype are developed quickly, demonstration to the management is possible to check feasibility and usefulness of the application.
10. If proper tools are used, low cost is required for development of prototype.

- Gordon and Bieman studied 39 different prototyping projects and found following benefits of using prototypes in the software process in 1995:
  - Improved system usability.
  - A closer match of the system to the users need.
  - Improved design quality.
  - Improved maintainability.
  - Reduced development effort.

4.5.2 Tools for Prototyping

- The tools for prototyping are listed below:
  1. **Screen generators:** Automatically input validation screens are prepared. It is useful to show the location of data entry field, display fields, headings of columns, labels, messages, colours, fonts etc.
  2. **Report generators:** The records from various files are extracted from the existing database and their reports are generated with some format.
  3. **Application generators:** There are software programs that permits the specification of an entire application at a very high level. They can accept input, validate data, perform calculations, interact with files and produce output.
  4. **4 GL:** We will see it in detail in next point.

Classical Model (Oct. 10)

- In the classical or traditional approach, SDLC concentrates on feasibility analysis, cost-benefit analysis, project management, hardware and software selection and personnel consideration.
- The basic idea of SDLC is that there is a well defined process by which a system is conceived, develop and implemented.
- System development is an interactive process. This includes following stages or activities:
  - Preliminary investigation.
  - System analysis.

-
    - System design.
    - System development/coding.
    - System testing.
    - System implementation and Evaluation.
    - System maintenance.
- This is referred as **classical SDLC**. These activities are shown in Fig. 4.8.

Fig. 4.8: Classical SDLC

- In practice, these steps may or may not be clearly defined in a given system. These stages may overlap. It is similar that while working on a particular stage, system analyst also considers possible solution related to the next phase. He may take review or revise the decision taken earlier in previous phase.

4GL Approach

- The majority of business applications involve manipulating data from a database and producing outputs which again organize and format that data. To support the development of these applications, all commercial database management systems now support database programming.
- The database programming is carried out using a specialized language which uses knowledge of database and includes database manipulation operations.
- This language provides a tool to support user interface definition, numeric computation and report generation. The term **fourth generation language** is used to refer both the database programming language and its supportive environment.
- Fourth generation language techniques are based on Non-Procedural Language (NPL) technique. In procedural language we have to specify about **what** is required and **how** to do it whereas, non-procedural language specify **what** is required only.

- 4GL technique uses software tool which automatically generates source code based on the developers specifications. This also focuses on the ability to specify software using specialized language forms or a graphic notation that describes the problem to be solved which a customer can understand.
- The fourth generation technology includes the tools like non-procedural language for database query, report generation, screen interaction, data manipulation and code generation. It means that 4GL technology fulfills the need to end-users.
- The user interface usually consists of a set of standard forms or a spreadsheet. The tools which are included in a 4GL are shown in Fig. 4.9.

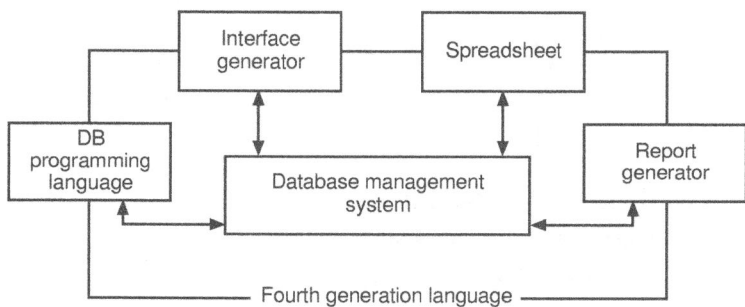

Fig. 4.9: 4GL components

- A database programming language is a query language which is to create forms filled in by the end-user so that system can take input.
- An interface generator which is used to create forms for data input and display.
- A spreadsheet is needed for the analysis and manipulation of numeric information. A report generator is used to create reports from the database. The examples of 4GL are FOCUS, SQL, NOMAD, MYSQL, POSTGRESQL etc.
- The 4GL technology begins with a requirement gathering step. Then the operational prototype is prepared using tools. **CASE tools** i.e. computer aided software engineering tools offers a credible solution to many software problems. Using 4GL lot of time required for modeling, coding can be saved to increase the productivity.

4.6 RAD MODEL (Oct. 09; April 11)

- Rapid Application Development (RAD) is a linear sequential software development model that emphasizes an extremely short development.
- Used primarily for information system's applications, the RAD approach encompasses the following phases, illustrated in following Fig. 4.10.
    - Business Modeling (BM),
    - Process Modeling (PM),

- Testing and Turnover (TT),
- Data Modeling (DM), and
- Application Generation (AG).

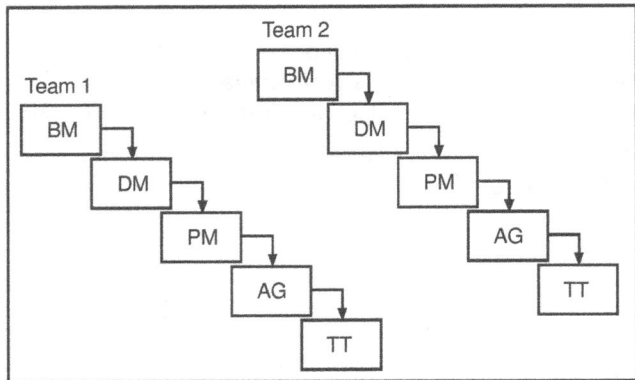

Fig. 4.10: RAD Model

1. **Business Modeling (BM) :** The information flow among business functions is modeled in a way that answers the following questions :
   - What information drives the business process ?
   - What information is generated ?
   - Who generates it ?
   - Where does the information go ?
   - Who processes it ?

2. **Data Modeling (DM) :** The information flow defined as part of the business modeling phase is refined into a set of data objects that are needed to support the business. The characteristics (called attributes) of each object are identified and the relationships between these objects are defined.

3. **Process Modeling (PM) :** The data objects defined in the data-modeling phase are transformed to achieve the information flow necessary to implement a business function. Processing descriptions are created for adding, modifying, deleting, or retrieving a data object.

4. **Application Generation (AG) :** RAD assumes the use of the RAD fourth generation techniques and tools like VB, VC++, Delphi etc rather than creating software using conventional third generation programming languages. The RAD works to reuse existing program components (when possible) or create reusable components (when necessary). In all cases, automated tools are used to facilitate construction of the software.

5. **Testing and Turnover (TT) :** Since, the RAD process emphasizes reuse, many of the program components have already been tested. This minimizes the testing and development time.

- **Advantages of RAD model are :**
  1. Flexible and adaptable to changes.
  2. Prototyping applications gives users a tangible description from which to judge whether critical system requirements are being met by the system. Report output can be compared with existing reports. Data entry forms can be reviewed for completeness of all fields, navigation, data access (drop down lists, checkboxes, radio buttons, etc.).
  3. RAD generally incorporates short development cycles - users see the RAD product quickly.
  4. RAD involves user participation thereby increasing chances of early user community acceptance.
  5. RAD realizes an overall reduction in project risk.
- **Disadvantages of RAD model are :** (W - 08)
  1. For Large (but scalable) projects, RAD requires sufficient resources to create the right number of RAD teams.
  2. RAD projects will fail if there is no commitment by the developers or the clients to 'rapid-fire' activities necessary to get a system complete in a much abbreviated time frame.
  3. If a system cannot be properly modularized, building components for RAD will be problematic.
  4. RAD is not appropriate when technical risks are high, e.g. this occurs when a new application makes heavy use of new technology.

Incremental Model

- The incremental model combines elements of the linear sequential model (with the iterative philosophy of prototyping, (See Fig. 4.11). Each linear sequence produces a deliverable increment of the software.

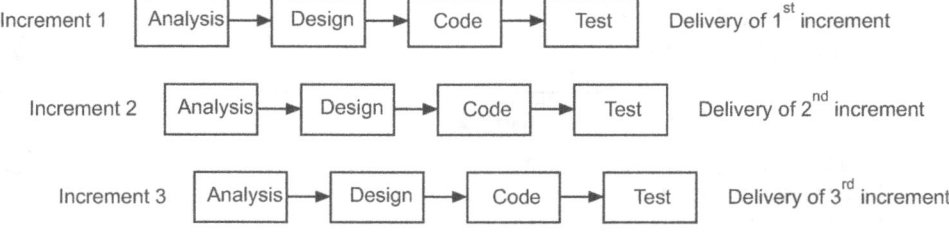

Fig. 4.11: Incremental Model

- The incremental model, is iterative in nature. When an incremental model is used, the first increment is often a "core product". That is, basic requirements are addressed, but many supplementary features remain undelivered.
- Incremental development is useful when staffing is unavailable for a complete implementation by the business deadline that has been established for the project.
- A problem with incremental development is that the system architecture has to be established before the requirements are complete.

- This means that the requirements tend to be constrained by the architecture that is established. Another, non-technical problem is that this approach to development does not fit well with established contractual models for software developers.
- Contracts for the development must be flexible and established before the requirements are fixed.

Practice Questions

1. What is SDLC ?
2. Explain the classical SDLC model.
3. Explain steps of SDLC.
4. Explain SDLC waterfall model.
5. Explain spiral model in detail.
6. Explain major activities involved in spiral model.
7. What is prototyping ? Explain the steps in prototyping.
8. What are the benefits of prototyping ?
9. Explain the importance of 4GL technique.
10. Write a short note on 4GL.
11. Explain RAD model with suitable diagram.
12. Briefly explain incremental model.

University Questions & Answers

October 2009

1. State advantages of waterfall model. [2 M]
Ans. Please refer to Section 4.3.
2. What is prototyping ? Explain steps in prototyping. [4 M]
Ans. Please refer to Section 4.5.
3. Write short note on: Spiral model. [4 M]
Ans. Please refer to Section 4.4

April 2010

1. Explain advantages of prototyping model. [2 M]
Ans. Please refer to Section 4.5.1.
2. Explain waterfall model in detail. [4 M]
Ans. Please refer to Section 4.3.
3. Write a short note on: Maintenance of system. [4 M]
Ans. Please refer to Section 4.2 phase (6).

October 2010

1. Explain classical SDLC [4 M]
Ans. Please refer to Section 4.5.2.
2. Write short note on: Spiral Model. [4 M]
Ans. Please refer to Section 4.4.

April 2011

1. State advantages of waterfall model. [2 M]
Ans. Please refer to Section 4.3.
2. What is prototyping ? [4 M]
Ans. Please refer to Section 4.5.
3. State stages in SDLC. [2 M]
Ans. Please refer to Section 4.2.1.
4. Discuss spiral model of software development. [2 M]
Ans. Please refer to Section 4.4.

October 2011

1. State advantages of prototype model. [2 M]
Ans. Please refer to Section 4.5.1.
2. Explain waterfall model in detail. [4 M]
Ans. Please refer to Section 4.3.
3. Write short note on: Spiral model. [4 M]
Ans. Please refer to Section 4.4.
4. Write short note on maintenance of system. [4 M]
Ans. Please refer to Section 4.2 phase (6).

April 2012

1. Explain waterfall model in detail. [4 M]
Ans. Please refer to Section 4.3.

October 2012

1. What is economical feasibility? [2 M]
Ans. Please refer to Section 4.2.1.
2. What are advantages of waterfall model ? [4 M]
Ans. Please refer to Section 4.3.
3. Implementation and maintenance. [4 M]
Ans. Please refer to Section 4.2.1.

April 2013

1. Explain prototyping model. [4 M]
Ans. Please refer to Section 4.5.

April 2014

1. Define technical feasibility. [4 M]
Ans. Please refer to Section 4.2.1.
2. Explain waterfall model.
Ans. Please refer to Section 4.3.

❖❖❖

Chapter 5...
Analysis and Design Tools

Contents ...

This chapter gives basic concepts of system such as:

5.1 INTRODUCTION

5.2 ENTITY-RELATIONSHIP DIAGRAMS
- 5.2.1 Entity
- 5.2.2 Entity Set
- 5.2.3 Attribute
- 5.2.4 Relationship
- 5.2.5 Relationship Set
- 5.2.6 Mapping Cardinality

5.3 DECISION TREES AND DECISION TABLES
- 5.3.1 Decision Trees
- 5.3.2 Decision Tables

5.4 DATA FLOW DIAGRAMS (DFDs)
- 5.4.1 Characteristics
- 5.4.2 Symbols of DFD
- 5.4.3 DFD Principles
- 5.4.4 Types of DFD

5.5 DATA DICTIONARY
- 5.5.1 Elements of Data Dictionary

5.6 PSEUDO CODE
- 5.6.1 What is Pseudocode?
- 5.6.2 Why is Pseudocode Necessary ?
- 5.6.3 Rules for Pseudocode
- 5.6.4 How to write Pseudocode ?
- 5.6.5 Advantages
- 5.6.6 Disadvantages

5.7 INPUT AND OUTPUT DESIGN
- 5.7.1 Input Design
- 5.7.2 Output Design

5.1 INTRODUCTION

- A Software Engineering begins with a series of modeling tasks which will give a complete specification of requirements and a design representation for the software to be built.
- The starting contains determining the system requirements. System requirements contain identifying the features needed in a system.
- The analyst understands the system first and find outs inputs, outputs and the processes. Here, we are going to study the analysis and design tools. It helps us in understanding large and complete systems.

5.2 ENTITY RELATIONSHIP DIAGRAMS (Oct. 09, 10; April 10, 12)

- Entity Relationship (E–R) diagrams is a design tool.
- E-R diagarams is a graphical representation of the database system which provides a high-level conceptual data model and supports the user's perception of the data.

5.2.1 Entity (April 12)

- An entity is an object in the real world that is distinguishable from all other objects.
- An entity is a thing in the real world with an independent existence.
- An entity has a set of properties or attributes and the values for some set of attributes or properties may uniquely identify an entity.
- An entity can be concrete or abstract.

    For example: Student, Account, Person are the entities.

    Student is an entity with properties (attributes) roll_no and class, of a student uniquely identifies the student (entity).

    Student is concrete entity whereas Day, Class are abstract entities.

    Entity Student:

    | Ashwin | 4320 | S.E. |

    Fig. 5.1: An Entity

5.2.2 Entity Set

- Entity set is a set of entities of the same type that share the same properties or attributes.
- Entity sets need not be disjoint.

    For example, the set of all students is defined as entity set student.

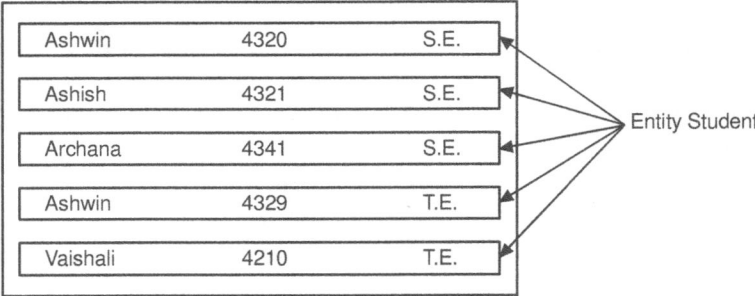

Student entity set

Fig. 5.2: An entity set

5.2.3 Attribute

- Each entity has a set of attributes. Each attribute has a domain from which the values for this attribute are drawn.
- Following are the attribute types:

    1. **Simple and Composite Attribute:** Simple attributes can not be divided into subparts, on the other hand composite attributes can be divided into subparts.

       For example, Consider customer entity with following attributes:

       ```
       Customer_no.
       Customer_address
       ```

       Here, customer_no. is simple attribute, and customer_address is composite attribute, which can be further divided into following components.

       ```
       Street_address
       Street_no.
       Apt_number
       ```

    2. **Single-valued and Multi-valued Attributes:** Single-valued attribute has single value for a particular entity.

       Multi-valued attribute has a set of values for a specific entity.

       For example, Consider the entity customer with attributes.

       ```
       Customer_no.
       Customer_address
       ```

       Where one may have two addresses.

       Here, customer_no. is a single-valued attribute. It refers to only one customer.

       But customer_address is multi-valued attribute. Customer_address may have any number of values.

3. **Null Attribute:** Null value is used when an entity does not have a value for an attribute.

   Null can also designate that an attribute is unknown. (i.e. missing or not known).

4. **Derived Attribute:** The value for this type of attribute can be derived from the values of other related attributes or entities.

5.2.4 Relationship   (Oct. 12)

- **Relationship is an association among several entities.**
- Consider the following two entity sets.

  Customer with attributes: (name, address, social_security)

  Account with attributes: (acc_no. balance, type)

  Cust_Acc is a relation between two entities customer and account, which specifies which account belongs to which customer.

5.2.5 Relationship Set

- It is a set of relationships of same type.
- Formally, it is mathematical relation on n ≥ 2 (possibly non distinct) entity sets.

  If $E_1, E_2, ..., E_n$ are entity sets, then a relationship set R is a subset of {$(e_1, e_2, ..., e_n)$ | $e_1 \in E_1, e_2 \in E_2, e_n \in E_n$} where $(e_1, e_2, ..., e_n)$ is a relationship.

  Consider the following two entity sets.

  Account = {acc_no., balance, type}

  Customer = {name, city, social_security}

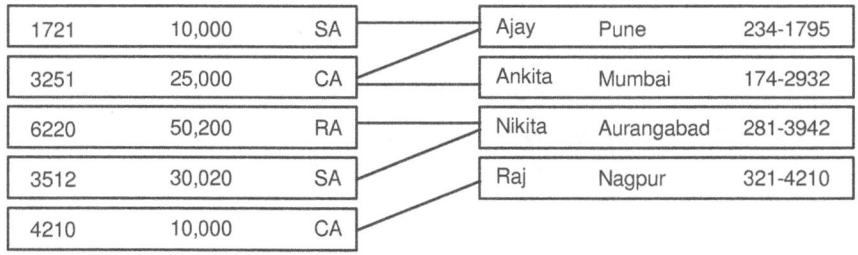

Fig. 5.3: Customer account relationship set

- Binary Relationship Set relates two entity sets. n-ary Relationship Set relates 'n' number of entity sets. n-ary relationship set can be replaced by binary relationship set.

5.2.6 Mapping Cardinality

- Mapping cardinality or cardinality ratio expresses the number of entities to which another entity can be associated via a relationship set.
- Mapping cardinalities are most useful in describing binary relationship sets.

- For a binary relationship set R between two entity sets A and B, the mapping cardinality must be one of the following.

  1. **One-to-One:** An entity in 'A' is associated with at most one entity in 'B' and an entity in 'B' is associated with at most one entity in 'A'.

     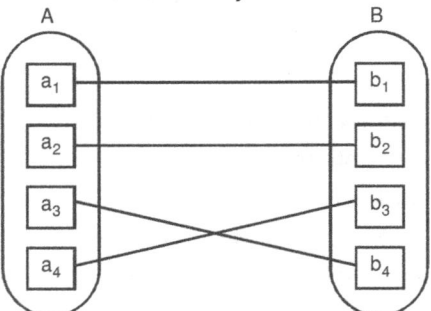

     Fig. 5.4: One-to-One

  2. **One-to-Many:** An entity in 'A' is associated with any number of entities in 'B'. An entity in 'B', however, can be associated with at most one entity in 'A'.

     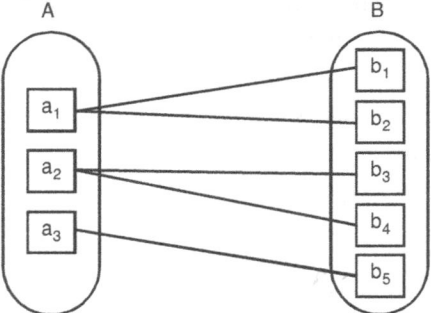

     Fig. 5.5: One-to-Many

  3. **Many-to-One:** An entity in 'A' is associated with at most one entity in 'B'. An entity in 'B', however can be associated with any number of entities in 'A'.

     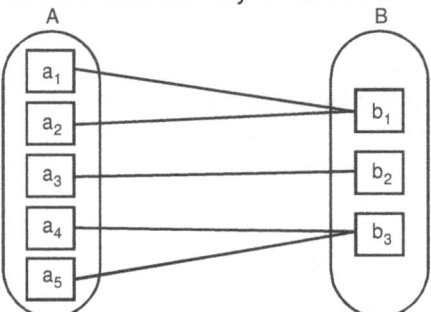

     Fig. 5.6: Many-to-One

4. Many-to-Many: An entity in 'A' is associated with any number of entities in 'B' and an entity in 'B' is associated with any number of entities in 'A'.

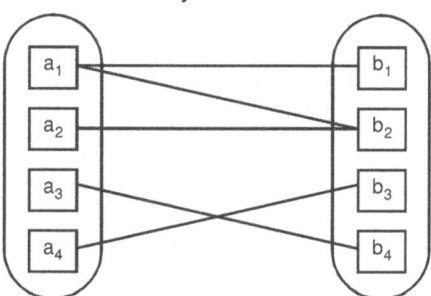

Fig. 5.7: Many-to-Many

- Following are the symbols used in E-R diagram. **(Oct. 10, 11)**

1.	Rectangles	:	Represent entity set.
2.	Ellipses	:	Represent attributes.
3.	Diamonds	:	Represent relationship set.
4.	Lines	:	Link attributes to entity sets and relationship sets.
5.	Double ellipse	:	Represent multi-valued attribute.
6.	Dashed ellipse	:	Represent derived attribute.
7.	Double lines	:	Indicate total participation of an entity in a relationship set.
8.	Double rectangle	:	Represent weak entity set.

Representation of Mapping Cardinalities

- Mapping cardinality is indicated by directed line (→) or undirected line (—).
- Consider two entities,

   Customer – {cust_name, social_security, address}

   Account – {acc_no, balance}

   Relationship set is depositor with attributes {social_security, acc_no}.

1. If the relationship is many-to-many i.e. one customer may have any number of accounts and one account can be shared by any number of customers, then this cardinality is represented as follows.

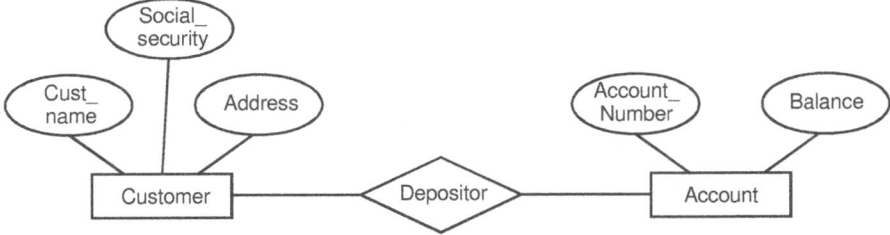

Fig. 5.8: Many-to-Many

2. If the relationship is one-to-many i.e. one customer may have any number of accounts, but one account belongs to only one customer then this cardinality is represented as follows:

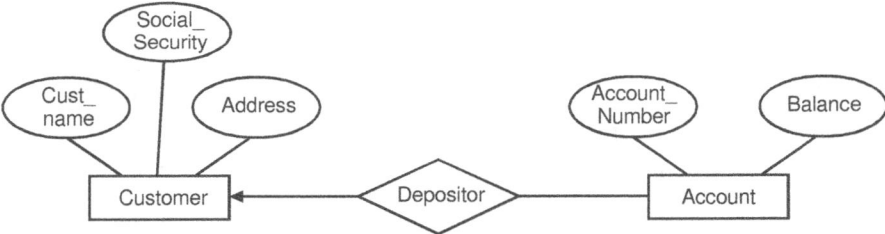

Fig. 5.9: One-to-Many

3. If the relationship is many-to-one i.e. many customers can share one account, then this cardinality is represented as follows:

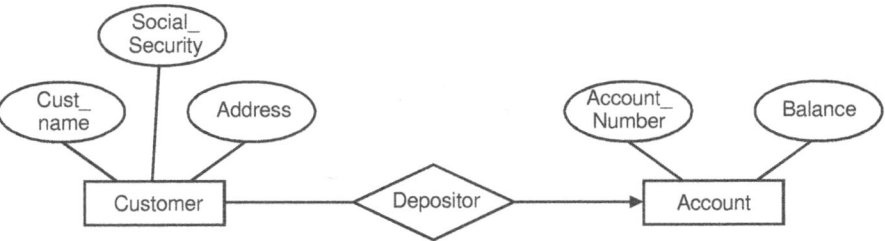

Fig. 5.10: Many-to-One

4. If the relationship is one-to-one i.e. each customer has one account and each account belongs to one customer, then this cardinality is represented as follows:

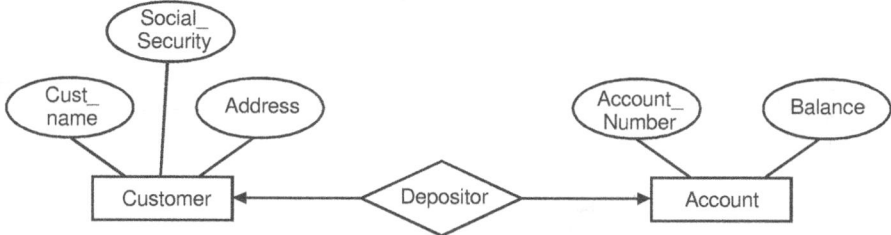

Fig. 5.11: One-to-One

Representation of Non-Binary Relationship:

Consider a ternary relationship set CAB which relates three entities.

Customer – {cust_name, social_security, street, city}

Account – {acc_no., balance}

Branch – {branch_name, city, assets}

Here, one customer may have several accounts, one account may belong to several customers.

Representation of weak entity set:

Weak entity sets are represented by a doubly outlined box.

Consider entity sets.

Account – {Account_no. balance}

Transaction – {transaction_no, date, amount}

where transaction is a weak entity set which is dependent on account entity. This can be represented as:

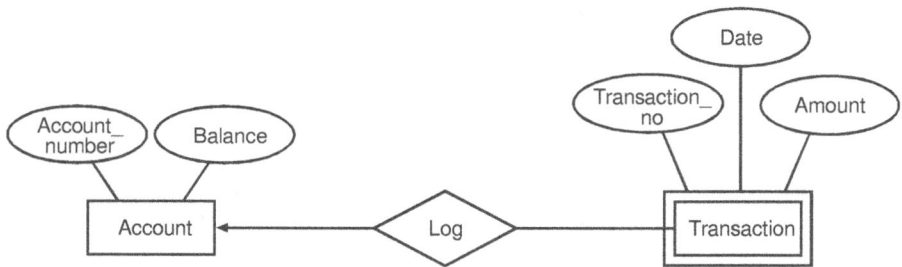

Fig. 5.12: Weak entity set

Weak entity set can also be represented as a multi-valued composite attribute of strong entity set.

SOLVED EXAMPLES

Example 1: Construct an E-R diagram for a car-insurance company that has a set of customers, each of whom owns one or more cars. Each car has associated with it zero to any number of recorded accidents.

Solution:

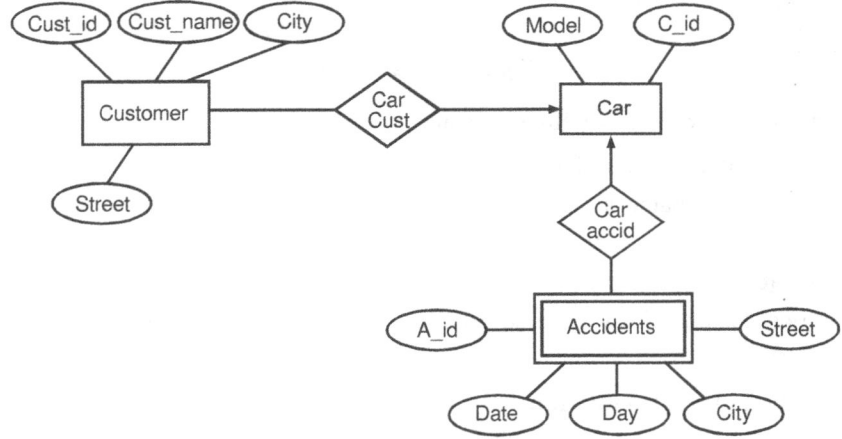

Fig. 5.13: E-R diagram - Car-insurance company

Example 2: Construct an E-R diagram for a hospital with a set of patients and a set of medical doctors. Associate with each patient a log of the various tests and examination conducted.

Solution:

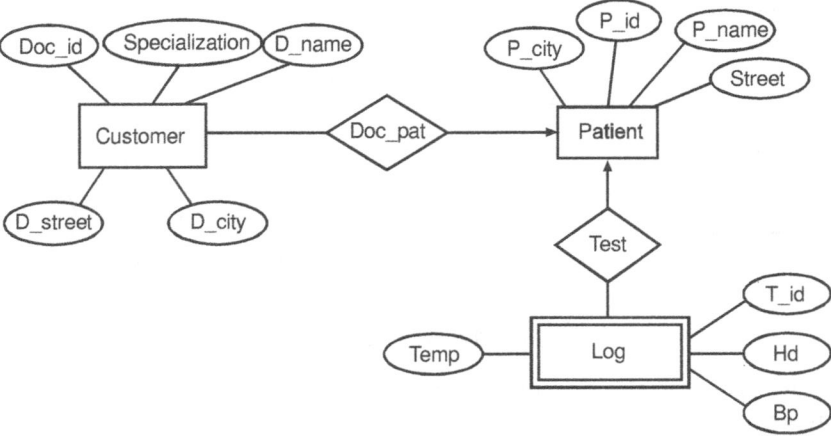

Fig. 5.14: E-R diagram - Hospital

Example 3: An insurance agent sells insurance policies to clients. Policies can be of different types such as vehicle insurance, life insurance, accident insurance etc. The agent collects monthly premiums on the policies in the form of cheques of local banks. Appropriate attributes must be assumed for various entities such as agents, vehicles, policy.

Draw an E-R model for above system. Your E-R model should take advantage of extended E-R notation where relevant.

Solution:

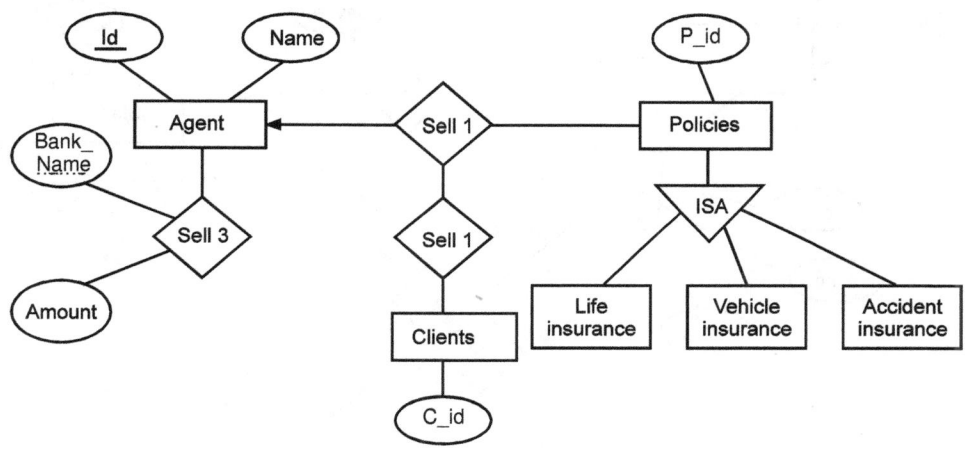

Fig. 5.15: E-R diagram - Insurance

Example 4: Following information is maintained manually in a library.

Books (Accession_number, name, authors, price, book_type, publisher)

Borrowers (membership_no., name, address,
 category, max_no of books that can be issued,
 Accession_number of books borrowed)

The following constraints are observed:

1. Each book has unique accession-number.
2. A book may have more than one author.
3. There may be more than one copy of a book.
4. The category of borrower determines the max. Number of books that may be issued to borrower.

Identify the entities, relationship and draw E-R diagram.

Provide for issue and return of book, fine calculation and claiming of an issued book.

Solution:

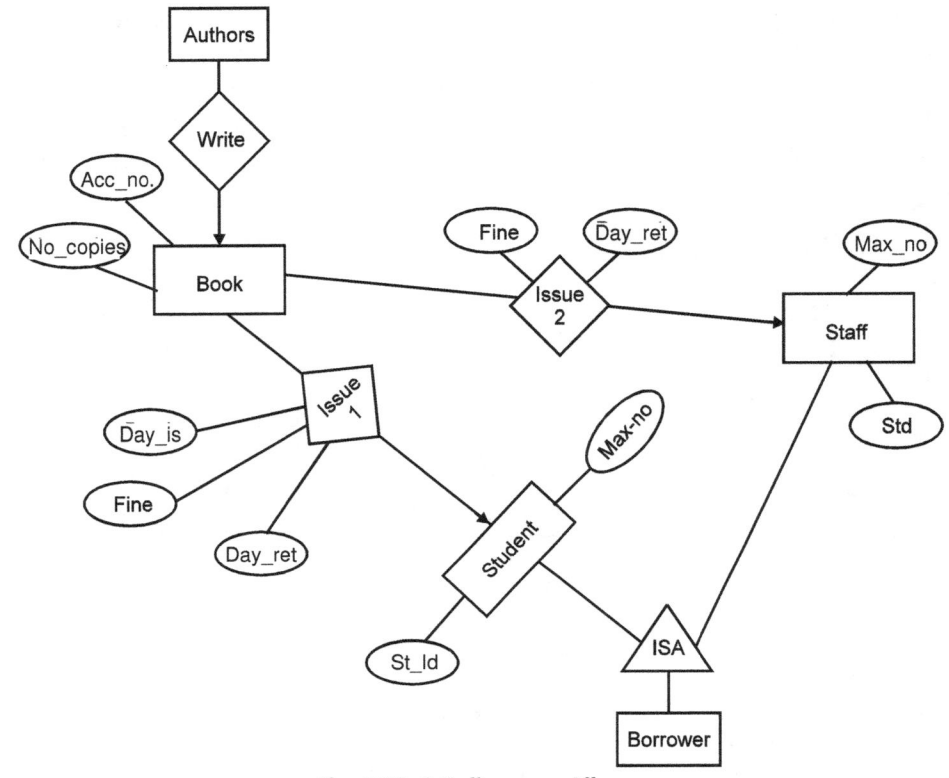

Fig. 5.16: E-R diagram - Library

Example 5: It is required to set-up medical record database system, given the following data.

- Patients identification number name, address date of birth, blood group.
- Physician identification number name, address and their specialties
- Data about patients visit to physician like the date of visit, the medicine prescribed, the dose of each medicine, tests ordered at the visit, result of those tests, temperature, blood pressure.

Give an E-R diagram for the database.

Solution:

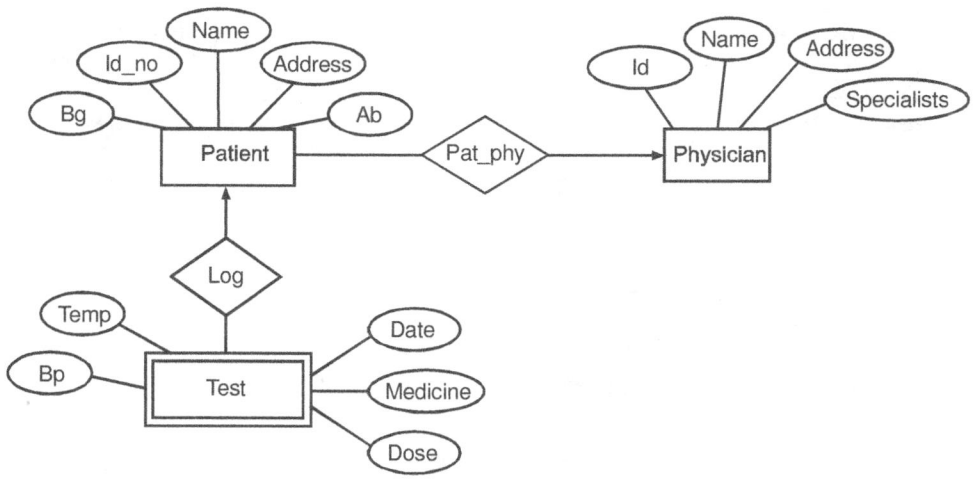

Fig. 5.17: E-R diagram - Hospital database

Example 6: A post office has few postmen who go everyday to distribute letters. Every morning post office receives a large number of registered letters. The post office intends to create a database to keep track of these letters.

- Every letter has a sender, an origin post office from where it was sent, a destination post office to which it is to be sent, a date of registration, date of arrival at destination post office, receiver and a status.
- Every sender has a name, an address.
- Every receiver has a name and an address.
- Every postman has a designated area where he delivers letters.
- The area consists of a set of streets under the jurisdiction of the post office.
- Every street consists of a set of buildings.
- Every building has a number and may be a name. It may be housing more than one family.
- The status of the letter can be not yet taken for delivery, delivered, addressee not available, address not known; addressee did not accept the letter, redirected to the new address of the addressee and sent to the sender.

Draw the E-R diagram.

Solution:

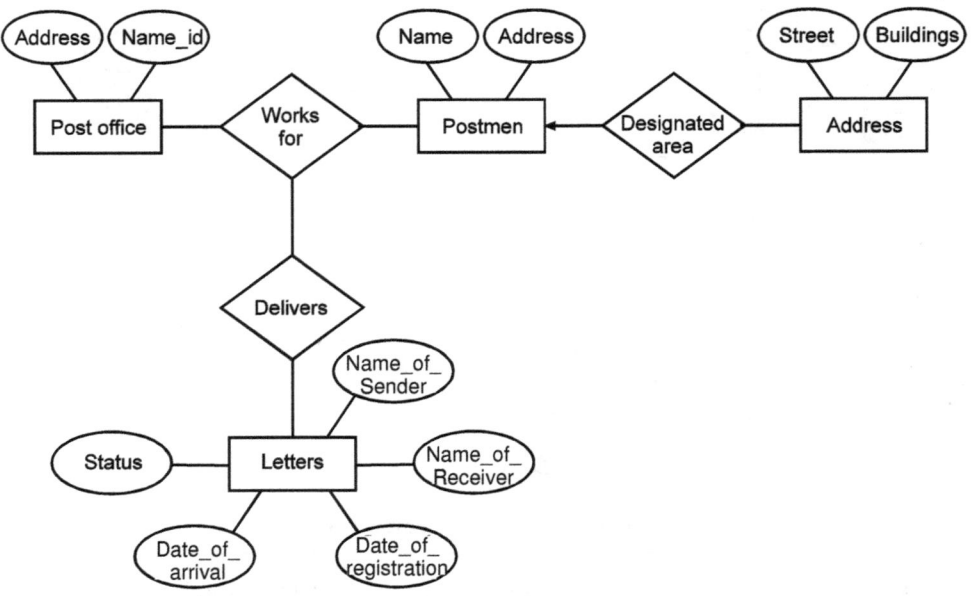

Fig. 5.18: E-R diagram - Post office

Example 7: A university database contains information about professors and courses. For each of the following situations, draw an E-R diagram that describes it.

1. Professors can teach the same course in several semesters, and only the most recent such offerings need to be recorded.
2. Professors can teach the same course in several semesters, and each offering is to be recorded.
3. Every professor must teach some course.
4. Every professor teaches exactly one course.
5. Every professor teaches exactly one course and each course must be taught by one professor.
6. Now suppose that team of professors can teach certain courses jointly, but it is possible that no one professor in a team can teach the course. Model this situation, introducing additional entity sets and relationship sets if necessary.

Solution:

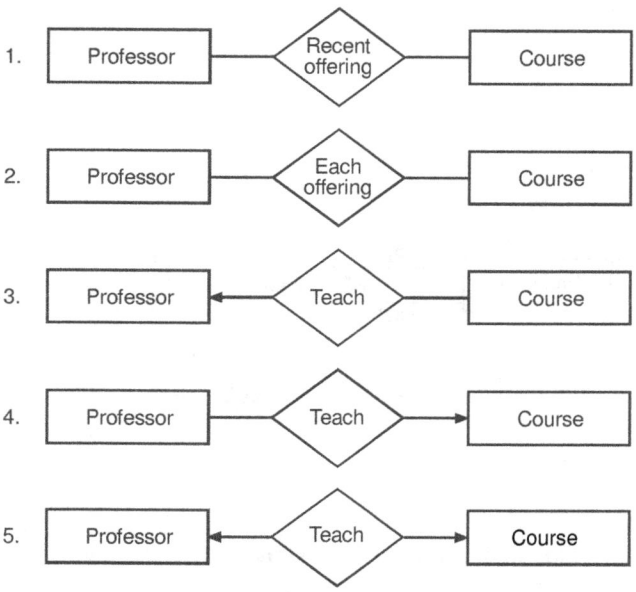

Fig. 5.19: E-R diagram - Professor

Example 8: Consider the following information about a university database.

- Professors have an id, a name, an age, a rank and a research area.
- Projects have a project number, a funding agency, a starting date, and finish data and a budget.
- Under-graduate students have an id, a name, an age, a course.
- Each project is managed by one professor, called as Principal Investigator.
- One or more professors, called as Co-investigators, work each project on.
- When graduate students work on a project, a professor must supervise their work on the project.
- Graduate students can work on multiple projects in which case they will have different supervisor for each one.
- Departments have a department number, department name and an office.
- Departments have a professor known as HOD.

Design and draw the E-R diagram.

Solution:

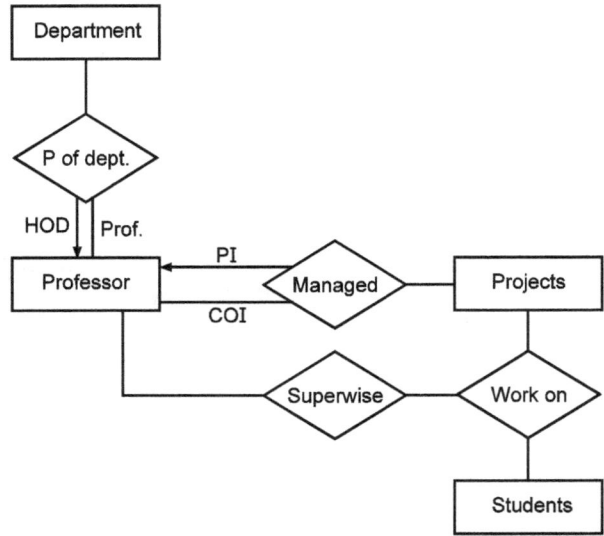

Fig. 5.20: E-R diagram – University department

Example 9: Draw an E-R diagram for a relational database that represents the current term enrollment at Pune University with following assertions. There are 2000 instructors, 4000 courses and 30,000 students.
1. An instructor may teach none, one or more courses in a given term (average 2.0 courses).
2. An instructor must direct the research of at least one student(average 2.0 students).
3. A course may have none, one or two prerequisite courses.
4. A course may exists even if no student has currently enrolled for that.
5. All courses are taught by only one instructor.
6. The average enrollment in E-R a course is 30 students.
7. A student must select at least one course per term.

Solution:

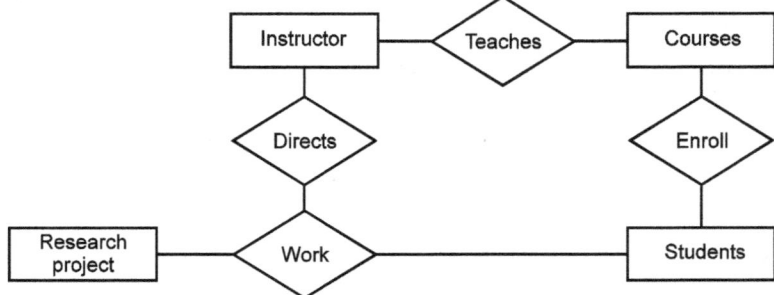

Fig. 5.21: E-R diagram - Team enrollment at Pune University

Example 10: The people's bank offer five types of accounts: Loan, Checking,, Premium Savings, daily interest saving, and money market. It operates a number of accounts. Account can be joint, i.e. more than one client may be able to operate a given account.

Identify entities and draw E-R Diagram.

Solution:

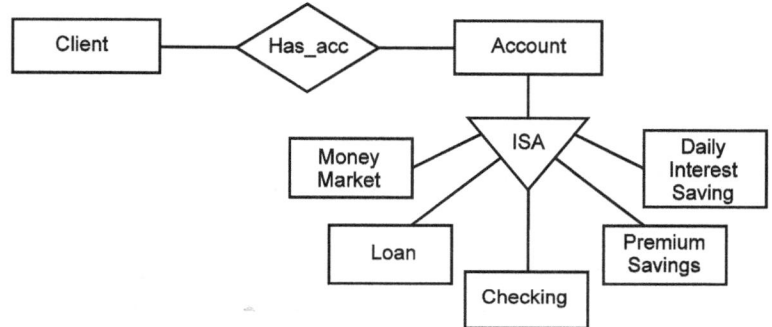

Fig. 5.22: E-R diagram - Bank Account

5.3 DECISION TREES AND DECISION TABLES

5.3.1 Decision Trees (Oct. 09, 11, 12; April 10, 11, 12, 13, 14)

- It is a tool which is used to portary the logic of the policy.
- It shows the detail request by using a tree like structure, in which number of branches and level are used. Decision trees are easy to conduct and easy to update.
- **Conditions:** If analyst is finding out a possibility or if the analyst is searching for what can happen then he is asking about conditions i.e. the possible set of an entity. The condition always vary and depending on the condition analyst need to take certain action.
- **Action:** When all possible conditions are known then analyst next determines what to do when certain condition occurs ? This is action. Actions are alternatives, the steps, activities or procedures that an individual many decide to take.
- For example, People often have different ways of saying the same thing.
  1. Greater than ₹ 10,000, ₹ 5000 but less than or equal ₹ 10,000 and below ₹ 5000.
  2. Not less than ₹ 10,000, not more than 10,000, but at least ₹ 5000 and not ₹ 5000 or more having different ways of saying the same thing can create the difficulties in communication during system analysis. Therefore, three exist number of tools to avoid such difficulties in communication.

5.3.1.1 Definition

- A decision tree is a diagram that presents condition and action sequentially thus show which condition is consider first, which second and so on. Decision trees are also a method of showing the relationship of each condition and its possible actions.

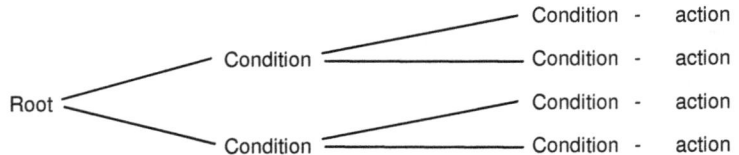

Fig. 5.23: Decision tree

- The root of the tree to the left of the diagram is the starting point of decision to be followed depends on the condition that exist and the decision to be made. Progression from left to right along a particular branch is a result of making series of decisions.
- The nodes of the trees represent condition and indicate that a determination must be made about which condition exist before next path can be selected.
- The right side of the tree lists action to be taken, depending on sequence of condition that is followed.

5.3.1.2 Developing Decision Trees

- Developing decision trees is beneficial to analyst in 2 ways first of all, they need to describe condition and action, forces the analyst to formally identify the actual decision that must be made.
- Therefore, it becomes difficult for analyst to overlook an integral step in the decision process. Decision trees also force analyst to consider the sequence of decisions.

5.3.1.3 Problems with Decision Trees

- Decision Trees may not always be a best tools for decision analysis. The decision trees growth for complex system in which many sequences of steps and combinations of conditions is uncontrollable.
- A large number of branches with many path always confused the analyst rather than helping. By observing such big decision trees, analyst can not find out whether, the actual problem arises.
- For example, Consider the company which gives discounts based on amounts on three different values as follows.
- If payment is made within 10 days and the purchasing amount more than 10,000 then company offers 3% discount on invoice. If the purchasing amount is between 5000 to

10,000 then company offer 2% discount and if amount < 5000 then no discount offer and customer has to pay full invoice amount. If customer is not paying within 10 lays then if he is regular customer then 1% discount is offer for amount more than 10,000 else no discount is offer and customers has to pay full invoice amount.

Draw decision tree for the above problem.

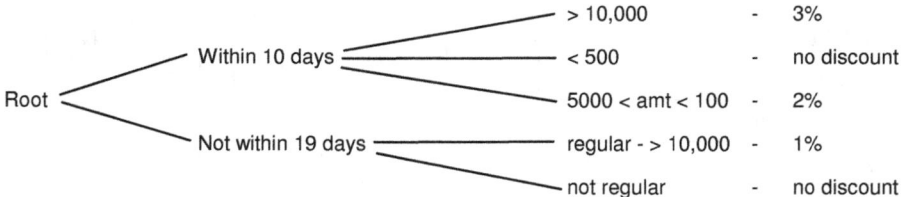

Fig. 5.24: Decision tree of company on discounts

5.3.2 Decision Tables (Oct. 09, 10, 11, 12, 13; April 10, 11, 12, 13, 14)

- It is a matrix of rows and columns, rather than a tree, that shows conditions and actions.
- Decision rules included in decision tables state what procedure to follow when certain condition exist.

    Decision table made up of four sections:

    (i) Condition statements

    (ii) Condition entries

    (iii) Action statements

    (iv) Action entries

- Condition statement identifies the relevant condition. Condition entries tells which value if any applies for particular condition.
- Action statements list set of all steps that can be taken when certain condition occur. Action entries show what specific action is the set to take when selected conditions or combinations of conditions are true.
- Sometimes, nodes are added below the table to indicate when to use a table or to distinguish it from other decision tables.
- The columns of the right side of the table, linking conditions and action forms the decision rule, which states the condition that must be satisfied for particular set of actions to be taken. The decision rules incorporates all the conditions that must be true and not just one condition at a time.
- The format of decision table is as on the next page.

Condition Rules	Decision Rules					
Decision Rules	Condition entries					
Action statement	Action entries					
1. Within 10 days	Y	Y	Y	N	N	
2. Over 10,000	Y	N	N	Y	N	N
3. 5000 to 10,000	N	Y	N	N	Y	N
4. Below 5000	N	N	Y	N	N	Y
1. 3% discount	X					
2. 2% discount		X				
3. Pay full invoice			X	X	X	X

- Develop a decision table which declares the student examination result using the following rules. There are two subjects in the examination called main and ancillary. If a person gets 50% or more in the main subject and 40% or more in the ancillary he passes. If he gets less than 50% in the main he must get 50% or more in the ancillary to pass. However, there are a group of students in the class who are granted special consideration. Their pass percentage 40% in the main and 40% in the ancillary. If they get less than 40% in the ancillary they are allow to repeat that subject if they obtain 40% or more in the main subject.

    1. ≥ 50% in main and ≥ 40% in ancillary
    2. < 50% in main and > 50% in ancillary
    3. ≥ 40% in main and ≥ 40% in ancillary
    4. ≥ 40% in main and < 40% in ancillary
    5. Special category.

< 40% in main and < 40% in anci.	N	N	N	N	N	Y
< 50% in main and < 40% in anci.	N	N	N	N	Y	N
1. ≥ 50% in main and ≥ 40% in anci.	Y	N	N	N	N	N
2. < 50% in main and > 50% in anci.	N	Y	N	N	N	N
3. ≥ 40% in main and ≥ 40% in anci.	N	N	Y	N	N	N
4. ≥ 40% in main and < 40% in anci.	N	N	N	Y	N	N
5. Special category.	N	N	Y	Y	N	Y
Pass	X	X	X			
Repeat				X		
Fail					X	X

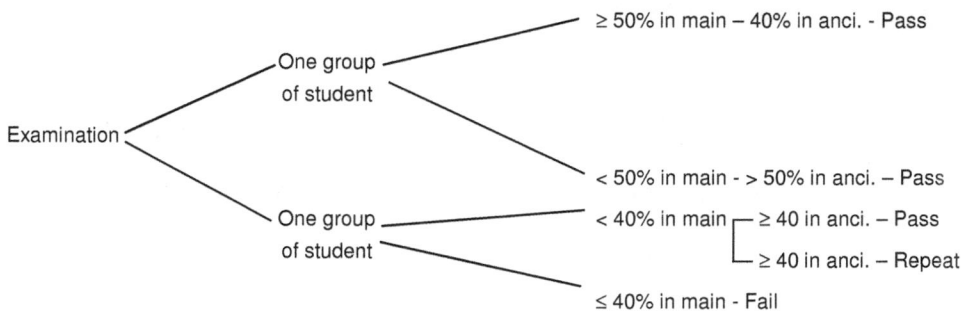

Fig. 5.25: Decision tree of examination

- Same as before problem, consider a company which is offering certain discount on the total amount of purchase. If the purchase amount is > 10,000 and the customer is making the payment within 10 days then 3% discount is offer on the total invoice amount. If the total purchase amount is < 10,000 and the payment is made within 10 days then the total of 2% discount is offer and the total amount is < 5000 and person is paying within 10 days then no discount is offer on the invoice. If the person is taking more than 10 days to pay then he has to pay full invoice amount. Draw decision tree for this.

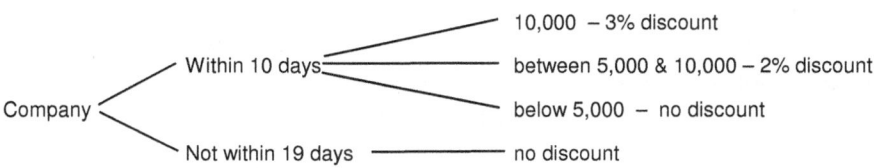

Fig. 5.26: Decision tree of examination

Condition Rules	Decision Rules					
	1	2	3	4	5	6
1. Within 10 days	Y	Y	Y	Y	N	N
2. More than 10,000	N	N	N	Y	N	N
3. Between 5,000 and 10,000	N	Y	N	N	Y	N
4. Below 5,000	N	N	Y	N	N	Y
1. 3%	X					
2. 2%		X				
3. No discount			X	X	X	X

5.3.2.1 Building Decision Tables

- For building a decision table follow the following steps:

    Step - 1: Determine the most relevant factors to be considered in making a decision. This identifies the conditions in the decision. Each selected condition should have the potential to either occur or not occur. That is partial occurrence is not possible.

    Step - 2: Determine the most feasible steps or activities and under varying condition. This identifies the actions.

    Step - 3: Study the combinations of conditions that are possible. For every number N of conditions there are 2^N combinations to be considered.

    For example: For 3 conditions we need to consider 23 i.e. 8 combinations.

    Step - 4: Fill in the table with decision rules.

    Step - 5: Mark action entries with X to indicate actions to take. Leave other cells of action either blank or mark it with - (dash).

    Step - 6: Examine the table for redundant rules or for contradiction within rules.

5.3.2.2 Checking Decision Tables

- After constructing a table, analyst verify it for completeness and correctness, to ensure that the table includes all the conditions along with the decision rules that relate them with the action.

- Analyst should also examine the table for redundancy and contradictions.

1. **Eliminating Redundancy:** Decision tables can become too large if we allow them to grow in an uncontrolled fashion. Removing redundant entries can help us to manage the table size.

- Redundancy occurs when both of the following conditions are true:

    (i) Two decision rules are identical except for one condition row.

    (ii) The actions for the two rules are identical.

- The condition row where they differ can be replace by a blank or a dash to show that the condition does not matter and because the decision rules are redundant we can combine them into one rule.

Decision Rules					
1	2	3	4	5	6
Y	Y	-	N	N	N
Y	N	N	Y	N	N
N	Y	N	N	Y	N
N	N	Y	N	N	Y

Redundancy between 3 and 6.

∴ One row is different and action is same.

2. **Removing Conditions:** Decision rules contradict each other when two or more rules have the same set of conditions and the actions are different.
- Contradictions means either the analyst information is incorrect or there is an error in the construction in the table.

5.3.2.3 Types of Table Entries

1. **Limited Entry Form:** The table structure consisting only of Y, N and blank entries in the condition entry section and X in the action entry section is a limited entry form table. It is one of the most commonly used format. For example, refer above table.

   Volume $\Rightarrow$ Total Transaction.

2. **Extended Entry Form:** The extended entry form replaces Y and N with action entries. In this format the condition and action statements themselves are not-complete.

   $\therefore$ The entry sections contained more details than Y or N.

   For example:

Condition	Decision Rules					
Time	Within 10 days	Within 10 days	Within 10 days	Not within 10 days	Not within 10 days	Not within 10 days
Business volume	Over 10,000	Between 5 and 10,000	Below 5000	Over 10,000	Between 5 and 10,000	Below 5000
Action	3%	2% discount	No discount	No	No	No

3. **Mixed Entry Form:** Analyst may combine the features of both the above form in the same table.

Condition	Decision Rules		
Time	Within 10 days	Within 10 days	Within 10 days
Business volume	Over 10,000	Between 5 and 10,000	Below 5000
3% discount	X		
2% discount		X	
No discount			N

4. **Else form:** This form is used to avoid repetition in table. To build an else form decision table analyst need to specify the rules with condition entries to cover all set

of actions except for 1, which will be the rule to follow when none of the other conditions is true. This rule is in the final column on the right of the table.

For example,

Condition	Decision Rules		
Time	Within 10 days	Within 10 days	Else
Business volume	Over 10,000	Between 5 and 10,000	Else
3% discount	X		
2% discount		X	
No discount			N

5.3.2.4 Multiple Tables (Oct. 09)

- Multiple table is the way by which we can link together multiple decision tables. Depending on the actions selected on the first table, additional actions are explained by one or more additional tables. Each additional table, provides more details about the actions to take.

- Multiple tables also enables the analyst to state what repetitive action should occur after same decisions have been made and will continue until certain condition has been reached.

- To use this method system analyst construct a separate decision table that meet all of the normal requirement and deal with specific decision.

- The tables are linked together in hierarchical fashion.

- A top level table contains the measure condition which determines what conditions, additional actions and tables to refer for further details.

- A transfer statement such as goto, perform are used to direct the routine to the lower tables. There are two types of transfers:

  1. Direct,
  2. Temporary.

1. Direct Transfer: This transfer uses one time transfer i.e. the referenced table does not refer back to the original table. The action statement goto indicate which table to examine next.

For example: (This is only paper work for analyst)

Table - 1:

Condition Rules	Decision Rules					
1. C1						
2. C2						
3. C3						
1. A1						
2. A2						
3. Go to Table 2	X					

Table - 2:

Condition Rules	Decision Rules					

2. Temporary transfer: In this method the second table can use the return statement to go back in the calling table.

Table - 3:

Condition Rules	Decision Rules					
1. C1						
2. C2						
3. C3						
1. A1						
2. Return		X				

- Return statement sends control back to the statement following the goto in the table 1.

5.3.2.5 Decision Table Processors

- Decision table have been partially automated. Table processors are computer programs that handle actual table formulation on the basis of input provided by the analyst.
- They also do all the checking for redundancy and consistency. Same table processors convert the decision table into actual computer program instruction.

- The usefulness of decision table processors is in saving programming time and checking for errors.
- **Flowcharting:** Flow-chart is the pictorial representation of logical flow of the program. It uses following symbols, to represent the logical processing.

1. **Processing symbols:**

1.		Computer processing. Use to indicate any processing perform by computer.
2.		Predefined processing. Use to indicate any process not specifically defined in the flow-chart but defined elsewhere in another flowchart.
3.		Any input and any output operation.
4.		Decision/Condition
5.		Sorting
6.		Manual operation
7.		Manual input i.e. any input operation that is not mechanical.
8.		Auxiliary operation/extra operation. Use to indicate any mechanical process which supplements the main computer processing.

2. Descriptive symbols:

1.	→ ←	Indicates directional flow.
2.	(zigzag)	Communication link. i.e. It is used to show any transmission of data by communication method/data through satellite.
3.	(rounded rectangle)	Terminal. Start and end of the computer processes.
4.	○	Use to connect different entry and exit points in the flow chart.
5.	(pentagon)	Off page connector. Use to connect parts of flow charts continued on separate pages.

3. Media symbols:

1.	(punch card shape)	Punch card.
2.	(document shape)	It is used to show any printed document input or output.
3.	(paper tape shape)	Paper tape. Use to represent any data on the paper.
4.	(cylinder horizontal)	Magnetic drum. Use to represent data on magnetic drum.
5.	(cylinder vertical)	Magnetic disk.

6.	◯	Magnetic tape.
7.	▢	On-line storage. Use to represent any on-line storage device.
8.	▽	Off-line storage. Used to represent any data stored off-line. (Floppy etc.)

5.4 DATA FLOW DIAGRAMS (DFDs) (Oct. 09, April 10, 13)

- DFD (Data Flow Diagram) is a graphic representation of system that shows data flows to, from and within the system, processing functions that change the data in some manner and the storage of this data.
- DFD provides a logical model of the system and show the flow of data and the flow of logic involved.
- Data flow diagrams are nothing but more than network of a related system functions (processing of data) that indicate from where information (data) is received (inputs) and to where it is sent (outputs).
- It is also called as bubble charts.
- DFDs are used to depict specific data flows (movement of inform) from both the physical view point (how it is done) and the logical view point (what is done).

5.4.1 Characteristics

- Various characteristics of DFD are given below:
    1. DFD shows the passage of data through the system.
    2. It supports top-down approach.
    3. DFD focus on the process that transforms incoming data flows i.e. inputs to outgoing data flows i.e. outputs.
    4. The processes that perform this transformation normally create as well as use data.
    5. External entities in DFD send and receive data flows from the systems.

5.4.2 Symbols of DFD

- Data flow diagram use a number of symbols to represent systems. Most data flow modeling methods use four kinds of symbols. These symbols are used to represent four kinds of system components:

- DFD shows how the data flows in the system.
- Fig. 5.27 shows symbols of DFD.
    1. **Process:** A component of DFD that describes how input data is converted to output data.
    2. **Data store:** A component of DFD that describes the repositories of data in a system.
    3. **Data flow:** Data flowing between processes data stores and external entities.
    4. **External entity:** An object outside the scope of system.

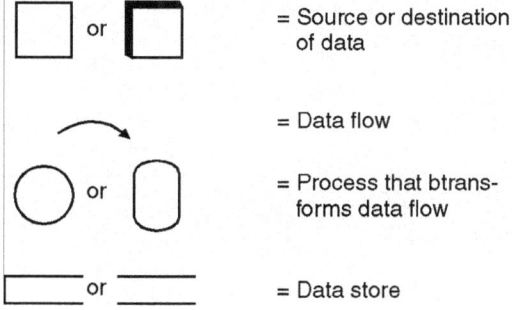

Fig. 5.27: Symbols of DFD

- Fig. 5.28 shows symbols of DFD with example.

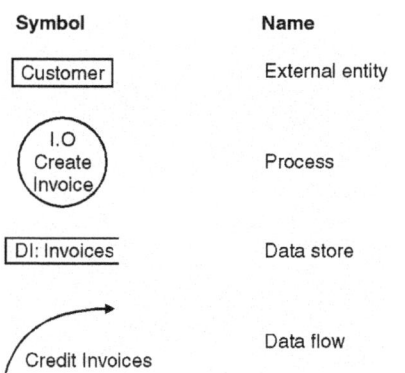

Fig. 5.28

- Fig. 5.29 present next level of detail (i.e. next level of data flow diagram). We see that the first action is to check the inventory to see if the software program ordered is in stock. If so, we place the order in a file "to be filled".

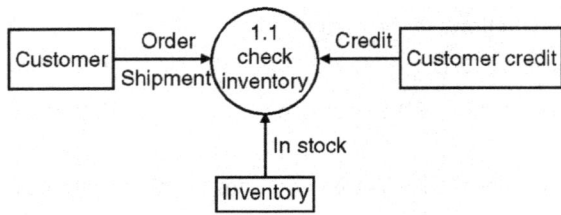

Fig. 5.29: Overview of mail-order business (1st level of data flow diagram)

- The warehouse staff removes order from this file, finds the items in inventory, packages the order and sends it to the customer.

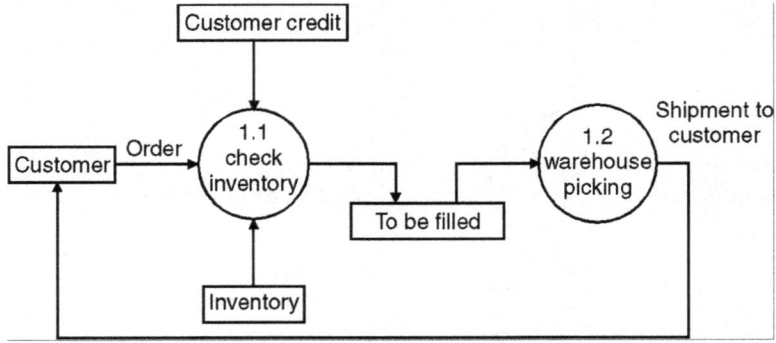

Fig. 5.30: Next level of detail DFD

- The numbers in the process symbols on the data flow diagram refer to levels. Note that a number like 1.0 means that we are on the first level; subsequent breakdowns into more detail carry numbers like 1.1, 1.11 etc. to show that we are at a lower level of detail.

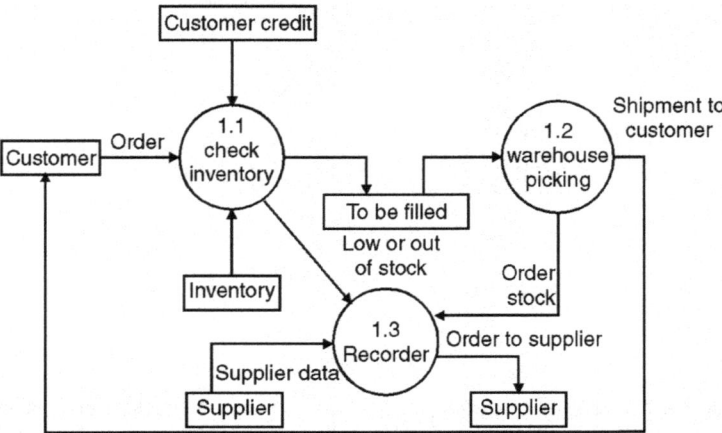

Fig. 5.31: Reorder plan

- In Fig. 5.31 the designer addresses the questions of what to do when items are out of stock. Management has made the decision that back ordering is probably not feasible because the customer is likely to look elsewhere for the program rather than to wait.
- However, it is important to reorder when stock is low or entirely gone. If more merchandise is needed, an order must be placed with a supplier. There is also a path from warehouse picking to the reorder process in case the inventory records do not match the warehouse contents neatly.
- Here, we want to check the warehouse carefully and then reorder if in fact there is nothing in inventory.
- Note that the "Check Inventory" process comes at level 1.1 in Fig. 5.31 under the step "Process Order", number 1.0 in Fig. 5.29. In checking inventory we encounter the process "Reorder" which is process 1.3 (Fig. 5.30).

5.4.3 DFD Principles

- The general principle in Data Flow Diagramming is that a system can be decomposed into subsystems and subsystems can be decomposed into lower level subsystems and so on.
- Each subsystem represents process or activity in which data is processed. At the lowest level, processes can no longer be decomposed.
- Each 'process' (and from now on, by 'process' we mean subsystem and activity) in a DFD has the characteristics of a system.
- Just as a system must have input and output (if it is not dead) so a process must have input and output.
- Data enters the system from the environment; data flows between processes within the system; and data is produced as output from the system.

5.4.4 Types of DFD

- The data flow diagrams are of two types:
    1. **Physical DFD:** DFDs shows how things happen or the physical component is called physical DFD. Typical processes is that appear in physical DFDs are methods of data entry, specific data transfer or processing methods and processes that depends on the physical arrangement of data. Physical DFD describes the flow of logical data components between physical operations in systems. **(Oct. 10)**
    2. **Logical DFD:** Logical DFD describes the flow of logical data components between logical DFD helps designer to gain a clear idea of what the system is to achieve without getting confused by its current implementation details. A diagram that shows the data object types output by one activity and later used by another activity. A logical data flow diagram is representation of the flow of data into, out of and between procedures, subsystems or systems. The diagram is similar to the process dependency diagram. **(Oct. 10)**

5.5 DATA DICTIONARY (Oct. 09, 10, 11, 12; April 11, 13, 14)

- When a team of analyst works for a particular system then the task of coordinating data definitions becomes more complex. Data dictionary solves this problem.
- It provides the additional information of the system. All definitions of the elements in the system, data flows processes and data stores are described in detail in data dictionary.
- If any member wants to know the definition of a data item name or the contents of particular data flow there information should be available in data dictionary.

What is Data Dictionary? (Oct, 09, 10)

- A data dictionary is a catalogue a repository of the elements in a system. These dictionary mainly talks about data and the way they are structured to meet user requirements and organizational needs.
- It is basically, the list of all the elements and data flowing through the system.
- The data dictionary stores detailed information about these elements.
- The main parts of data dictionary are data flows, data stores and processes.
- Data dictionary is basically, the answers to the questions such as:
  1. What is width of data item?
  2. What are the other names it is referenced in the system?
  3. Where it is used in the system?
- The data dictionary is built up during data flow analysis. But it is used during. The system design also.
- Following are the use of data dictionary:
  1. **To manage the details:** Normally, the systems have very large amount of data flowing through the system. Such as, documents reports etc. Similarly, the new data is created. Using the existing data. This volume goes on increasing in same years.
  2. **To communicate common meaning for all system elements:** Data dictionary gives common meaning for system elements and activities. The common words are used in the business and known to everyone. But the actual meaning with data that defines the common word is recorded in the data dictionary. It completely describes the data used or produced in the system. It also records additional information as to how data flows in the system.
  3. **To document the features of the system:** Features includes parts components and the characteristics that distinguish them. It records under what situations each process is performed and how often the situation occurs.
  4. **To facilitate analysis of the details:** It is needed to evaluate characteristics and determine where system changes to be made the characteristics can be:
     - **Nature of Transactions:** The business activities that will be carried out while using the system.

For example: Student will be given a admission transaction where payment is by credit card ?

- **Inquiries:** The retrieval of data where joining of two tables is needed to consumer the query.
- **Output and Report Generation:** Results of the system should be presented to users in an acceptable form.
- **Files and Databases:** Details of transactions close and master records should be done properly.
- **System capacity:** The ability of a system to accept, process and store transactions of data.

5. **Locate Errors and Omissions:** After recording information about transactions, inquiries, data and capacity use should be guaranteed that the information is complete and accurate. So automated data dictionary can evaluate them and present the difficulties or errors in a report.

Components of Data Dictionary: (Oct. 09, 11; April 11)

- The transactions, inquiries reports and output, file and database everything depends on a data.
- The data dictionary has two types of descriptions:
    1. **Data Elements:** Data element is the fundamental level or the elementary item.

       For example: Invoice number, invoice date and amount due are the data elements.

       Data elements are building blocks for all other data in the system. Only data elements will not mean anything. Only date will not have any meaning. But when it is put on the invoice it tells on what date the invoice was issued.

    2. **Data Structures:** Data elements are grouped together to makeup a data structure. A data structure is a set of data items that are related to are another and collectively describe a component in a system, (See Fig. 5.32).

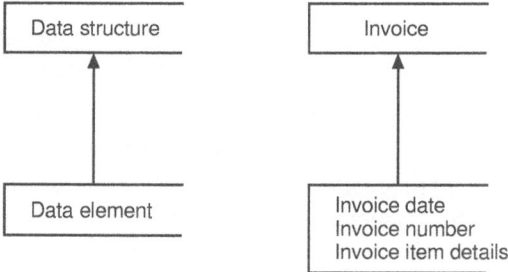

Fig. 5.32: Data structure and Data element

- Data flows and data stores are nothing but the data structures.

5.5.1 Elements of Data Dictionary (Oct. 09)

- It describes data used or produced in the system.
- The data elements are identified by:
    1. **Data Name:** To distinguish data from one another the meaningful name is assigned. These names are used throughout the system. Therefore, meaningful names should be chosen. For invoice data, the data names can be Date-of-invoice, Invoice-data etc. instead of AAA or BBB. The names should not be more than 30 characters. It should not contain any blank spaces. It should be consisting of A-Z, 0-9 and hyphen.
    2. **Data Descriptions:** It tells what data item represents in the system.

       For example: Data of invoice means that the data on which the invoice was prepared. Data descriptions should be written without any assumption and words. It should be understood to the common man who does not know about the system.
    3. **Aliases:** The same data item can be referred to by different names depending on who is using the data. These additional names are called as aliases.

       For example: Invoice may be called as statement bill etc. The data dictionary should include all the aliases.
    4. **Length:** It will record the amount of space needed for each data item. Length describes the number of spaces required but without knowing how they are stored.
    5. **Data values:** The data item may have some values which are permissible. It will allow only permissible values to be given to the particular data item no other values are allowed. So here the data values are restricted to a specific range. Example the invoice number should be a five digit numbers.

5.6 PSEUDO CODE (Oct. 10, 12; April 12)

- Pseudocode is a compact and informal high-level description of a computer programming algorithm that uses the structural conventions of some programming language, but is intended for human reading rather than machine reading.
- Pseudocode typically omits details that are not essential for human understanding of the algorithm, such as variable declarations, system-specific code and subroutines.
- The programming language is augmented with natural language descriptions of the details, where convenient, or with compact mathematical notation.
- The purpose of using pseudocode is that it is easier for humans to understand than conventional programming language code, and that it is a compact and environment-independent description of the key principles of an algorithm.
- It is commonly used in textbooks and scientific publications that are documenting various algorithms, and also in planning of computer program development, for sketching out the structure of the program before the actual coding takes place.

- Flowcharts were the first design tool to be widely used, but unfortunately they do not reflect some of the concepts of structured programming very well.
- Pseudocode, on the other hand, is a newer tool and has features that make it more reflective of the structured concepts. The drawback is that the narrative presentation is not as easy to understand and/or follow.

5.6.1 What is Pseudocode? (Oct. 10)

- It is quite difficult to define the pseudo code exactly. It is a kind of structured English for describing algorithms. It allows the designer to focus on the logic of the algorithm without being distracted by details of programming language syntax.
- The pseudo code describes the logic of the program and acts as a blueprint for the source code to be written by the programmer.
- Pseudocode consists of short, English phrases used to explain specific tasks within a program's algorithm.
- Pseudocode should not include keywords in any specific computer languages. It should be written as a list of consecutive phrases.

5.6.2 Why is Pseudocode Necessary ?

- The programming process is a complicated one. You must first understand the program specifications, of course, then you need to organize your thoughts and create the program. This is a difficult task when the program is not trivial (i.e. easy).
- You must break the main tasks that must be accomplished into smaller ones in order to be able to eventually write fully developed code. Writing pseudocode will save you time later during the construction and testing phase of a program's development.

5.6.3 Rules for Pseudocode

- A pseudocode consists following rules:
    1. Write only one statement per line.
    2. Capitalize initial keyword.
    3. Indent to show hierarchy.
    4. End multiline structures.
    5. Keep statements language independent.

5.6.4 How to Write Pseudocode ?

- First you may want to make a list of the main tasks that must be accomplished on a piece of scratch paper. Then, focus on each of those tasks.
- Generally, you should try to break each main task down into very small tasks that can each be explained with a short phrase. There may eventually be a one-to-one correlation between the lines of pseudocode and the lines of the code that you write after you have finished pseudocoding.

- It is not necessary in pseudocode to mention the need to declare variables. It is wise however to show the initialization of variables. You can use variable names in pseudocode but it is not necessary to be that specific.
- The word "Display" is used in some of the examples. This is usually general enough but if the task of printing to a printer, for example, is algorithmically different from printing to the screen, you may make mention of this in the pseudocode.
- You may show functions and procedures within pseudocode but this is not always necessary either.
- Overall, remember that the purpose of pseudocode is to help the programmer efficiently write code. Therefore, you must honestly attempt to add enough detail and analysis to the pseudocode.
- In the professional programming world, workers who write pseudocode are often not the same people that write the actual code for a program. In fact, sometimes the person who writes the pseudocode does not know beforehand what programming language will be used to eventually write the program.
- **Example:** Write a program that obtains two integer numbers from the user. It will print out the sum of those numbers.
- **Pseudocode:**

    Prompt the user to enter the first integer.
    Prompt the user to enter a second integer.
    Compute the sum of the two user inputs.
    Display an output prompt that explains the answer as the sum.
    Display the result.

5.6.5 Advantages

- Some advantages of using pseudo code to specify an algorithm rather than immediately writing program code are:

    1. **Reduced complexity:** For any complicated development whether it be constructing a program or a building. It is important that every effort is taken to reduce complexity. Breaking a single task into two simpler tasks generally results in a reduction in overall complexity. Writing pseudo code and program code separately simplifies the overall task by splitting it into two simpler tasks. While writing the algorithm the developer can focus on solving the problem, not how it is written in a a particular language. Having written the pseudo code and checked it, writing the code becomes much simpler, the programmer is only concerned with converting the pseudo code into the appropriate program code.

2. **Increased flexibility:** Pseudo code is written so that code based on it should be able to be written in any language (*language independent*). Using the algorithm the program could be written in Visual Basic or Java or C...

3. **Ease of understanding:** You don't have to understand a particular programming language to understand Pseudo Code. It is written in semi-structured, somewhat English like manner.

5.6.6 Disadvantages (April 13)

- Pseudocode consist of following disadvantages:
  1. Not visual and
  2. No accepted standard, varies from company to company.

5.7 INPUT AND OUTPUT DESIGN (April 10, 12; Oct. 12)

5.7.1 Input Design

- A major step in design is the preparation of input and the design of output reports in a form acceptable to the user.
- Inaccurate input data are the most common cause of errors in data processing. Errors entered by data entry operators can be controlled by input design.
- Input design is the process of converting user oriented inputs to a computer based format. In system design phase, the expanded data flow diagram identifies logical data flows, data stores, sources and destinations. A system flowchart specifies master files, transaction files and computer programs.
- Input data are collected and organized into groups of similar data. Once identified, appropriate input media are selected for processing.

5.7.1.1 Methods and Issues for Data Capture and Input

- The input design is the link that lies the information system into the world of its users.
- Input design consists of developing specifications and procedures for data preparation, those steps necessary to put transaction data into a usable form for processing and data entry, the activity of putting the data into the computer for processing.
- The five objectives guide the design of input, which are:
  1. Controlling amount of input,
  2. Avoiding delay,
  3. Avoiding errors in data,
  4. Avoiding extra steps, and
  5. Keeping the process simple.

5.7.1.2 Data Capture, Data Entry, Data Input

1. **Data capture:** Data Capture is the capture the data from the outside world other than the system which has been developed. There are general guidelines that will assist the analyst in formulating an input design. The analyst should start by **capturing** only those items that must actually be input. There are two types of data that must be input when processing transactions:

    (a) **Variable data:** Those data items that change for each transaction handled or decision made.

    (b) **Identification data:** The element of data that uniquely identifies the item being processed.

2. **Data Entry:** Data entry is to store or enter the data in the database of the existing system when the data input is been alone. What not to enter is equally important. Input procedure should not require entry of the following:

    (a) **Constant data:** Data that are the same for every entry.

    (b) **Details that the system can retrieve:** Stored data that are quickly retrievable from system files.

    (c) **Details that the system can calculate:** Results that can be produced by having the system use combinations of stored and entered data.

- Identifying Data Entry requirements and system responsibilities.

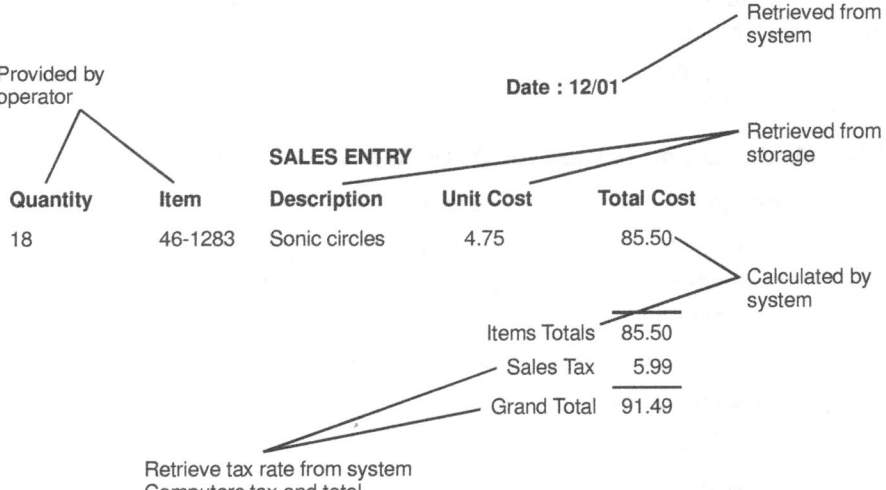

Fig. 5.34 : Data entry

- In the Fig. 5.34, to compute the cost of items sold, the system can require the operator to provide the item number and quantity purchased. The design then specify that the system will retrieve the unit price and multiply it by the quantity to produce the cost extension for one item. It also total all the extensions for an order, calculate sales tax and draw a grand total. Only a few items need be entered for this processing to occur. Hence, data entry is the data that the user has to enter to complete the transactions.

3. **Data Input:** To actually input the data in the existing way of format provided by the system. The goal of designing input data is to make data entry as easy, logical and free from errors as possible. In entering data, operators need to know the following:

   1. The allocated space for each field.
   2. Field sequence, which must match that in the source document.
   3. The format in which data fields are entered.

- For example: filling out the data field is required through the edited format mm/dd/yy.

5.7.1.3 Data Capture (Issues and Methods)

- The source document is the form on which data are initially captured i.e. recorded.
- A well-designed source document is easily completed and allows the process of actually recording the data to be rapid.
- There are four commonly used methods for data capture.
   1. Source data capture with key punching.
   2. Source data capture with key-to-storage.
   3. Source data capture with scanner.
   4. Direct entry through intelligent terminals.

5.7.1.4 Input Methods and Media

- Source data are input into the system in a variety of ways. The following media and devices are suitable for operation.
   1. **Punch Cards** are either 80 or 96 columns wide. Data are arranged in a sequential and logical order. Operators use a keypunch to copy data from source documents onto cards. This means that the source document and card design must be considered simultaneously.
   2. **Key-to-diskette** is modelled after the keypunch process. A diskette replaces the card and stores upto 3, 25,000 characters of data-equivalent to the data stored in 4,050 cards. Like cards, data on diskettes are stored in sequence and in batches. The approach to source document and diskette design is similar to that of the punch card. Data must be in sequence and logically cohesive.

3. **MICR** translates the special fonts printed in magnetic ink on checks into direct computer input.

4. **Mark-sensing readers** automatically convert pencil marks in predetermined locations on a card to punched holes on the same card.

5. **Optical Character Recognition (OCR)** readers are similar to MICR readers, except that they recognize pencil, ink or characters by their configuration rather than their magnetic pattern. They are often used in remote locations as free-standing input preparation devices or direct input media to the system.

6. **Optical Bar Code Readers (OBCR)** detect combination of marks that represent data. The most widely known system is the Universal Product Code (UPC), which codes retail items in the store. OBCR automatically read the codes and is an ideal way to collect unit inventory information fast, accurately and economically.

7. **Cathode Ray Tube (CRT)** screens are used for online data entry. CRT display's 20, 40 or 80 characters simultaneously on a television-like screen. They show as many as 24 lines of data.

5.7.1.5 Online Data Entry

- Online data entry makes use of a processor that accepts commands and data from the operator through a keyboard or a device such as a touch-sensitive screen or voice input.
- The input received is analyzed by the processor. It is then accepted or rejected or further input is requested.
- The request for inputs is in the form of a message displayed on the screen or by audio output. Care should be taken that the hardware facilitates easy data entry into the system.
- There are three major approaches for entering data into the computer: Menus, formatted forms and prompts.
    1. **Menu:** A menu is a selection list that simplifies computer data access or entry. Instead of remembering what to enter, the user chooses from a list of options and types the option letter associated with it. A menu limits the user's choice of responses but reduces the chances for error in data entry.
    2. **Formatted form:** A formatted form is preprinted form or a template that requests the user to enter data in appropriate locations. It is till in the blank type form. After the user responds by filling in appropriate information, the curser automatically move to the next line, an so until the form is completed. The system requests information about the customers' name, address, renewal data and so on.

- An example of formatted form:

```
Set up
Office
(0)    Open date: 8/12/82
(1)    Last /_ /_
(2)    Customer:
       Last name _____
       First name _____
(3)    Address:  1 _____
                 2 _____
                 3 _____
(4)    Renewal month _____
(5)    Account number _____
```

3. **Prompt (Conversational mode):** In prompt the system displays one inquiry at a time, asking the user for a response. Most systems edit the data entered by the user for a response.

   Most system edit the data entered by the user. The prompt method also allows the user to key questions that determine the next response of system. The main limitation with many of the available menus or prompt is that they require only one item to be entered at a time rather than a string of data items simultaneously.

5.7.1.6 End-user considerations for Input Design

- Considering End-user, some of the following points are taken care during input design.
    1. **Controlling amount of input:** By reducing input requirements, the analyst can speed the entire process from data capture to processing to providing results to users.
    2. **Avoiding delay:** A processing delay resulting from data preparation or data entry operations is called a bottleneck. Avoiding bottlenecks using turnaround documents can also help the user.
    3. **Avoiding error in data:** The smaller the amount of data to input, the fewer opportunities for errors. The manner in which data must be entered can affect the incidence of error. Another aspect of error control is the need to detect errors when they do occur checks and balances in the data entry programs, called input validation techniques, also detect errors in input.
    4. **Avoiding extra steps:** Sometimes, the volume of transactions and the amount of data preparation or data entry jobs resulting from them cannot be controlled. The experienced analyst will avoid designs that cause extra steps.
    5. **Keeping the process simple:** The experienced analyst keeps all the process simple as simplicity works and it is accepted by users. Hence, complexity is avoided considering the end-user.

Internal controls for inputs, implement and requirements

- Internal controls are been implemented for inputs so as there is a requirement for avoid errors in the input.
- Three main categories of methods are concerned with checking the transaction data and changing the transaction data.
- **Checking the transaction:** It is essential to identify any transactions that are not valid, that is not acceptable. Transactions can be invalid because they are incomplete, unauthorized or even out of order.
    1. **Batch controls:** Batch processing means delaying processing by accumulating the transactions into batches or groups of records. To control the error rate, batch control uses fixed both size. At the end of all the batches, the batch totals the number of batches which are processed. That number should be equal to the number of batches and hence, controls the processing.
    2. **Transaction validation:** The steps of system takes to ensure that the transaction is acceptable are called transaction validation.
    3. **Sequence Test:** Sequence tests use codes in the data serial numbers to test for either of two different conditions, depending on the characteristics of the application. In some systems, the order of transactions is important. In a bank if a series of withdrawals is mistakenly processed before a deposit that actually occurred first, the customer could be penalized for overdrawing the account when in fact that did not actually happen. Sequence tests also point out missing items.
- **Checking the transaction data:** Even valid transactions can contain invalid data. Therefore, analysts should be sure to specify methods for validating the data when developing input **procedures**. There are four data validation methods.
    1. **Existence test:** It examines those essential fields, determine that they contain data.
       For example, some data fields in transactions are designed to not be left empty or blank.
    2. **Limit and Range tests:** These tests verify the reasonableness of the transaction data. Limit tests validates either the minimum or maximum amount acceptable for an item. Range tests validate both minimum and maximum values.
    3. **Combination test:** Combination tests validate that several data items jointly have acceptable values, that is the value for one element of data determines whether other data values are correct.
    4. **Duplicate processing:** In this, data is processed more than once either on different equipment or in different ways. The results are then compared for agreement and accuracy. Duplicate processing ensures upmost accuracy.

- **Changing the transaction data:** A third way of validating data involves modifying the data themselves. Two methods are:
  1. **Automatic correction of errors:** In this method some such programmes has been used which detect an error and make the correction automatically.

     This input validation method is used to minimize the number of separate error correction steps or rejection of transactions during processing.
  2. **Self-checking digits on key fields:** Two of the most common errors in handling data occur with data that are captured correctly but entered incorrectly into processing.
     (i) Transcription errors occur if data are inadvertently copied incorrectly by the data entry person.
     (ii) With, transposition errors, two or more digits are reversed so that their positions in the data are incorrect.
- Since, the chance of these errors occurring is high, the method devised to help detect them during computer processing is called check digit method. It adds an additional digit to a data element being used for identification purposes.
- Adding an additional number to the data improve the quality of data entering the system by helping to eliminate transposition and transcription errors.

5.7.2 Output Design (April 10)

- The output from an information system should accomplish one or more of the following objectives.
  1. Convey information about past activities, current status or projections of the future.
  2. Signal important events, opportunities, problems or warnings.
  3. Trigger an action.
  4. Confirm an action.
- There are many guidelines that will make the analyst's job easier and more important, ensures the users of receiving an understandable report.
  1. Report and documents should be designed to read from left to right and top to bottom.
  2. The most important items should be the easiest to find.
  3. All pages should have a title and page number and show the date the output was prepared.
  4. All columns should be labeled.
  5. Abbreviations should be avoided.

5.7.2.1 Choices for Media and Formats of Computer, Generated Outputs

- The output of the system is the primary contact between the system and most users. The quality of this output and its usefulness determines whether the system will be used, so

it is essential to have the best possible output.
- Computer output is the most important and direct source of information to the user. Efficient, intelligible output design should improve the system's relationships with the user and help in decision-making.
- A major form of output is a hard copy from the printer. Printers should be designed around the output requirements of the user.
- The output devices to consider depend on factors such as compatibility of the device with the system, response time requirements, expected print quality and number of copies needed.
- The following media devices are available for providing computer based output.
    1. MICR Readers
    2. Line, matrix and laser printers.
    3. Computer output micro film.
    4. CRT screen display.
    5. Graph plotters.
- Computer output is for people. Hence, the format of the computer output should be approved by the people.
- Whether, the output is a formatted report or a simple listing of the contents of a file, a computer process will produce the output.
- System output may be:
    1. A report
    2. A document
    3. A message.
- Depending on the circumstances and the contents, the output may be displayed or printed. Output contents originate from these sources:
    1. Retrieval from a data store.
    2. Transmission from a process or system activity.
    3. Directly from an input source. The information can be represented in a:
        (a) Tabular format
        (b) Graphic format
            (i) To facilitate effective presentation of data.
            (ii) To manage a volume of information.
            (iii) To fulfill personal preference.
        (c) Printed output
        (d) Visual display output

5.7.2.2 Internal Controls for Outputs

- Internal controls for outputs govern the pattern of outputs. It defines the representation of outputs either on VDU or printed form.
- The controls applied on outputs are such as:
  1. The size of paper or screen in which the output should fit in.
  2. The type of font or color used.
  3. Display or print should be in tabular form or graphic form. In graphics Pie chart or Bar chart.
  4. If printed format, then how many number of copies should be printed.
  5. Carbonless copies or interleaved carbon copies.
  6. Deciding the layout of display screens.
- All the above forms the internal controls of outputs.
- **Examples of Output's Generated:**

  1. **Types of business graphics:**

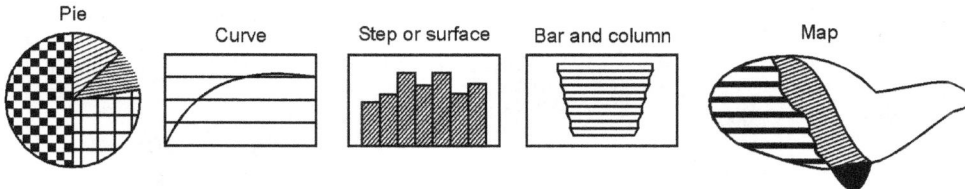

Fig. 5.35: Types of business graph

  2. **Tabular:**

Month	Million
1	1.8
2	1.94
3	1.76
4	1.70
5	1.81
6	1.85
7	1.76
8	1.74
9	1.51
10	1.53
11	1.46
12	1.35
1	1.58

2	1.75
3	1.85
4	1.91
5	1.93
6	1.61
7	1.58
8	1.71
9	1.61
10	1.68
11	1.47
12	1.41

3. **Preprinted forms for computer output:**

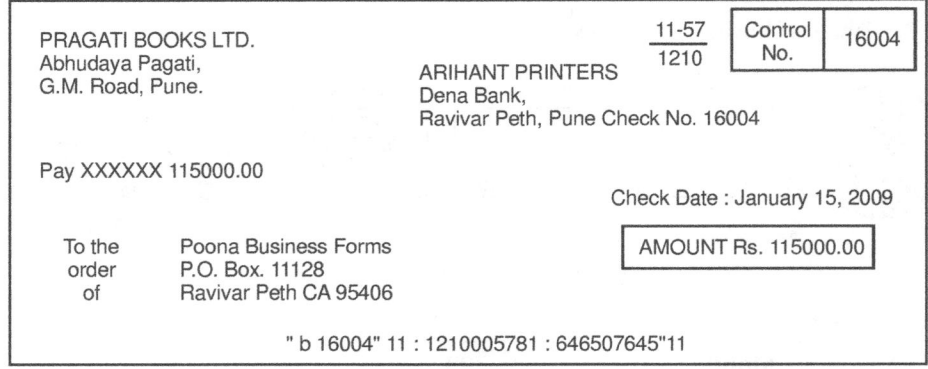

Fig. 5.36: Preprinted form

4. **Effective placement of in formation on visual display unit.**

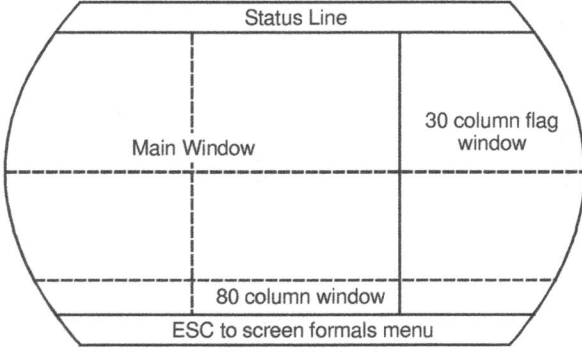

Fig. 5.37: Visual display

5.7.2.3 Steps involved to Prototype and Design Computer Outputs

- For many end-users output is the main reason for developing the system and the basis on which they will evaluate the usefulness of the application.
- When designing output, systems analysts must accomplish the following:
  1. Determine what information to present.
  2. Decide whether to display, print, or "speak" the information and select the output medium.
  3. Arrange the presentation of information in an acceptable format.
  4. Decide how to distribute the output to intended recipients.
- To accomplish the activities listed above will require specific decisions, such as whether to use preprinted forms when preparing reports and documents, how many lines to plan on a printed page or whether to use graphics and color.

Practice Questions

1. What is meant by Analysis.
2. Write short note on: Analysis tools.
3. Explain pseudo code in detail.
4. Write short notes on:
   (a) Decision table, (b) Decision tree
5. What is the problem with Decision tree?
6. Explain DFD.
7. List out various types of DFD's.
8. Explain in detail Data Dictionary.
9. Explain Decision table processors.
10. Explain how to develop a DFD.
11. List out component of data dictionary.
12. Explain the term input design in detail.
13. Explain the term output design in detail.
14. With suitable diagram describe physical DFD.
15. With suitable diagram describe logical DFD.
16. Enlist various components of Data dictionary.
17. Explain the following terms:
    (a) Data capture,
    (b) Data entry
    (c) Data input

18. What do you mean by Data flow and Data entry.
19. Compare logical and physical DFD.
20. Enlist various internal controls of output design.

University Questions & Answers

October 2009

1. State different types of Decision Tables and explain any one. [2 M]

Ans. Please refer to Section 5.3.2.

2. What is Data Dictionary ? Explain its various elements. [4 M]

Ans. Please refer to Sections 5.5 and 5.5.1.

3. Design an Output Screen for Bill of purchased items from a shop, maximum for 5 items. [8 M]

Ans. Please refer to Section 5.7.2.

4. ABC company decides to give Diwali Bonus to all employees for which the management has divided employees into three categories namely. Administrative Staff (AS), Office Staff (OS), Workers (W) and considered the following rules: [8 M]

   (i) If the employee is permanent and in the AS Category the bonus amount is three months salary.

   (ii) If the employee is permanent and in the OS Category the bonus amount is two salaries.

   (iii) If the employee is permanent and in the W Category the bonus amount is one month salary.

   (iv) If the employee is temporary, then half of the amount given to permanent employee as bonus is given to them.

   Represent above study using:

   (i) Decision Tree

   (ii) Decision Table

Ans. Please refer to Sections 5.3.1 and 5.3.2.

5. Write short note on: Entity Relationship Model. [4 M]

Ans. Please refer to Section 5.2.

6. Ranbaxy Pharmaceutical Ltd., distributes a range of products in 5 regions spread over 5 States in India. The regions are further subdivided into 4-5 zones each. Each zone has 30 to 40 sales-representatives. The company's product range includes 20 different items. For each item, sales-representative wise targets for quantity to be sold each month are

established. The targets are set at the beginning of the quarter. The actual sales made by each of the sales-representatives are built up from invoices, which alongwith other information carry unique sales-representative number.

The company desires to have an information system to monitor sales performance of the representative with respect to targets and product wise sales, similar performance reports for the zones, for the regions and for the company as a whole are also required. Variation in targeted and actual sales beyond 10% on either side is to be highlighted. Analyse problem from the specifications given above.

(i) Identify all entities, **[16 M]**

(ii) Draw Context Level Diagram, and

(iii) First Level DFD for the system.

Ans. Please refer to Sections 5.2 and 5.4.

April 2010

1. Define decision tree and decision table. **[2 M]**

Ans. Please refer to Sections 5.3.1 and 5.3.2.

2. Explain E-R model. **[4 M]**

Ans. Please refer to Section 5.2.

3. Design an output screen for Indian Railway Ticket format including passenger details (name, male/female, age, phno.), Source and Destination for traveling, total fare and class. **[8 M]**

Ans. Please refer to Section 5.7.2.

4. XYZ Company divides its customers into 2 categories for the purpose of determining delivery charges:

   (a) Those whose sales region code is 50 and above and those with code of less than 50.

   (b) If the code is less than 50 and the invoice amount is less than ₹ 5,000, the delivery charge to be added to the invoice amount is ₹ 150. But if the invoice value is for ₹ 5,000 or more the delivery charge is ₹ 75.

   (c) If the code is equal to or greater than 50 the corresponding delivery charges are ₹ 200 and ₹ 100 respectively.

   Draw Decision Tree and Decision Table. **[8 M]**

Ans. Please refer to Sections 5.3.1 and 5.3.2.

5. Write short note on: Design guidelines (for input/output forms). **[4 M]**

Ans. Please refer to Sections 5.7.

6. Indian Bank provides fixed deposit schemes through which people can deposit money for a certain period of time. The bank pays interest for this period and returns money when FD period is over. Interest rate depends upon the period.

   The depositor may choose to renew FD.

   The depositor may get loan against deposits.

   A maximum of 75% of the deposit amount is allowed as loan amount.

   Analyse problem from the specifications given above:

   (i) Identify all entities and data stores. [3 M]

   (ii) Draw Context Level Diagram. [6 M]

   (iii) Draw First Level DFD for System. [7 M]

Ans. Please refer to Sections 5.2 and 5.4.

October 2010

1. What is data dictionary. [2 M]

Ans. Please refer to Section 5.5.

2. What is E-R diagram? Draw various symbols of E-R diagram. [2 M]

Ans. Please refer to Section 5.2.

3. What is decision table. [2 M]

Ans. Please refer to Section 5.3.2.

4. What is Pseudocode. [2 M]

Ans. Please refer to Section 5.6.1.

5. Compare logical and physical DFD with suitable example. [4 M]

Ans. Please refer to Section 5.4.

6. Design an output screen layout for electricity bill containing period, customer name, address number, previous and current reading, rate, amount (per unit), penalty, gross amount etc. Suggest validation for screen. [8 M]

Ans. Please refer to Section 5.7.2.

7. The discount policy of a manufacturer, producing two products:

   (a) Mechanical Typewriter and

   (b) Electronic typewriter, and who has three types of customers, (R) Retailer, (D) Dealer, (I) Institution, is given below:

   Rules: In case of Mechanical Typewriter.

   (i) If the order is from retailer for amount up to ₹ 5,000, he allows 6% discount.

   (ii) If the order is from dealer for amount up to ₹ 5,000, he allows 7.5% discount.

Software Engineering (BCA-III)   5.50   **Analysis and Design Tools**

    (iii) On retail exceeding ₹ 5,000, 7.5% discount.

    (iv) If the order is from dealer for an amount exceeding ₹ 5,000, 11% discount is given.

    (v) In all of the above cases a flat discount of 7.5% is given to Institution.

    (vi) In the case of Electronic Typewriter a flat discount of 6% is given regardless of amount. **[8 M]**

Ans. Please refer to Sections 5.3.1 and 5.3.2.

8. Consider a system for Swimming Tank Management. Applicants fill admission form containing details like address, date of birth, age, father's/guardian's name and also submit two photographs, medical certificate and fees. Then Swimming Tank Management issues I Card to the applicant. **[16 M]**

    (i) Identify all Entities.

    (ii) Draw Context Level Diagram and

    (iii) First Level DFD for the System.

Ans. Please refer to Section 5.4.

April 2011

1. Define decision tree and decision table. **[2 M]**

Ans. Please refer to Sections 5.3.1 and 5.3.2.

2. What is data dictionary? **[2 M]**

Ans. Please refer to Section 5.5.

3. Discuss contents of data dictionary. **[4 M]**

Ans. Please refer to Section 5.5.1.

4. Design a screen layout for creating user account on Internet (with personal details, user_id and password, save, cancel commands etc.) **[8 M]**

Ans. Please refer to Sections 5.6 and 5.7.

5. A co-operative Bank XYZ will grant loans under the following conditions:

    (1) If a customer has an account with the bank and has no loan outstanding, loan will be granted.

    (2) If a customer has an account with the bank but some amount is outstanding from previous loans, then loan will be granted if special approval is obtained.

    (3) Reject loan applications in all other cases.

Represent above study, using:

    (a) Decision Tree.

    (b) Decision Table. **[8 M]**

Ans. Please refer to Sections 5.3.1 and 5.3.2.

6. Write short note on: Decision tree. [4 M]

Ans. Please refer to Section 5.3.1.

7. Prepare a Context Level Diagram and First Level Diagram for the Saving Bank Deposit and Withdrawal System in a Nationalized Bank. Also involve calculation of Interest.

Ans. Please refer to Section 5.4.

October 2011

1. What is E-R diagram ? Draw various symbols of E-R diagram. [2 M]

Ans. Please refer to Sections 5.2.

2. Define decision tree and decision table. [2 M]

Ans. Please refer to Section 5.3.1 and 5.3.2.

3. What is data dictionary ? Explain its various elements. [4 M]

Ans. Please refer to Sections 5.5 and 5.5.1.

4. Design an Input Form for College Admission System. [4 M]

Ans. Please refer to Section 5.7.

5. Material is issued to the department by considering whether the Material Requisition Note (MRN) is signed or not, it contains valid items or not it is given within 8 hrs. or not. [4 M]

   Draw Decision Tree and Decision Table.

Ans. Please refer to Sections 5.3.1 and 5.3.2.

6. Consider a Hospital Management System in which the hospital has Inpatient Department (IPD), Outpatient Department (OPD) the system maintains patient records and bills of patient it also manages, information of various wards in the hospital like ICU, General, Private, Semi-private and Delux. [16 M]

   (a) Identify all entities
   (b) Draw Context Level Diagram
   (c) First Level DFD for the System

Ans. Please refer to Sections 5.2 and 5.4.

April 2012

1. Define decision tree and decision table. [2 M]

Ans. Please refer to Sections 5.3.1 and 5.3.2.

2. Define the term entity. [2 M]

Ans. Please refer to Section 5.2.1.

3. Define Pseudocode. [2 M]

Ans. Please refer to Section 5.6.1.

4. Design an input form for employees salary slip with following details. [2 M]
   - Employee Number, Name and designation.
   - Earning (Basic, DA, HRA, TA) and deductions (PF, PT and others)

Ans. Please refer to Section 5.7.

5. Material is issued to the department by considering whether the Material Requisition Note (MRN) is signed or not, it contains valid items or not and it is given within 8 hours or not. Draw decision tree and decision table. [4 M]

Ans. Please refer to Sections 5.3.1 and 5.3.2.

6. Write short notes on:
   (i) E-R diagram.
   (ii) Physical and logical DFDs. [4 M]
   (iii) Advantages of Data dictionary [4 M]

Ans. Please refer to Sections 5.2, 5.4 and 5.5.2.

7. The Railway Reservation System functions as follows:

   The passenger is required to fill in a reservation form giving details of his journey. The counter clerk ensures whether the place is available. If so, entries are made in the register, tickets are prepared amount is computed and cash is accepted. A booking statement is prepared in a triplicate from the reservation register. One copy of it is retained as office copy, the other is pasted on the compartment and the third is passed on to the train conductor. Besides booking statements, cash statement is prepared at the end of each shift.

   (i) Identify all entities.
   (ii) Draw content level diagram
   (iii) Draw First level DFD for the system.

Ans. Please refer to Sections 5.2 and 5.4.

October 2012

1. Define entity and relationship with diagram. [2 M]

Ans. Please refer to Sections 5.2.4.

2. Define decision tree and decision table. [2 M]

Ans. Please refer to Section 5.3.

3. What is data dictionary? [4 M]

Ans. Please refer to Sections 5.5.

4. What are design principles. [4 M]

Ans. Please refer to Sections 5.7.

5. Draw a prototype of input screen for entering patients information in hospital, including patient information, doctor information and treatment information. **[8 M]**

Ans. Please refer to Sections 5.7.1.

6. A STARFISH Company is offering certain discount on the total amount of purchase. If the purchasing amount is more than 5,0000 and the customer is making the payment within 5 days then company offers 5% discount on invoice. If the purchase amount is between 3,000 to 5,000 and the customer is making the payment within 5 days then compnay offers 3% discount. If the amount is less than 3,000 and customer is making the payment wihtint 5 days then no discount offered and customer has to pay full amount. if customer is not able to pay within 5 days then no discount is given.

   Draw decision tree and decision table. **[8 M]**

Ans. Please refer to Sections 5.3.1 and 5.3.2.

7. Write short note on pseudocode. **[4 M]**

Ans. Please refer to Sections 5.6.

April 2013

1. Explain data dictionary with example. **[2 M]**

Ans. Please refer to Section 5.5.

2. What are symbols of DFD ? **[2 M]**

Ans. Please refer to Section 5.4.

3. Define an Screen layout for mark sheet format. **[8 M]**

Ans. Please refer to Section 5.7.

4. If customer is within Maharashtra State and has Sales Tax Exemption Certificate no Sales Tax s levied; otherwise 8% Sales Tax is charged on the sales value. If the customer is outside Maharashtra Sate 4% Central Sales Tax in place of Sales Tax, is charged.

   Draw decision tree and decision table. **[8 M]**

Ans. Please refer to Section 5.3.1 and 5.3.2.

5. Write short note on Data validation. **[4 M]**

Ans. Please refer to Section 5.6.6.

April 2014

1. Define data dictionary. **[2 M]**

Ans. Please refer to Section 5.5.

2. Design screen layout for registration at "Vyoms.com". The information of registered persons will be later saved in company's database. [8 M]

Ans. Please refer to Section 5.7.

3. Draw decision tree and table fro co-operative tank. If the customer has account with the bank and has no dues then sanction loan. If customer has account with the bank but has previous dues then check for management approval. If customer has management approval then sanction loan otherwise reject loan. [8 M]

Ans. Please refer to Section 5.3.1 and 5.3.2.

4. Write short note on Decision tree.

Ans. Please refer to Section 5.3.1.

5. Write short note on E-R diagram.

Ans. Please refer to Section 5.2.

❖❖❖

Chapter 6...
Structured System Design

Contents ...

This chapter gives basic concepts of system such as:

6.1 INTRODUCTION
    6.1.1 Structured Design
    6.1.2 Qualities of Good Design
    6.1.3 Additional Design Guidelines

6.2 MODULES CONCEPTS AND TYPES OF MODULES
    6.2.1 Modularization Criteria
    6.2.2 Advantages and Disadvantages of Modular Programming
    6.2.3 Graphical Representation of a Module
    6.2.4 Connections between Modules
    6.2.5 Module Concepts
    6.2.6 Types of Modules

6.3 STRUCTURED CHART

6.4 QUALITIES OF GOOD DESIGN
    6.4.1 Coupling
    6.4.2 Cohesion

6.1 INTRODUCTION

- Design is the mental process, a kind of thinking.
- The process of design involves conceiving and planning out in mind and making a drawing, pattern or sketch of the system. The design evolves from observing, modelling and thinking about a problem.
- The design process may involve developing several models of the system at different levels of abstraction.
- As the design is decomposed, errors and omissions in earlier stages are discovered. Therefore the designer should consider ease of software implementation, testing and maintenance as guiding criteria in the application of these concepts.
- The general model of design process is shown in Fig. 6.1

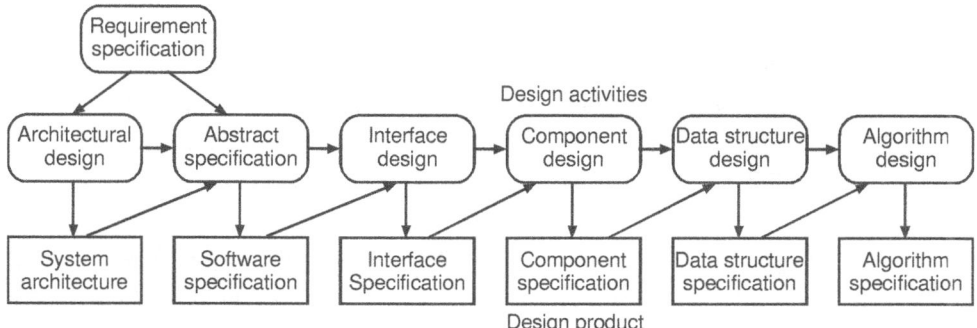

Fig. 6.1: A general model of design process

- Fig. 6.1 suggests that the stages of design process are sequential and all the activities are interleaved.
- The specific design process activities are:
  - Architectural design.
  - Abstract specification.
  - Interface design.
  - Component design.
  - Data structure design.
  - Algorithm design.
- Therefore, the design is simply acts like a bridge between the analysis of a problem and implementation of the solution of that problem.

6.1.1 Structured Design   (Oct. 10, 11)

- Structured design was developed by Ed Yourdon and Larry Constantine.
- This technique deals with the size and complexity of a program by breaking up the program into a hierarchy of modules which result in a computer program that is easier to implement and maintain.
- The structured design is a disciplined approach to computer system design.
- The structured design is the software design method which closely parallels the current trend in technology towards systems which are easy to maintain and expensive at least cost effective to construct.
- Structured system design is a step-by-step methodology which produces a software structure.
- The software structure is the specification of the components of the system [modules] and interconnection between these components.

- The structured design has following five aspects :
  1. It uses a definition of problem to guide definition of solution.
  2. It partitions the system into 'black boxes' and organizes a suitable computer implementation for each black box.
  3. It uses graphics to make system understandable.
  4. It offers set of strategies for developing a design solution.
  5. It offers a set of criteria for evaluation of quality into the design solution.
- In short, structured design produces the systems which are easy to understand, reliable, flexible, long lasting, smoothly developed and efficient to operate. It actually produces inexpensive systems.

6.1.2 Qualities of Good Design (Oct. 10, 11)

- The structure chart does not tell about the quality of a particular design because it is simply a tool for showing a module in the system and their relationship to one another.
- But the fundamental aim of structured design is to partitioned large systems into manageable modules. This partitioning should be carried out independently and each module should carry out a single problem related function.
- These two purposes are solved through coupling and cohesion respectively. Coupling and cohesion were described by Stevens, Constantine and Myers.
- There are some more guidelines or qualities which are needed to improve the design quality.
- There are various qualities followed for good design:
  1. The design process should not suffer from "tunnel vision".

     A good designer should consider alternative approaches based on requirement of the problem.
  2. The designs should be traceable to the analysis model. A single element of design model may have multiple requirements.
  3. The design should minimize the intellectual distance between system and the problem of real world. The design of a system should be such that which gives the structure of the problem domain.
  4. The design should exhibit uniformity and integration. Even if work has been done as a team, the rules, style and format should be uniform.
  5. The design should be structured to accommodate change.
  6. The design should be assessed for quality.
  7. The design should be revised to minimize conceptual errors.

- In order to evaluate the quality of design representations, we must establish some criteria's for good design.
  1. A design should exhibit an architectural structure or a hierarchical organization.
  2. A design should be modular.
  3. A design should contain distinct and separable representation of data and procedure.
  4. The design should lead to modules for example, subroutines, procedures, macros etc. which shows independent functional characteristics.
  5. A design should lead to interfaces which reduce the complexity of connections between modules and with the external environment.
  6. A design should be derived using a repeatable method.

6.1.3 Additional Design Guidelines

- The structure design needs some more criteria's. There are various criteria's other than cohesion and coupling.
  1. Factoring,
  2. Fan-in,
  3. Fan-out,
  4. System shape,
  5. Error reporting, and
  6. Generality/Restrictivity.

1. **Factoring:** Factoring is the separation of a function contained as code in one module into a new module of its own. This is done for any of the following six reasons:
   (i) To reduce module size.
   (ii) To get the modular advantage of classic top-down design. So it makes the systems easier to understand and making modification to the system more localized.
   (iii) To avoid having same function carried out in more than one module.
   (iv) To separate work (i.e. calculating and editing) from management (calling and deciding).
   (v) To provide more generally useful modules.
   (vi) To simplify implementation.

2. **Fan-In:** It is a module where the number of immediate bosses it has (See Fig. 6.2). The High fan-in is the reward for intelligent factoring and the removal of restrictive modules. At programming time, one function is called by several bosses. This avoids the need of coding practically the same function in several places. So avoids redundancy at maintenance time.

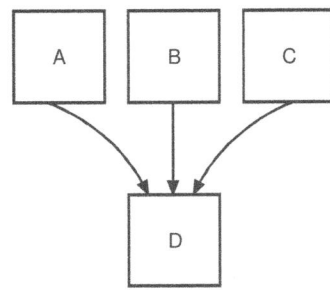

Fig. 6.2: Module D has a fan-in of three (A, B and C)

- Do not be afraid of the situation shown in Fig. 6.3 where modules bosses are at different levels. If a module has a truly useful function, then it can be used by the module anywhere in the system.

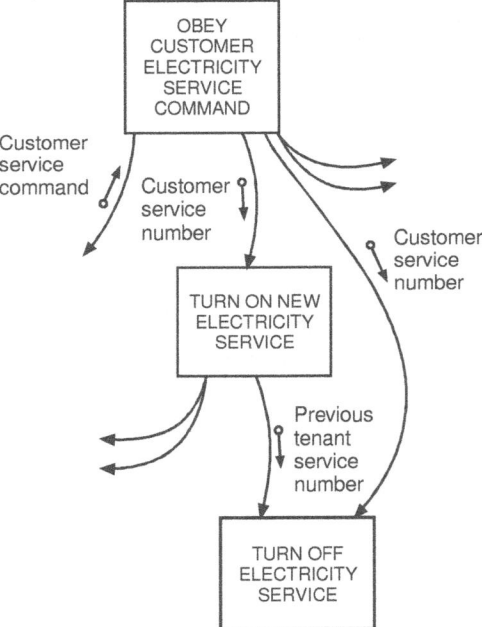

Fig. 6.3: Different level in fan-in

- There are two rules to restrict the use of fan-in.

    (i) Modules with fan-in must have good cohesion, preferably functional but at least communicational or sequential. Any fool can create a coincidentally cohesive module with a fan-in of 100.

(ii) Each interface to a single module must have the same number and types of parameter. For example, Fig. 6.4 makes no sense.

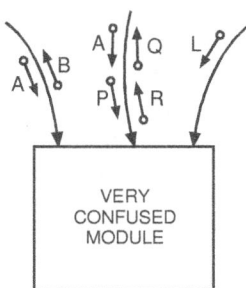

Fig. 6.4: Interface in single module

3. **Fan-out:** The fan-out from a module is the number of intermediate subordinates to that module. This is shown in Fig. 6.5.

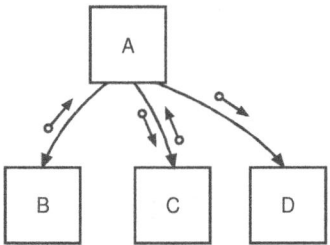

Fig. 6.5: Module A has fan-out of three modules

- In 1960, the concept of modularity becomes popular, a software design technique known as main-line design was very famous. This design called for a single boss (control) module with every other module as its subordinates. This is shown in Fig. 6.6.

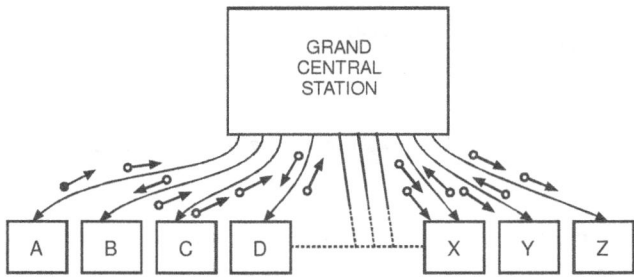

Fig. 6.6: Single boss module

- There was a well-intentioned purpose of main-line design: to reap the benefits of modularity by isolating a single change to a single module. Almost every non-trivial change that was made to the system required a change.

- Because almost every non-trivial function in the system was being carried out by that unhappy module. Even from the structure chart in Fig. 6.6 alone, you can visualize that the main-line module must contain a maelstrom of code, for all the pieces of data in the system are dashing in and out like Keystone Kops.

- The adulation of main-line design turned to sneers, and the bouquests of roses to cabbages. Main-line design was booed off the software stage and almost dragged modularity with it.

- To avoid repeating, try to limit the fan-out from a module to no more than seven. A module with too many subordinates can be easily curved by the old familiar remedy of factoring.

- Separate each subfunction within a main-line module into a module of its own, as shown in Fig. 6.7. It looks like a "pancake", which a symptom of a missing intermediate level. High fan-out is rectified by factoring out middle-management modules with strong cohesion and loose coupling, (See Fig. 6.8).

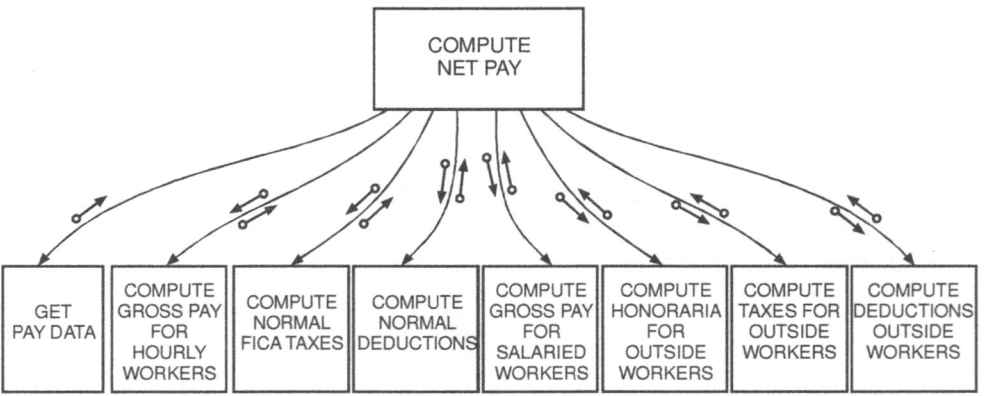

Fig. 6.7: Subfunctioning main-line module

- We should limit the number of immediate subordinates to a module as seven and not seventeen or twenty-seven. The number seven is not an unbendable standard, although a fan-out of more than seven from any module should cause warning bells to sound in your mind.

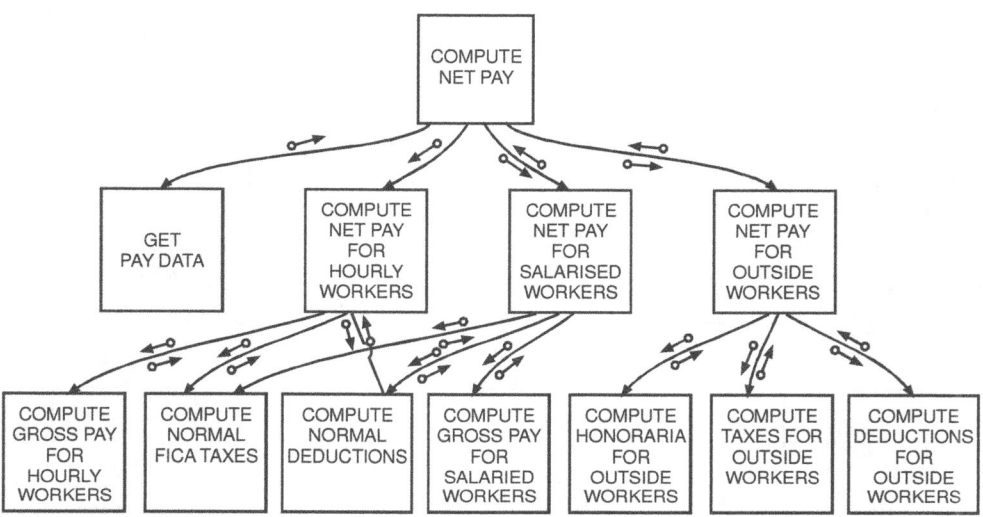

Fig. 6.8: Level of fun-out module

- Seven is a very important number in human psychology. If you try to do more than seven activities at once, you probably become very flustered and prone to making errors. Reasonably scientific experiments have yielded the results shown in Fig. 6.9.

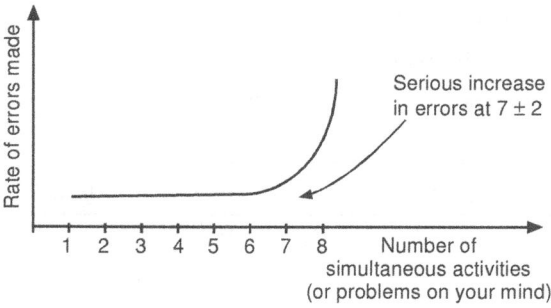

Fig. 6.9: Scientific result of more than seven activity

- Low fan-out is acceptable. It's rather like a department with one boss and one worker. Such a case may be a hint to factor out a module from the boss, as VALIDATE trans has been factored in the example in Fig. 6.10.

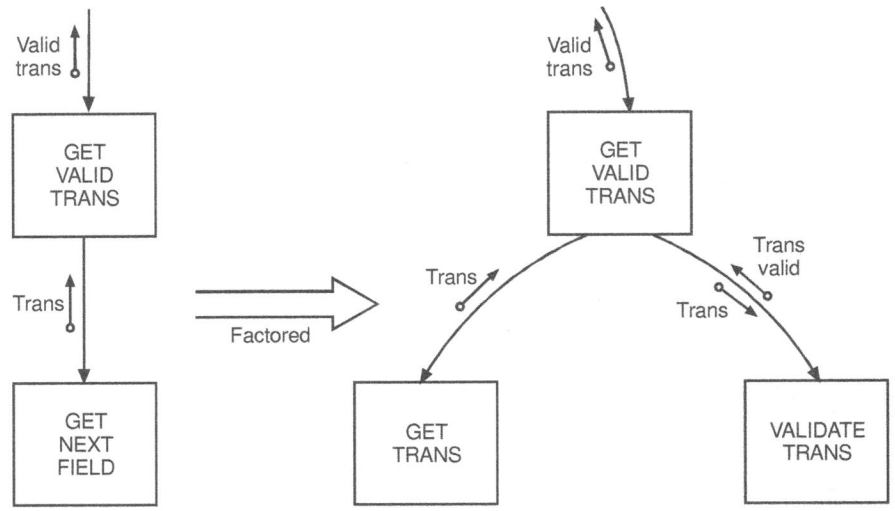

Fig. 6.10: Factor of validate trans

6.2 MODULE CONCEPTS AND TYPES OF MODULE

(Oct. 09, 10; April 10, 12, 14)

- When we ask a question "what is module?" the answer comes in our mind is, "**module is a number of statements that do some activity**". Obviously, we are talking about the concept of module in various programming language.

- Fig. 6.11 lists the examples of module in various languages.

Language name	Module
ALGOL	PROCEDURE
COBOL	PROGRAM (SECTION OR PARAGRAPH)
FORTRAN	SUBROUTINE, FUNCTION
C	FUNCTION
PASCAL	PROCEDURE FUNCTION
VISUAL BASIC	Code of each form object.

Fig. 6.11: Examples language module

- For structured design, the definition of a module of a black box is as follows:

- "**A module** is defined as a collection of program statements with four basic attributes i.e. input and output, function, mechanics and internal data", where
    1. Input means the accepted values; output means the returned or displayed values.
    2. Function means what it does to its input to produce the output.
    3. Mechanics means the logic or procedural code.
    4. Internal data means its own private workspace where it refers to data.
- A module also has other attributes like name by which it can be referenced as a whole unit and it can be invoked by other modules.
- For example, by giving call to a function.
- In structural design, we are concerned with the outside view of a module. That is we are concerned about what a module does rather than how it does it.

    For example: The module is part of airlines reservation system which assigns a seat to a passenger, based on his class of ticket and whether he likes to stare out the window. The module figures out a suitable seat and tries to maintain an even balance on plane. If no suitable seat is available, the module assigns the next best seat.
- Modular systems incorporate collections of abstraction in which each functional abstraction, each data abstraction and each control abstraction handles a local aspect of a problem being solved.
- **Abstraction** is the intellectual tool that allows us to deal with concepts apart from particular instances of those concepts.
- The **functional abstraction** involves the use of parameterized subprograms. The data abstraction involves specifying a data type or a data object by specifying legal operations on these objects.
- The **control abstraction** is used to state a desired effect without stating the exact mechanism of control.
- All three abstractions are commonly used in system design. Modular systems consist of well defined, manageable units with well-defined interfaces among the units.
- The properties of a modular systems are:
    1. Each processing abstraction is a well-defined subsystem which is useful in other applications.
    2. Each function in each abstraction has a single, well-defined purpose.
    3. Each function manipulates only one major data structure.
    4. Functions share global data selectively.
    5. Functions which manipulate instances of abstract data types are encapsulated.
- Modularity allows improving design clarity, easy implementation, debugging testing, documenting and maintenance of the software product.

6.2.1 Modularization Criteria

- A software module to be a normal entity which has following characteristics:
    1. Module contains instructions, processing logic and data structure.
    2. Modules can be separately compiled and stored into a library.
    3. Modules can be included in a program.
    4. Module segment can be used by invoking a name and some parameters.
    5. Module can use other modules.
- Modularity allows the design to decompose a system into functional unit. There are various criteria's used to guide modularization of the system.
    1. **Conventional criteria:** In this each module and its sub module corresponding to a processing step in the execution sequence.
    2. **Information hiding criteria:** In this each module hides a difficult or changeable design decision from the other modules.
    3. **Data abstraction criteria:** In this each module hides the representation details of a major data structure behind functions that access and modify the data structure.
- In practice, a software system can be modularized using single design criteria or several criteria.

6.2.2 Advantages and Disadvantages of Modular Programming

- Modularization is important to reduce the complexity. There are advantages and disadvantages available with modularization, these are given below:
- **Advantages:**
    1. It is easier and less costly to change features, add features or correct errors after deployment.
    2. It is easier to write and debug the program.
    3. It is easy to manage difficult and easy modules with help of experts and junior programmers respectively.
    4. We can divide a large, complex problem into number of modules. Each module manages the complexity.
    5. The modular concepts give top-down design.
    6. Formal module interface definition is helpful in organization and bottom-up design.
- **Disadvantages:**
    1. as there are very few formal design techniques. It is difficult to learn even if the principles are clear.
    2. Modular programming requires more design efforts.

3. Many programmers are reluctant to try new things, including modular design.
4. Modulator programming needs more memory space and run-time.
5. Modules should be available in the same machine page (which calls each other).

6.2.3 Graphical Representation of a Module

- The module is shown as a rectangular box with its name inside as shown in Fig. 6.12. The name of the module is a statement of its function.

- The module is called and completed after the process is finished. The process is the mechanics where actual logic is written.

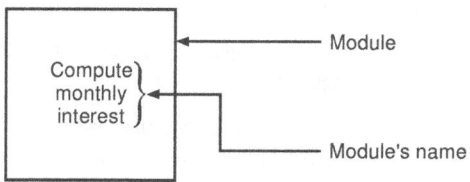

Fig. 6.12: A module

- A predefined module is shown graphically by adding lines inside which are parallel to the vertical lines. This is shown in Fig. 6.13. This module is a module or little subsystem which we do not have to write because it already exists into an application's library.

    For example: Validating telephone number from employee database.

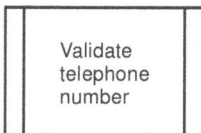

Fig. 6.13: Predefined module

- Most shops use the same symbol for modules in the operating system or database management systems.

6.2.4 Connections between Modules

- Fig. 6.14 shows A is calling B without saying anything to B. The communication is shown by arrow.

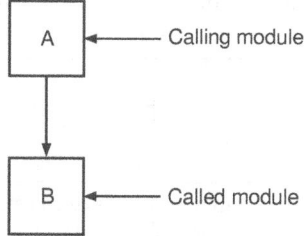

Fig. 6.14: Connections between modules

- If we call someone on phone, we speak to a person. This type of communication is shown in Fig. 6.15.

- In the Fig. 6.15 GET CUSTOMER DETAILS calls FIND CUSTOMER NAME. But these two modules communicate the information to each other.
- Consider the following.
  - The module GET CUSTOMER DETAILS sends data i.e. customer account number to FIND CUSTOMER NAME.
  - The Module FIND CUSTOMER NAME returns the data customer name to get CUSTOMER DETAILS and
  - FIND CUSTOMER NAME also returns a flag account number is ok to GET CUSTOMER DETAILS may inadvertently send an account number for a non-existent customer.
- Here, we have to use two different symbols for the communication between the modules:
  - ⤴ Is called a data couple.
  - ⤴ Is called a flag.
- The direction of arrow shows which module sends information to another.

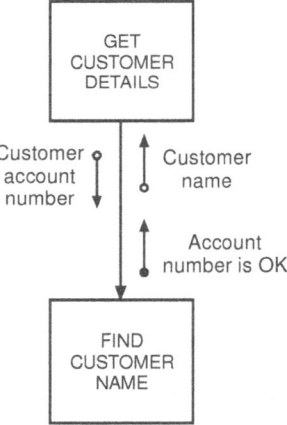

Fig. 6.15: Communication between two module

- The actual difference between data couple and flag are shown in Fig. 6.16.

⤴ Data	⤴ Flag
1. Data is processed.	1. It is not processed.
2. Data may be tested.	2. Flat typically tested and set.
3. Data relates to the problem itself, for example: insurance age of applicant for an insurance policy.	3. Flat communicates information about a piece of data, for example, (i) Zip code is valid. (ii) Pending orders.

Fig. 6.16: Difference between data couple and flag

6.2.5 Module Concepts

- A module is a logically separable part of a program which is discrete and identifiable with respect to compiling and loading.
- In the systems using functional abstraction, a module is usually a procedure of function or a collection of these.
- In modular design, some criteria must be used to select module so that it will support well-defined abstraction. In the system which uses functional abstraction, coupling and cohesion are the two criteria's for modularization.

6.2.5.1 Coupling

- The two modules are independent if they can function completely without the presence of other module. If they are independent, they are solvable and modifiable separately.
- In the system it is not possible to have all the modules independent. At least some interaction must be their.
- The notion of coupling attempts to capture coupling concept of "how strongly" different modules are interconnected.
- Coupling between modules is the strength of interconnections between modules.
- Suppose there are two modules A and B. If we know more about module A to understand module B the more closely connected A is to B. The strong interconnection shows highly coupled module and a weak interconnection shows loosely coupled module.
- Coupling is decided at the time of system design because the modules of the software system are created during system design.
- Coupling is an abstract concept and is not easily quantifiable.
- That is why no formulas can be given to determine the coupling between two modules.
- The most important thing between modules is connection between them, the complexity of interface and type of information flow.
- Coupling increases with the complexity and obscurity of the interface between modules. For having low coupling we should minimize the number of interfaces per module and also complexity of each interface. If one module passes the information to other module by parameter, it reduces coupling.
- Another factor affecting coupling is the complexity of interface.
- The degree of coupling is higher if the interface is complex. The third factor affecting coupling is the type of information flow along the interfaces.
- There are two kinds of information that can flow along an interface: data and control.

- Passing or receiving control information means the action of module will depends on the control information.
- The control information makes it more difficult to understand the module and provide its abstraction.
- Transfer of data information means that the module passes data to another module and also returns the data as output.
- The coupling is highest if the data is **hybrid**. It means some data items and some control items are passed between modules.

6.2.5.2 Cohesion

- Cohesion tells up about the bound of internal elements of the module.
- Cohesion gives an idea about whether the different elements of the module belong together in the same module to the designer.
- Cohesion and Coupling are related with each other. More or greater cohesion gives minimum coupling.
- The functional is the highest and coincidental is the lowest level. Functional binding is much stronger them the other levels. The highest level of cohesion is applicable to almost all the modules of the system.
- A module has **logical cohesion** if there is some logical relationship in the elements of a module. Temporal cohesion is same logical except elements are also related in time are executed together.

    For example: Initialization, clean-up and termination are the temporal bounds of the modules.

- A procedurally cohesive module contains the elements that belong to a common procedural unit.

    For example: A loop or a sequence of decision statements in a module may be combined to form a separate module. This type of cohesion occurs when modular structure is determined in the form of flowchart.

- We should know how to determine the cohesion level of module? There is no mathematical formula. For this we have to use our judgement. The following tests can be made:

    (a) If the sentence must be compound sentence, if it contains comma or having more than one verb, the module is probably performing more than one function and it probably has sequential or communicational cohesion.

    (b) If the sentence contains works which are related with time like 'first', 'next', 'when' and 'after', the module probably has sequential or communicational cohesion.

    (c) If a predicate of a sentence does not contain a single specific object following the verb for example, 'edit all data', the module probably has logical cohesion.

    (d) The words like 'initialize' and 'clean-up' imply temporal cohesion.

- The modules with functional cohesion can always be described by a simple sentence. If a description is a compound sentence, it does not mean that the module does not have functional cohesion.

6.2.6 Types of Modules   (Oct. 10, 12; April 13, 14)

- The designed shape of a system depends on the types of modules. The module consists of four basic types which determine the direction from that the data flows.
- The four basic types are shown below:
    1. Afferent module   (April 10)
    2. Efferent module
    3. Transform module, and
    4. Co-ordinate module.
- These four modules tell about 'what you give to a module and 'what you get back from it'.

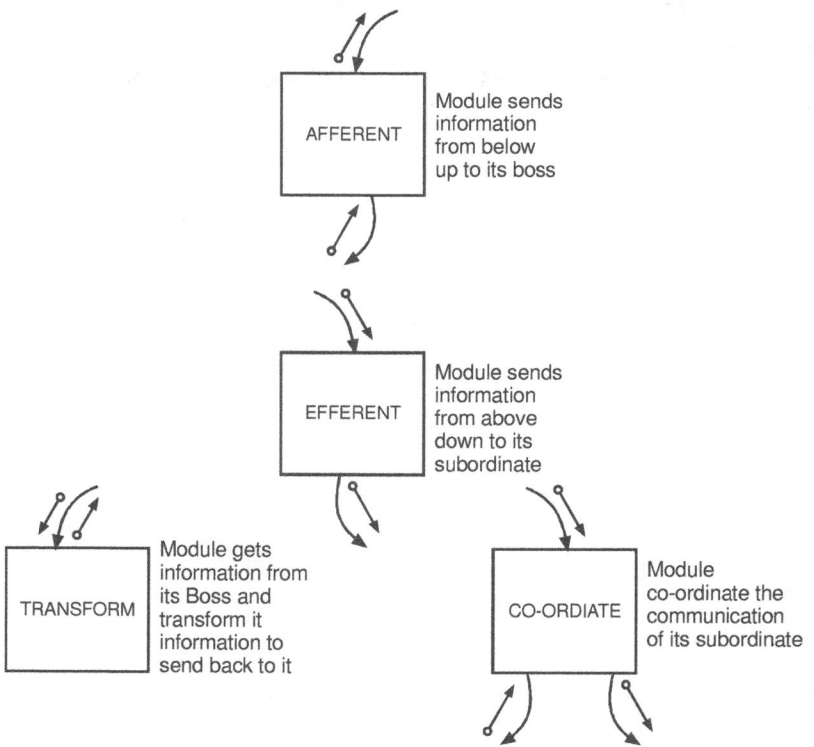

Fig. 6.17: Types of modules

- The term afferent and efferent are taken from human anatomy where it is defined as an afferent nerve sends information towards brain and an efferent nerve sending it away from brain. These module types are shown in Fig. 6.17.
    1. **Afferent modules:** This module gets data from sub-ordinates and forward it to super-ordinates (boss) modules. These are also called as input module. **(April 10)**
    2. **Efferent modules:** This module gets data from super-ordinates and forwards it to sub-ordinates. These are also called as output modules. **(Oct. 11)**
    3. **Co-ordinate modules:** This module manages the flow of data between different sub-ordinates. They are used for selection purpose and in decision making.
    4. **Transform modules:** This module gets data from super-ordinates, process that data and again forward it to super-ordinate modules. These modules are used for processing purpose.
- Let us see the example which allows us to understand this module type in detail. Fig. 6.18 shows this structure well defined.
- The module GET VALID CITY NAME, VALIDATE ALPHABETIC FIELD, PRINT ERROR MESSAGE shows efferent module.
- The module GET RECORD, GET VALID CITY NAME and GET CITY NAME shows afferent module.

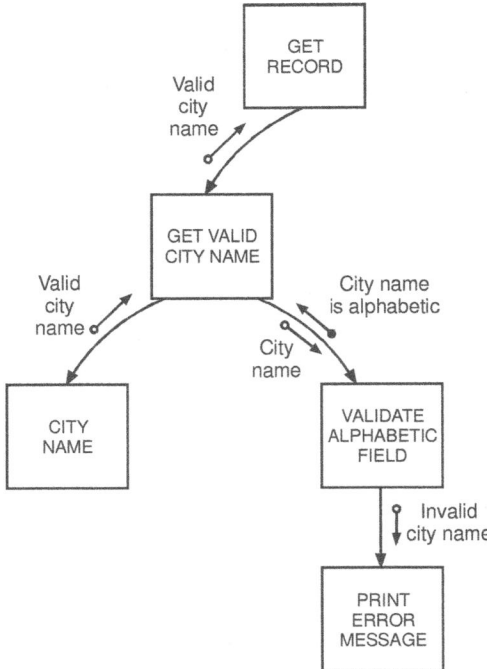

Fig. 6.18: Example which shows types of modules

- But this system is not balanced. Why? Because it prints error message only when it validate alphabetic field. If it takes the name of the city from module city name then it does not print error.
- So we can have other alternative design of a simple system. This design is shown in Fig. 6.19. Where, it specifies that when GET VALID CITY NAME executed it should accept **city** name, validate it and if it is not alphabetic print error message.

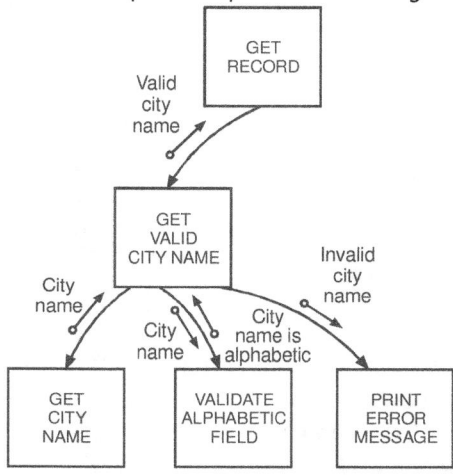

Fig. 6.19: Example of searching city

- The best example to show the transform module is shown in Fig. 6.20. This module does the pay calculations. GET EMPLOYEE PAY module gets the HOURLY EMPLOYEE TIME REPORT which is send to calculate employee pay.
- This returns the hourly employee pay to GET EMPLOYEE PAY module. This same information again sends back to the BOSS module.

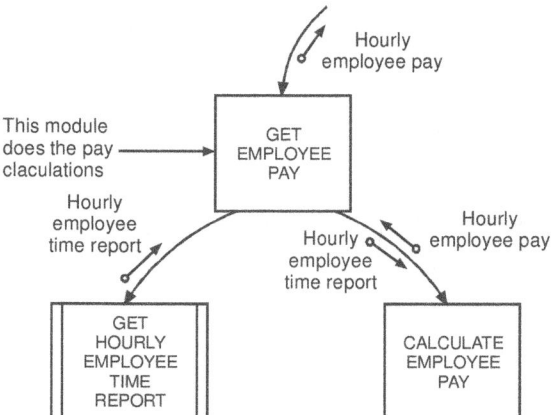

Fig. 6.20: Transform module

- Fig. 6.21 shows the best example of co-ordinate module where the module co-ordinates the communication of its subordinates.

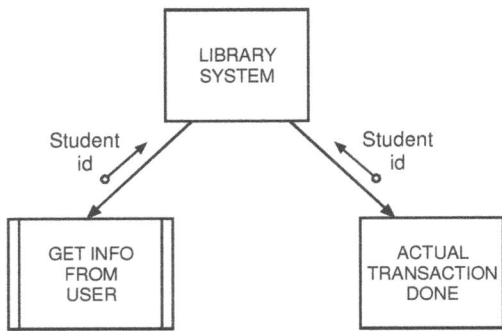

Fig. 6.21: Co-ordinate module

6.3 STRUCTURE CHARTS (Oct. 09, 10, 12; April 10, 13, 14)

- A structure chart is a hierarchy diagram.
- Structure charts are used to graphically depict a modular design of a program.
- Specially, they show how the program has been partitioned into smaller more manageable modules, the hierarchy and organization of those modules and the communication interface between modules.
- However, structure chart do not show the internal procedures performed by the module or the internal data used by the module.
- The structure charts concentrates on the black box aspect of modules, their external functions, input and outputs rather than their internal procedures and data.
- The structure of a hierarchical system can be specified using a structure chart is shown in Fig. 6.22.

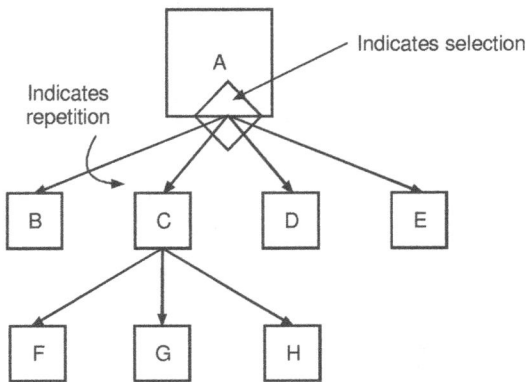

Fig. 6.22: Format of a structure chart

- To draw the structure chart, the following points are very important:
  1. The structure chart modules are depicted by named rectangles for example, A, B, C etc.
  2. The structure chart modules are presumed to execute in a top to bottom, left-to-right sequence.
  3. An arrow from upper module to lower module represents a module call.
  4. An **arc** shaped arrow located across a line which represents module call means that the module makes iterative call.
  5. A diamond symbol located at the bottom of the module means that the module calls one and only one of the other lower modules that are connected to the diamond.
  6. Program modules communicate with each other through passing of data.
  7. Program modules may also communicate with each other through passing of messages or control parameters called **flags**.
  8. Library modules are depicted on a structure chart as a rectangle containing a vertical line on each side.
- The best example of a structure chart is the ATM (All Time Money) system available in almost all the banks. The different modules which take part into ATM system are shown in Fig. 6.23.

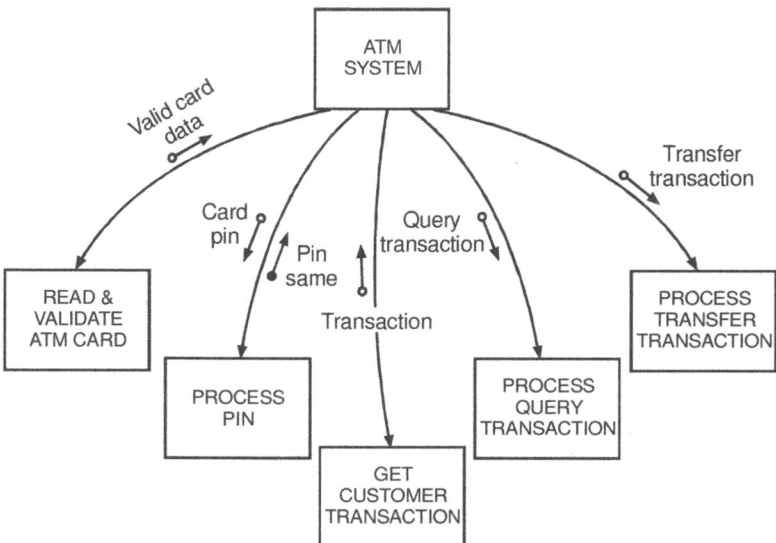

Fig. 6.23: ATM system

Examples:
1. **Phone bill system structure chart:**

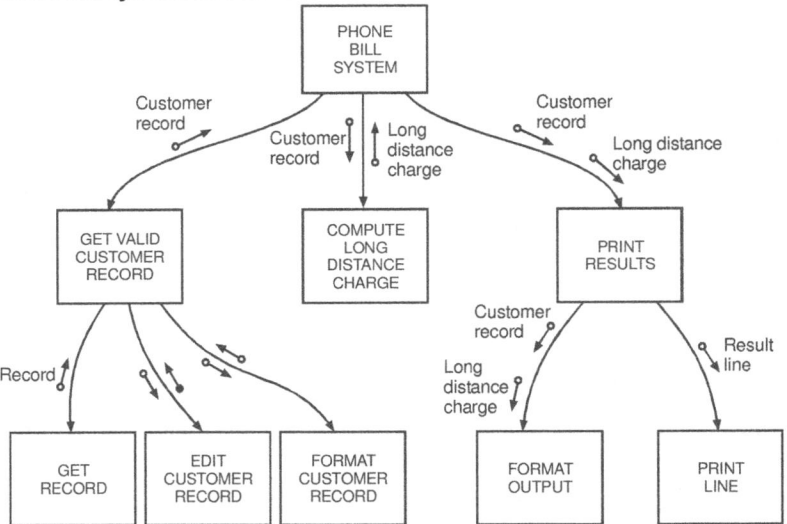

Fig. 6.24: Phone bill system

2. **Payroll system structure chart:**

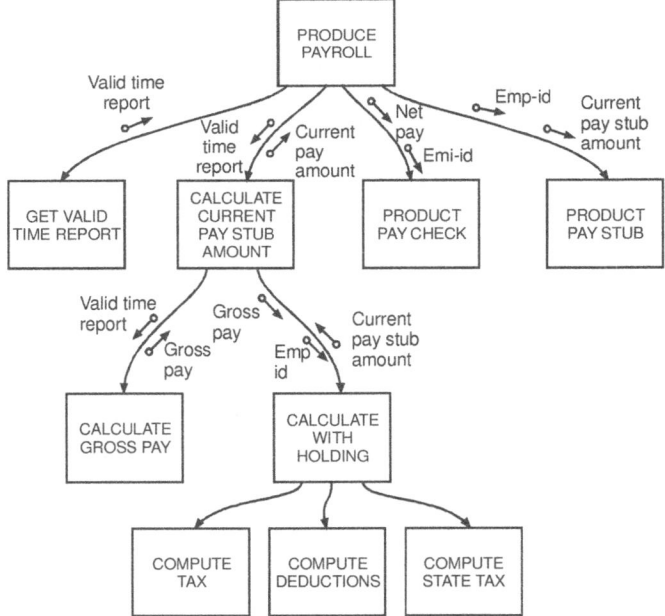

Fig. 6.25: Payroll system

6.4 QUALITIES OF GOOD DESIGN (Oct. 10, 11, 12; April 11, 12, 13, 14)

6.4.1 Coupling (April 13)

- It is a way of measuring design quality coupling is the degree of interdependence between two modules.
- Our main objective is to minimize the coupling i.e. our aim is to make modules independent. Low coupling between modules indicates a well-partitioned system.
- This can be attained in one of the following three ways:
    1. By eliminating unnecessary relationships.
    2. By reducing the number of necessary relationships.
    3. By easing the tightness of necessary relationships.
- The achieve low coupling between modules, the module should be more independent so that there is less chance for ripple effect.
- Ripple effect means a defect in one module appears as a symptom in another module.

Types of Coupling:

- The coupling is used to connect module, have various types. These are shown in Fig. 6.26.

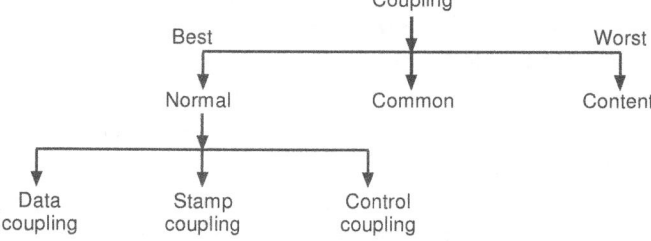

Fig. 6.26: Types of coupling

1. Normal Coupling (April 11)

- Consider, there are two modules normally coupled where A calls B and B returns to A. This is shown in Fig. 6.27.

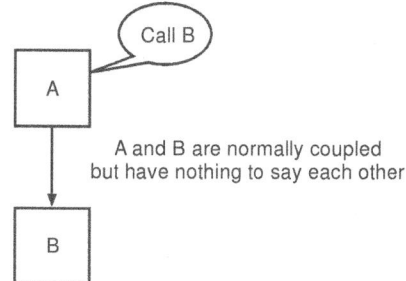

Fig. 6.27: Normal coupling

- All the information passed between them is by means of parameters. It is shown in Fig. 6.28. When no parameters passed, and nothing is written) then it makes zero coupling.

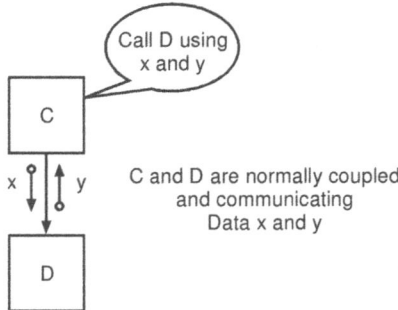

Fig. 6.28: Normal coupling (Data)

- As shown in Fig. 6.26, normal coupling has three main types:
    (i) Data coupling,
    (ii) Stamp coupling, and
    (iii) Control coupling.

(i) Data Coupling

- Fig. 6.28 shows the example of data coupling where data is shared by the module.
- Two modules are data coupled if they communicate by parameters; each parameter is an elementary piece of data.
- This coupling is the necessary communication of data between modules.
- Data coupling is unavoidable and harmless.

    For example: The module ASSESS HOUSE AFFORDABILITY uses term, interest rate, sum borrowed to calculate the second module called CALCULATE MORTGAGE REPAYMENT so receives the information about repayment rate. This is shown in Fig. 6.29.

- Data coupling shows all the best characteristics of coupling.
    (i) Create narrow connection.
    (ii) Create direct connection.
    (iii) Create local connection.
    (iv) Create obvious connection.
    (v) Create flexible connection.

- The narrow connection specifies the breadth of an interface between two modules.

    For example: Communicating only two pieces of data from one to another.

- The Direct connections show the interface without referring several other pieces of information first.

- For example, if a module uses piece of data called cust-details, which is defined as name, account number, address and balance. Then a person trying to understand the module connection to the outside world will consider only name, account number and balance. Address may be kept aside.
- The local connection shows the interface with parameter list.
- The obvious connection is easier to understand.

  For example: An assembly language routine (A) that communicates with routine B by modifying the contents of a table in B.
- The flexible connection, the information can be changed while passing.

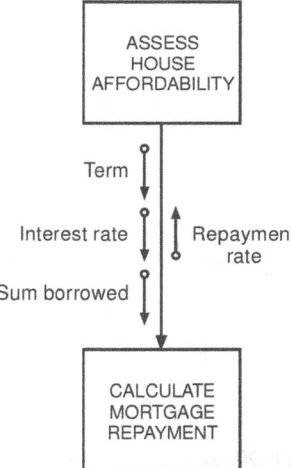

Fig. 6.29: Two data coupled modules

- Data coupling shows all the best characteristics of coupling.
    1. Data coupling is **narrow** because it avoids sending unnecessary junk.
    2. Data coupling is **direct** because what you see is what you get.
    3. Data coupling is **local**, in the code the actual coupling is shown along with the call and calling module.
    4. Data coupling is **obvious**, no trickery or sleigh of hand is at work.
    5. Data coupling is **flexible** because the called module can be quickly replaced by any other module.
- There are two warning about data coupling:
    1. Keep the interfaces as narrow as possible.
    2. A tramp i.e. a piece of information that shuffles aimlessly arounded a system, unwanted by and meaningless to most of the modules through which it passes.

(ii) Stamp Coupling

(Oct. 09)

- This term was introduced by Myers in 1975.
- Two normally coupled modules are stamp coupled if one passes to other with composite piece of data. That is a piece of data with meaningful structure is passes for example, the composite data might be a customer-record comprising many fields.
- Fig. 6.30 shows two stamp-coupled modules. In Fig. 6.30, the three parameters chess-board, move and new chess-board have rich internal structure.
- The data structure used is natural and there is no obscurity. Some indirectness is introduced.

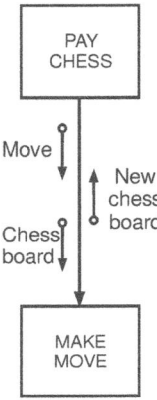

Fig. 6.30: Stamp coupled modules

- The good designers use stamp coupling well, bad designer do some wrong things. So there are two warnings.

  (i) Never pass records containing many fields to module that needs only one or two of those fields.

  Fig. 6.31 shows three stamp-couples modules.

- Customer rental record has many fields: License number, club membership, club number, gas used, car type, miles driven and days used. The module CALCULATE BASIC RENTAL CHANGE NEEDS last three fields but it receives the whole customer rental record.

- Therefore such injudicious stamp coupling broadens interfaces, introduces extra obscurity and reduces flexibility.

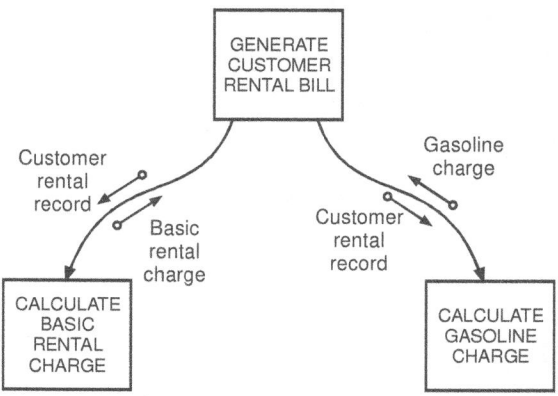

Fig. 6.31: Unnecessary stamp-coupling

(ii) Consider the fragment of a structure chart shown in Fig. 6.32. There are four fields passed to a module. These 4 fields can be replaced by a single data structure shown in Fig. 6.33. This idea of collecting unrelated data items into an artificial data structure is 27 as bundling.

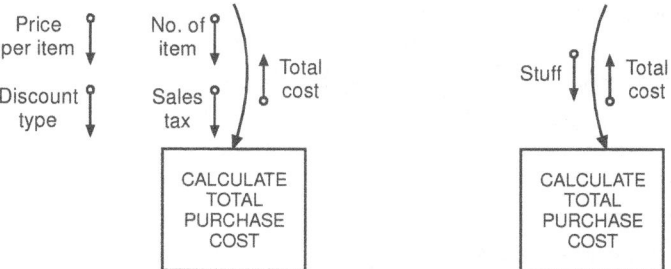

Fig. 6.32: Fragment of structure chart   **Fig. 6.33: Single data structure**

(iii) Control Coupling

- Two modules are control coupled if one passes a piece of information intended to control the internal logic of the other to the other module.
- Fig. 6.34 shows two control-coupled modules.
- The value of flag indicates to SYSTEM INPUT/OUTPUT CONTROL which record to read.
  For example, value of flag is 1 means get next control,
  Value of flag is 2 means master record,
  Value of flag is 3 means Trans record etc.

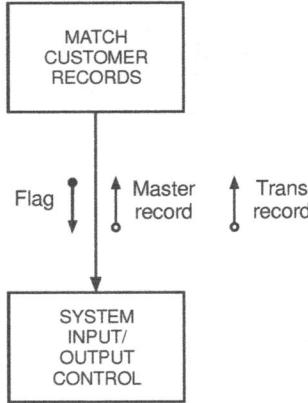

Fig. 6.34: Two control-coupled module

- All this leads to some indirectness and obscurity. If a control flag passes downward from a boss to subordinate, the boss must know something of the internals of the subordinates.

2. Common (Alias Global) Coupling

- This is the coupling which strays outside the bounds of good modularity. The two modules are common coupled if they refer to the same global data area.
- Fig. 6.35 FIND PART NAME and REMOVE STOCK are common coupled because they both refer to the same global area, which contains part table and error flag.
- These are the circle symbols called hoc notations; they are not typically used in structured design.
- Common coupling is bad for seven seasons.
    1. A defect in any module using a global area may show up in any other module using that global area. This is because global data does not reside in the protective heaven of a module.
    2. Global data is referred by explicit name.

For example: A telephone number editing module receive telephone number from a global piece of data called Tel no, it cannot edit a tel no which has some other name.

    3. Common coupling introduces and odd kind of remoteness into a system: remoteness in time.
    4. The global area may sometimes be drastically abused as for instance when different modules use the same area to store quote different pieces of information. In Fig. 6.35, error flags mean insufficient stock or no such part number. Due to this extra obscurity, maintenance efforts become hairy.

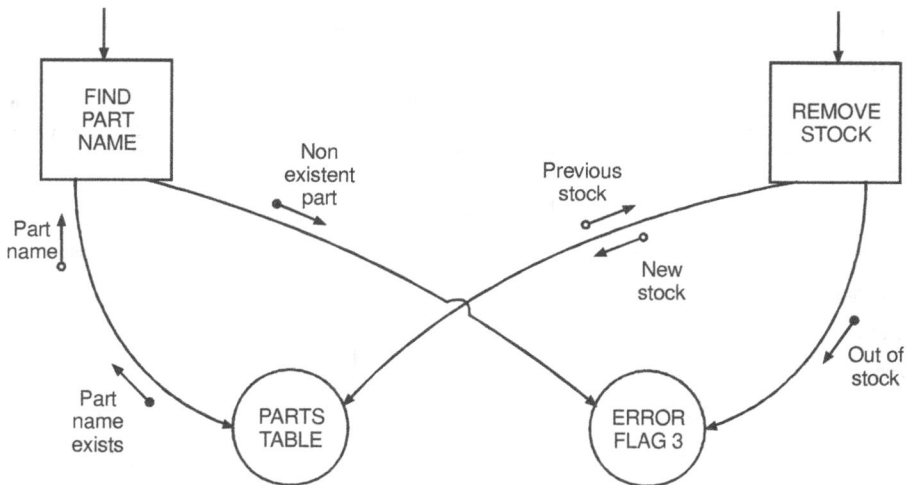

Fig. 6.35: Common-coupled modules

5. Programs with lot of global data are extremely tough for maintenance. Because what data used in a particular module is difficult to know. It is hard to tell what actual coupling is between any pairs of modules. Because one has to know which data is shared?

6. It is difficult to discover what data is changed if the module changed. Even it is also difficult to find out what module changed according to data change.

7. Common coupling is undesirable applies specifically to FORTRAN. In this language, modules refer to the data in common not by name but by location relative to the beginning of the common block.

- The use of small NAMED COMMON areas does largely alleviate this particular problem. However, the use of constant data in a common area in order to reduce redundancy is often permissible. COBOL is not strong in this respect.

3. Content (Alias Pathological) Coupling

- Two modules exhibit content coupling if one refers to the inside of the other module any way.
- For example, if one module branches through another, if one module refers or changes data within another. Such coupling makes non-sense of the concept of black box modules. Only assembler language allows designer to indulge in such sick practices.
- The higher level languages make it difficult to implement content coupling.
- The problem content coupling is that it defines the principle of modularity. It brings us back to the undisciplined mess of nonmodular coding.

- The comparison of coupling types i.e. shown in Fig. 6.36 which reviews the specific qualities.

Coupling type	Susceptibility to ripple effect	Modifiability	Under-stand ability	Modulus usability in other systems
Data	Variable	Good	Good	Good
Tramp	Poor	Medium	Medium	Poor
Stamp	Variable	Medium	Medium	Medium
Bundling	Variable	Medium	Poor	Poor
Control	Medium	Poor	Poor	Poor
Hybrid	Medium	Bad	Bad	Bad
Common	Bad	Medium	Bad	Poor
Content	Bad	Bad	Bad	Bad

Fig. 6.36: Comparison

6.4.2 Cohesion

(April, 13, 14)

- Another way to determine partitioning is to see how the activities within a single module are related to one another, this is called cohesion. Cohesion of the module determines how tightly it will be coupled to other modules in a system.

- Consider Fig. 6.37, which shows the heavy traffic between Ranjangaon and Pune which arises because of the way in which the Goodnight mousetrap company and Limca Soda Company have distributed themselves.

- Every morning the Goodnight mousetrap workers leave their homes in Pune and beat a path to the door of Goodnight Mousetrap Company in Ranjangaon. In the night, they all return back.

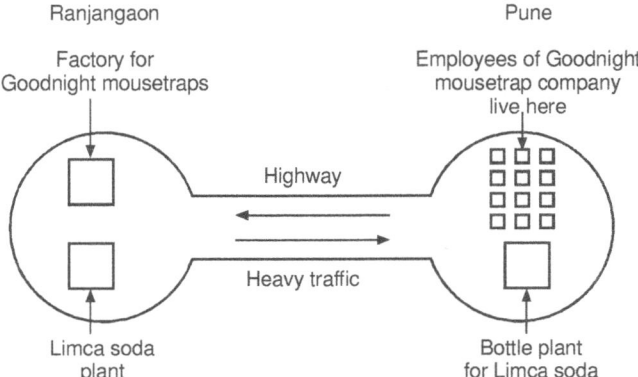

Fig. 6.37: Shows heavy traffic

- Day and night, trucks full of bottles rumble from Pune to Ranjangaon to be filled with sparkling, low calorie Limca soda.
- But if these two companies restricted themselves to one city, resulting in little or no traffic between the cities, shown in Fig. 6.38.

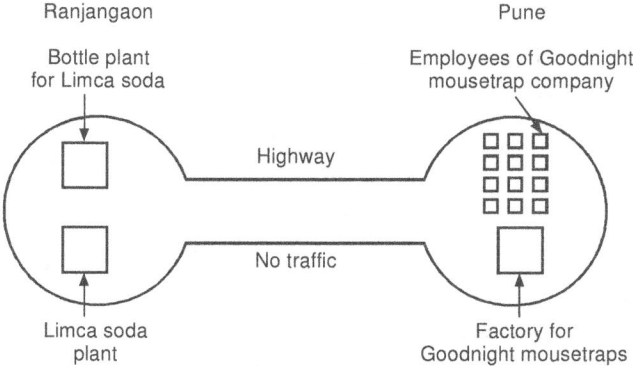

Fig. 6.38: No traffic

- Therefore, cohesion is the measure of the strength of functional relatedness of elements within a module. Elements mean an instruction.
- Designers should create strong, highly cohesive modules whose elements are strongly and genuinely related to one another.
- Cohesion is the second way to tell how well use has partitioned a system into modules.
- A good cohesion is the best way to minimize coupling between modules. The idea of cohesion came to Larry Constantine in mid 1960's.

Types of Cohesion:
- There are seven types of cohesion:
    1. Functional cohesion.
    2. Sequential cohesion.
    3. Communicational cohesion.
    4. Procedural cohesion.
    5. Temporal cohesion.
    6. Logical cohesion.
    7. Coincidental cohesion.
- Let's see all of them in detail. The scale of cohesion is shown in Fig. 6.39.

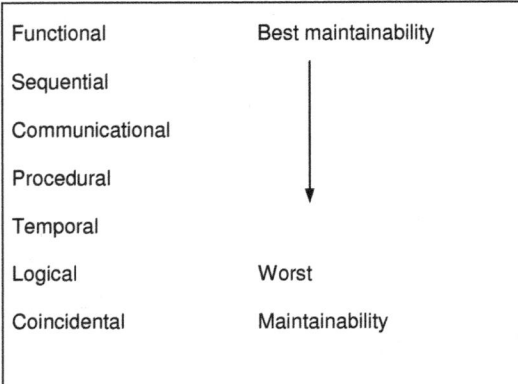

Fig. 6.39: Scale of cohesion

1. Functional Cohesion:

- It contains elements those contribute to the execution of one and only one problem related task.

    For Examples: Compute cosign at angle,

    Verify alphabetic symbol,

    Read transaction record,

    Compute point of impact of missile,

    Assign seat to airlines customer etc.

- Remember that each of these modules has a strong, single-minded purpose. When the boss calls it, carries out just one job to completion without getting involved into any extra curricular activity. The systems in which this cohesion occurs are easy to maintain.

2. Sequential Cohesion

- This module is one whose elements are involved in activities such that the output data from one activity serves as input data to the next activity.
- The sequence of steps might be something like this.
    1. Take a pot.
    2. Put sugar, tea powder, water.
    3. Put milk.
    4. Switch on gas.
    5. Put the pot on the flame.
    6. Switch off gas if it boils.
- This group of activities cannot be summed up as a single function. It means the module is not functionally cohesive.

- The sequentially cohesive module has good coupling and easily maintained. The disadvantage is it is not so readily reusable in the same system.

3. Communication Cohesion

- This is the module in which the elements contribute to activities that use the same input or output data. Suppose we want to find facts about a book, we may see following:
    - Find title of book.
    - Find price of book.
    - Find publisher of book.
    - Find author of book.
- All these four activities are related because they all work on the same input data, book which makes the module commnicatly cohesive. These modules are quite maintainable.

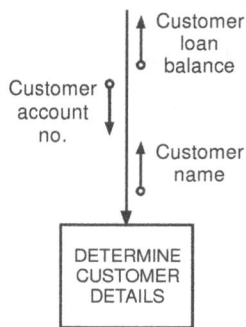

Fig. 6.40: Communication in cohesion

- For example in Fig. 6.40, it is possible that another module in the system wants to find customer name but not interested in his loan balance. This lead to dirty and redundant coupling.
- Another problem with this type of cohesion is to share code among the activities within it. It can make it tough to change one activity without destroying another.

    For example: In Fig. 6.41 EMPLOYEE SAL REPORT generates reports on all of the employee's salaries and calculates their average salary.

- The modules with communicational and sequential cohesion are similar because they both contain activities organized around the data in the original problem. They have clean coupling because some of their elements are related to the elements in other modules.
- The sequentially cohesive module operates like assembly line i.e. its individual activities must carried out in a specific order. But in communicatly cohesive module, order of it is unimportant.

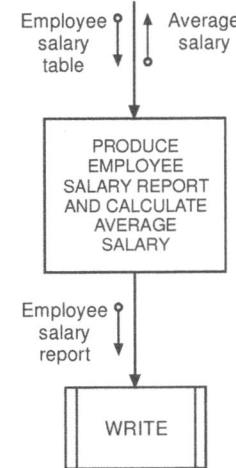

Fig. 6.41: Employee salary report

4. Procedural Cohesion
- This module is one whose elements are involved in different and possible unrelated activities in which control flows from each activity to the next.

    For example:
    1. Make a phone call.
    2. Take shower.
    3. Chop vegetables.
    4. Set table.

- All above are the modules. They all are happen in a particular day.
- The procedural cohesion modules tend to be composed of pieces of functions which have little relationship to one another. Therefore, this module contains different and unrelated activities and control flows sequentially from one activity to next activity.

5. Temporal Cohesion
- This module is one whose elements are involved in activities that are related in time.

    For example:
    1. Put out cat.
    2. Turn OFF T.V.
    3. Brush teeth.
    4. Go to bed.

- These activities are unrelated to one another except they carried out at a particular time. This module tend to be composed of partial functions whose only relationship is that they all happen to be carried out at a certain time. All activities are more closely and having tight coupling. The only problem is to share code among the activities related only by time. The module is difficult to reuse.

- The procedural and temporal modules are quite similar with respect to coupling. The difference between them is similar to the difference of sequential and communicational cohesion. This module tends to contain more straight-line code.

6. Logical Cohesion

- This is one whose elements contribute to activities of same general category in which the selected activities are form outside the module. For example, a journey might compile the following list:
    1. Go by car.
    2. Go by train.
    3. Go by boat.
    4. Go by plane.
- They all are means of transport. This module contains a number of activities of same type. These modules are forced to share only one interface. The name of this module is illogical cohesion.

7. Coincidental Cohesion

- This module is one whose elements contribute to the activities with no meaningful relationship to one another.

    For example:
    1. Fix car.
    2. Bake cake.
    3. Walk dog.
    4. Have a beer.
    5. Get out of bed.
- It is similar to logical cohesion. These activities are not in data flow and not by flow of control. This is rare. It causes misguided attempts to save time or memory. They have no well-defined functions.
- The comparison of cohesion is shown in Fig. 6.42.

Cohesion level	Coupling	Cleanliness of implementation	Modifiability	Under-standability	Effect on maintainability
Functional	Good	Good	Good	Good	Good
Sequential	Good	Good	Good	Good	Fairly good
Communicational	Medium	Medium	Medium	Medium	medium
Procedural	Variable	Poor	Variable	Variable	Bad
Temporal	Poor	Medium	Medium	Medium	Bad
Logical	Bad	Bad	Bad	Poor	Bad
Coincidental	Bad	Poor	Bad	Bad	Bad

Fig. 6.42: Comparison of cohesion

Practice Questions

1. What is meant by structured system design?
2. What is structured design? What are the various aspects of structured design?
3. Explain the modular system in detail.
4. Explain the modularization criteria.
5. What are advantages and disadvantages of modular programming?
6. What is coupling?
7. With suitable diagram describe normal coupling.
8. Explain different types of modules in detail.
9. Write a short note on structure chart.
10. Explain different symbols which are used to draw structure chart.
11. What is coupling? Explain any two types in detail?
12. Explain normal coupling.
13. Explain data coupling.
14. Explain stamp coupling.
15. Explain control coupling.
16. What is cohesion? Explain with example.
17. Explain different types of cohesion in detail.
18. Write short notes on:
    (a) Factoring.
    (b) Fan-out
    (c) Error reporting
    (d) Fan-in
    (e) System-shape
    (f) Generality/Restrictivity.
19. Explain the term functional cohesion.
20. Explain the term pseudocode.

University Questions & Answers

October 2009

1. What is stamp coupling? [2 M]

Ans. Please refer to Section 6.41 (Point 1 subpoint ii)

2. What is module? What are the different attributes of module? [4 M]

Ans. Please refer to Section 6.2.

3. Write short note on: Structure Chart. [4 M]

Ans. Please refer to Section 6.3.

4.	What is ripple effect?	[4 M]
Ans.	Please refer to Section 6.4.1.	

April 2010

1.	What is coupling? State any two types of coupling.	[2 M]
Ans.	Please refer to Section 6.4.1.	
2.	What is afferent module?	[2 M]
Ans.	Please refer to Section 6.2.6 (Point 1).	
3.	Define module and explain types of modules.	[4 M]
Ans.	Please refer to Section 6.2 and 6.2.6.	
4.	Write steps for converting DFD into structure chart.	[4 M]
Ans.	Please refer to Section 6.3.	

October 2010

1.	Define the terms: Coupling and cohesion.	[2 M]
Ans.	Please refer to Sections 6.4.1 and 6.4.2.	
2.	State different types of modules. Explain any one.	
Ans.	Please refer to Section 6.2.6.	
3.	What is structured design? What are the various aspects of structured design?	[4 M]
Ans.	Please refer to Section 6.1.1.	
4.	Write short notes on:	[4 M]
	(i) Qualities of good design	
Ans.	Please refer to Section 6.1.2.	
	(ii) Structure chart.	[4 M]
Ans.	Please refer to Section 6.3.	

April 2011

1.	What are the types of coupling?	[2 M]
Ans.	Please refer to Section 6.4.1.	
2.	Write short note on: Coupling	[4 M]
Ans.	Please refer to Section 6.4.1.	

October 2011

1.	What is ripple effect?	[2 M]
Ans.	Please refer to Section 6.4.1.	

2.	What is coupling and cohesion?	[2 M]
Ans.	Please refer to Sections 6.4.1 and 6.4.2.	
3.	What is afferent module?	[2 M]
Ans.	Please refer to Section 6.2.6 (Point 1)	
4.	What is structured design? What are the various aspects of structured design?	[4 M]
Ans.	Please refer to Section 6.1.1.	
5.	Write short note on: Qualities of good design.	[4 M]
Ans.	Please refer to Section 6.1.2.	

April 2012

1.	What is a module?	[2 M]
Ans.	Please refer to Section 6.2.	
2.	What is coupling?	[2 M]
Ans.	Please refer to Section 6.4.1.	

October 2012

1.	Explain co-ordinate module with diagram.	[2 M]
Ans.	Please refer to Section 6.2.6.	
2.	Explain different types of coupling.	[2 M]
Ans.	Please refer to Sections 6.4.1.	
3.	Write short note on Structured chart.	[2 M]
Ans.	Please refer to Section 6.3.	

April 2013

1.	What is preventive maintenance?	[2 M]
Ans.	Please refer to Section 6.4.2.	
2.	Explain cohesion with example.	[2 M]
Ans.	Please refer to Section 6.4.2.	
3.	What is ripple effect?	[2 M]
Ans.	Please refer to Section 6.4.	
4.	Explain different types of coupling.	[2 M]
Ans.	Please refer to Section 6.4.	
5.	Write a note on structured chart.	[2 M]
Ans.	Please refer to Section 6.3.	
6.	Write short note on types of modules.	[2 M]
Ans.	Please refer to Section 6.2.	

April 2014

1. Define preventive maintenance. **[2 M]**
Ans. Please refer to Section 6.4.2.

2. Define module. **[2 M]**
Ans. Please refer to Section 6.2.

3. Define cohesion. **[2 M]**
Ans. Please refer to Section 6.4.2.

4. Explain types of coupling. **[2 M]**
Ans. Please refer to Section 6.4.1.

5. Write a note on structured chart. **[2 M]**
Ans. Please refer to Section 6.3.

6. Write short note on types of modules. **[2 M]**
Ans. Please refer to Section 6.2.6.

❖❖❖

Chapter 7...
Software Testing

Contents ...

This chapter gives basic concepts of system such as:

7.1 DEFINITION, TEST CHARACTERISTICS
- 7.1.1 Definition
- 7.1.2 Testing Objectives and Principles
- 7.1.3 Testing Process
- 7.1.4 Software Testing Techniques
- 7.1.5 Testing Characteristics
- 7.1.6 Test Information Flow
- 7.1.7 Test Case Design

7.2 TYPES OF TESTING
- 7.2.1 Black-Box Testing
- 7.2.2 White-Box Testing
- 7.2.3 Unit Testing
- 7.2.4 Integration Testing

7.3 VALIDATION

7.4 VERIFICATION

7.1 DEFINITION, TEST CHARACTERISTICS (Oct. 10; April 12)

- Making perfect software system is the difficult job. This is because the development requires many activities where human errors are enormous.
- These errors are logical errors, carelessness or improper communication in software development. So we should find out the next best alternative in such situation to reduce the errors.
- This can be performed by an activity referred as quality assurance activity. It includes four sub activities into it as shown in Fig. 7.1
- The verification is performed by executing a program whereas validation is a process of using any software in order to find errors. But our main aim is testing.
- Software or system testing is highly complex activity. It is also very difficult to say when testing is complete.

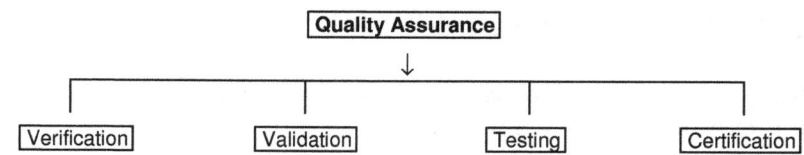

Fig. 7.1: Sub-activities

- In this chapter we will study the software testing, their objectives, and principles strategies for completion of testing.

7.1.1 Definition (Oct. 10)

- There are various definitions of Testing:

    Testing is the process which is performed to prove that there are no errors in a program.

    OR

    Testing is the process to prove that software works correctly.

    OR

    Testing is the process to detect the defects and minimize the risk associated with the residual defects.

- Out of above three definitions, the third definition is realistic.
- The objective of testing is to uncover as many bugs as possible.
- The testing should be done perfect and without any attachments to the software. The software testing is destructive than constructive.
- The software testing is must because the cost associated with a software failure and enormous.
- When the software product reached a mature stage of development, then start testing. We should keep track of the number of bugs which are detected and correct the software. When software is good enough then release it into the market.

Debugging

- Debugging is that activity which is performed after executing a successful test case.
- Debugging consists of determining the exact nature and location of the suspected error and fixing the error i.e. the process of removing errors.
- Debugging is probably the most difficult activity in software development from a psychological point of view because of the following reasons:
    1. Debugging is done by the person who developed the software, even though it is hard for that person to acknowledge that an error was made.
    2. Of all the software-development activities, debugging is the most mentally taxing because of the way in which most programs are designed and because of the nature

of most programming languages i.e. the location of any error in any statement in the program.

3. Debugging is usually performed under a tremendous amount of pressure to fix the suspected error as quickly as possible.
4. Compared to the other software-development activities, little research, literature, and formal instruction exist on the process of debugging.

7.1.2 Testing Objectives and Principles (Oct. 10, 11; April 12, 14)

- The testing objective is basically to test the code. This provides a high probability to find all the errors.
- The objective also demonstrates that the software functions are working according to the Software Requirement Specifications [SRS].
- The SRS is related with functionality, features, facilities and performance. It may be possible that there are certain requirement stipulated in SRS but the code is not written. Then the code does not generate any error.

7.1.2.1 Objectives or Goals of Testing

- Following goals are used to demonstrate the correctness of the software.
    1. To demonstrate that errors are not present.
    2. To show that intended functions are present.
    3. To gain confidence in the softwares ability to do what it is required to do.
    4. Discover the unnoticed errors.
    5. Increase the probability of discovering errors.

7.1.2.2 Testing Principles

- Before we enter into software testing, let us state the basic principles which govern software testing.
- A software engineer must understand these basic principles which guide software testing.
    1. All tests should be traceable as per the customer requirements. It follows that the most severe defects are those that cause the program to fail to meet its requirements. This is customers point of view.
    2. An overall testing schedule and resource planning must be made in advance. Therefore, all tests can be planned and designed before any code has been generated, i.e. immediately after the requirement model is complete.
    3. The pareto principle: The principle implies that 80% of all errors uncovered during testing are traceable to 20% of all program modules. Therefore, the problem is to isolate these suspect modules and to thoroughly test them.
    4. Testing should begin: "in the small" and progress towards testing "in the large". The first test planned and executed focuses on the individual program modules. As

testing progresses, it shifts focus in an attempt to find errors. This is in integrated clusters of modules and ultimately in the entire system.
5. Exhaustive testing is not possible.
6. Testing should be conducted by an independent people so that it is most effective.

- The testing principles in short are:
  - Tests should be traceable to the customer requirements shown in SRS.
  - Test cases should be designed when SRS are finalized.
  - Test cases should be planned from lower level components and take them to higher level.
  - Test cases should show all functions features, facilities and performance of SRS.

- The test ability can be increased if we use and follow the following guide-lines:
  1. Needs and relationships between input and output must be clearly present.
  2. The code of software must be structured.
  3. All the outputs should be traceable to SRS.
  4. Modular structure should be used for software design.
  5. Software testability must be improved by writing proper program structure, data structure and code.

7.1.3 Testing Process

- During design stage, the software is divided into modules and each module is divided into units. If we tests entire system then it is not good practice. A practical approach to divide testing process into different levels.
- So that we can test each unit separately. Then modules have to be built from the units and then they are tested. All these tested modules are combined together and the system is built and tested.

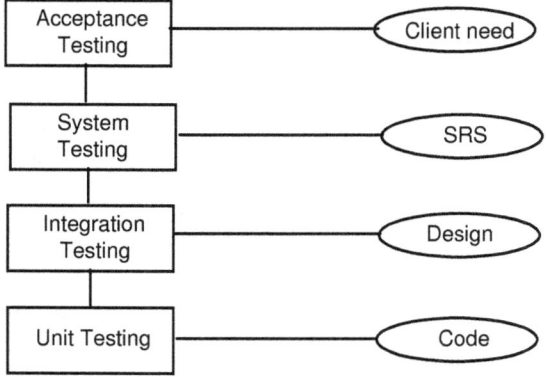

Fig. 7.2: Testing levels

- Fig. 7.2 shows each level of testing for testing specific entity. Unit testing is done to test source code, integration testing is done to test design, system testing is done to test SRS i.e. Software Requirement Specification whereas Acceptance testing is done to test client or user requirements.

1. **Unit Testing:** A Unit is the smallest entity of the software. These units are tested separately as per the specification. The additional code is written to test the units. So it is done by development engineers themselves. Individual components are tested to ensure that they operate correctly.

2. **Module Testing:** A module is an independent entity in the software like an object class, an abstract data types or collection of procedures or functions. The tested unit are integrated into a module. Each module is tested separately for specifications.

   For example, if software is database management system, the modules are database (back end) and user-interface (front end). So database can be tested separately by SQL command. After that a front-end can be tested.

   After module testing, a module-level test report is prepared.

3. **Integration and System Testing:** The modules are integrated and then start testing. Because debugging is very difficult. After integrating all the modules together, system testing can be performed on functional and non-functional requirements.

4. **Acceptance Testing:** This is the final test. It is sometimes referred as alpha testing. The software is tested by the client/user. If system is a software product then beta testing can be performed. Where defects can be detected and removed.

The various stages of system testing are shown in Fig. 7.3 and Fig. 7.4 shows complete testing process.

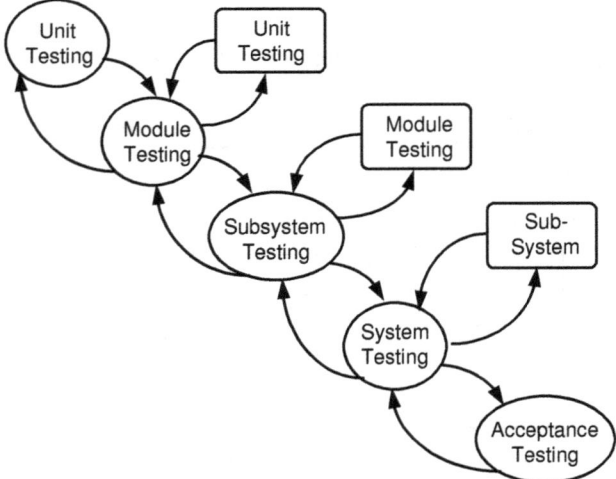

Fig. 7.3: Stages of system testing

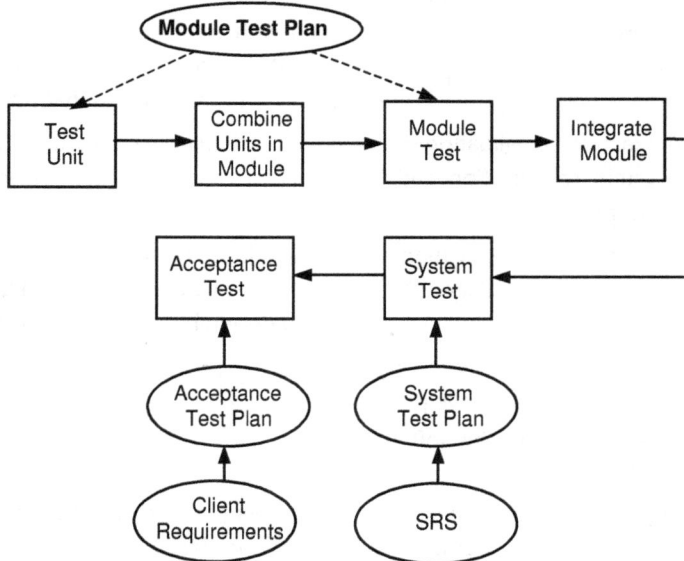

Fig. 7.4: Testing process

- The software quality assurance is achieved through designing test cases. These test cases should ensure the desired quality as shown below:

Test	Test case	The focus given
Unit test	Process	Code
Module test	Function	Design
Application test	Business operations	Design
Integration test	Various business operations	Interface

7.1.4 Software Testing Techniques

- The importance of software testing and its impact on software cannot be underestimated.
- Software testing is a fundamental component of software quality assurance and represents a review of specification, design and coding.
- The greater visibility of software systems and the cost associated with software failure are motivating factors for planning, through testing.
- It is not uncommon for a software organization to spent 40% of its effort on testing.

1. Validation and Verification are two of the most important activities that occur on a software project. The former is concerned with ensuring that an evolving software system matches user requirements. The latter is concerned with ensuring that the output of a project phase is a correct reflection of the input to that phase.
2. A good example of validation is the software requirements review. This takes place during system specification and its aim is to check that the system specification matches user requirements.
3. A good example of verification is testing effort on the smallest unit of software design i.e. each module. Here, the conformance of a coded program unit (subroutine or procedure) is checked against its detailed design by executing it with test data.

- During testing the software engineering produces, a series of test cases that are used to "rip apart" the software they have produced.
- Testing is the one step in the software process that can be seen by the developer as destructive instead of constructive.
- Software engineers are typically constructive people and testing requires them to overcome preconceived concepts of correctness and deal with conflicts when errors are identified.

7.1.5 Testing Characteristics

- A number of rules that act as testing characteristics are:
    1. Testing is a process of executing a program with the intent of finding an error.
    2. A good test case is one that has a high probability of finding an as yet undiscovered error.
    3. A successful test is one that uncovers an as yet undiscovered error.
    4. Testing cannot show the absence of defects, it can only show that software defects are present.

7.1.6 Test Information Flow

- Information flow for testing follows the pattern shown in the Fig. 7.5. Two types of input are given to the test process:
    1. A software configuration,
    2. A test configuration.
- Tests are performed and all outcomes considered, test results are compared with expected results. When erroneous data is identified, error is implied and debugging begins.
- The debugging procedure is the most unpredictable element of the testing procedure.

- An "error" that indicates a discrepancy of 0.01 percent between the expected and the actual results can take hours, days or months to identify and correct.
- It is the uncertainty in debugging that causes testing to be difficult to schedule reliability.

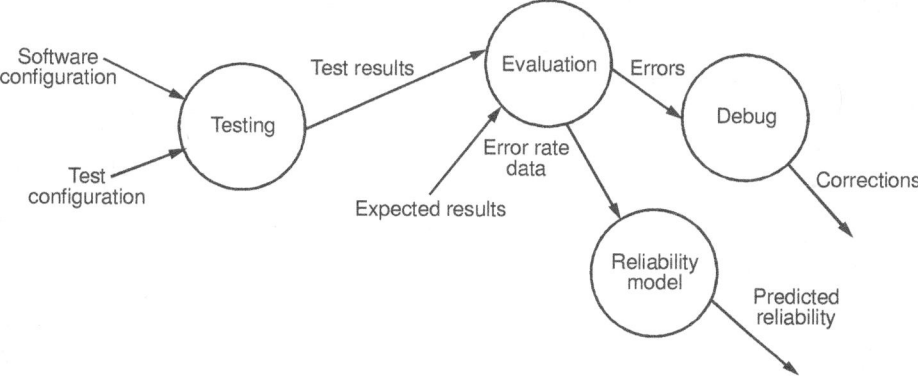

Fig. 7.5: Test information flow

7.1.7 Test Case Design

- The design of software testing can be a challenging process. However, software engineers often see testing as an after thought, producing test cases that feel right but have little assurance that they are complete.
- The objective of testing is to have the highest likelihood of finding the most errors with a minimum amount of timing and effort.
- A large number of test case design methods have been developed that offer the developer with a systematic approach to testing. Methods offer an approach that can ensure the completeness of tests and offer the highest likelihood for uncovering errors in software.
- Any engineering product can be tested in two ways:
  1. Knowing the specified functions that the product has been designed to perform, tests can be performed that show that each function is fully operational.
  2. Knowing the internal workings of a product, tests can be performed to see if they jell. The first test approach is known as a **black-box testing** and the second **white-box testing**.
- Black-box testing relates to the tests that are performed at the software interface.
- Although they are designed identify errors, black box tests are used to demonstrate that software functions are operational; that inputs are correctly accepted and the output is correctly produced.

- A black-box test considers elements of the system with little interest in the internal logical arrangement of the software.
- White-box testing of software involves a closer examination of procedural detail. Logical paths through the software are considered by providing test cases that exercise particular sets of conditions and/or loops.
- The status of the system can be identified at diverse points to establish if the expected status matches the actual status.

A Strategic approach to Software testing and Testing issues

- Testing is a set of activities that can be planned in advance and conducted systematically.
- A number of software testing strategies have the following generic characteristics:
    - Testing begins at the module level and works "outward' toward the integration of the entire computer-based system.
    - Different testing techniques are appropriate at different points in time.
    - Testing is conducted by the developer of the software and an independent test group.
    - Testing and Debugging are different activities, but debugging must be accommodated in any testing strategy.
    - Software testing is often referred to as verification and validation (v and v). Verification refers to the set of activities that ensure that software correctly implements a specific function.
    - Validation refers to a different set of activities that ensure that the software that has to be built is traceable to customer requirements.
    - The activities required to achieve the software quality may be viewed as a set of components depicted in Fig. 7.6.

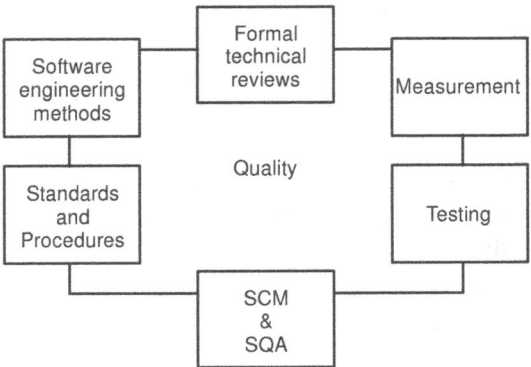

Fig. 7.6: Software Quality Management Activities

- **Organization for software testing:**
  - From a psychological point of view, software analysis and design are constructive tasks. From the point of view of the builder, tests can be considered to be (psychologically) destructive.
  - The software developer is always responsible for testing the individual units (modules) of the program, ensuring that each performs the function for which it was designed.
  - In many cases, the developer also conducts 'integration tests the testing step that leads to the construction (and test) of the complete does an independent test group become involved.
  - The role of an Independent Test Group (ITG) is to remove the inherent problems associated with letting the builder test the thing that has been built.
- **A software testing strategy:**
  - The software engineering process may be viewed as a spiral, as illustrated in Fig. 7.7.

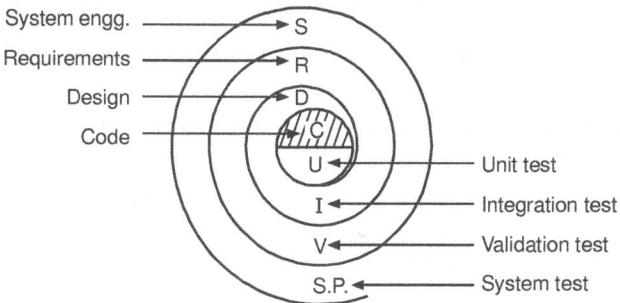

Fig. 7.7: Testing Strategy

  - A strategy for software testing may also be viewed in the context of the spiral of Fig. 7.7.
    - Unit testing begins at the vertex of the spiral and concentrates on each unit of the software as implemented in the source code.
    - Integration testing focusses on the design and the construction of the software architecture.
    - In validation testing, requirement analysis are validated against the software that has been constructed.
    - In system testing, the software and the other system elements are tested as a whole.

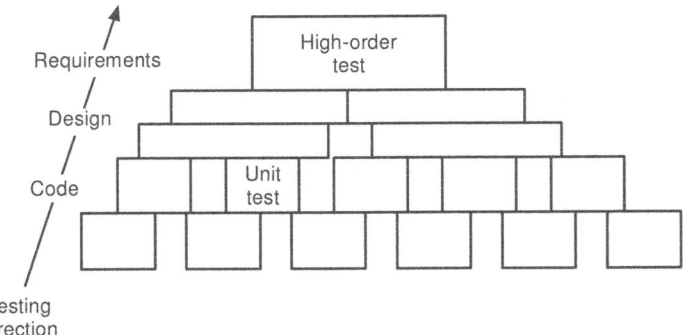

Fig. 7.8: Software Testing Steps

Failure model: (Logarithmic Poisson execution-time model)

$$f(t) = \left(\frac{1}{P}\right) \ln(l_0 \, Pt + 1) \qquad \ldots (1)$$

where, f(t) = Cumulative number of failures that are expected to occur once the software has been tested for a certain amount of execution time t.

l_0 = The initial software failure intensity (failures per unit time) at the beginning of testing.

P = The exponential reduction in failure intensity as errors are uncovered and repairs are made.

- The instantaneous failure intensity, $l(t)$, can be derived by taking the derivative of

$$f(t): l(t) = \frac{l_0}{l_0 \, Pt + 1} \qquad \ldots (2)$$

(i) Failure intensity as a function of execution time.

■ → data collected during test.

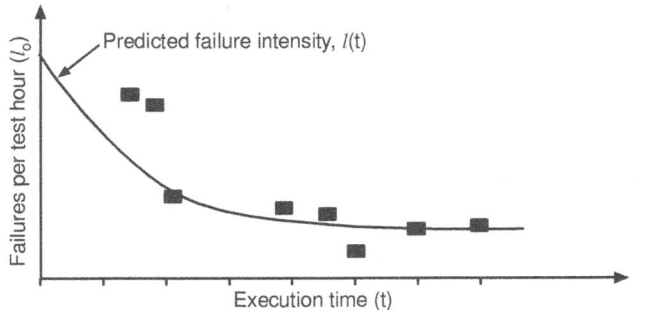

Fig. 7.9: Failure intensity as a function of time

- A strategy for software testing integrates software test case design techniques into a well-planned set of steps that cause the production of software.
- A software test strategy provides a road map for the software developer, the quality assurance organization and the customer. Any testing strategy needs to include test planning, test case design, test execution and the resultant data collection evaluation.
- A software test strategy should be flexible enough to promote the creativity and customization that are required to adequately test all large software-based systems.

7.2 TYPES OF TESTING (Oct. 10)

7.2.1 Black-Box Testing (Oct. 09, 10, 11; April 10, 11, 12)

- Black-box testing relies on the specification of the system or component which is being tested to drive test cases.
- The system is a 'black-box' whose behaviour can only be determined by studying its inputs and the related outputs.
- Another name for this is **'functional testing'** because mathematical functions can be specified using only their inputs and outputs.
- Fig. 7.12 illustrates the model of a system which is assumed in black-box testing. This model is the same as that used for reliability testing.
- The key problem for the defect tester is to select inputs that have a high probability of being members of the set Ie. In many cases, the selection of these test cases is based on the previous experience of test engineers. They use domain knowledge to identify test cases which are likely to reveal defects.

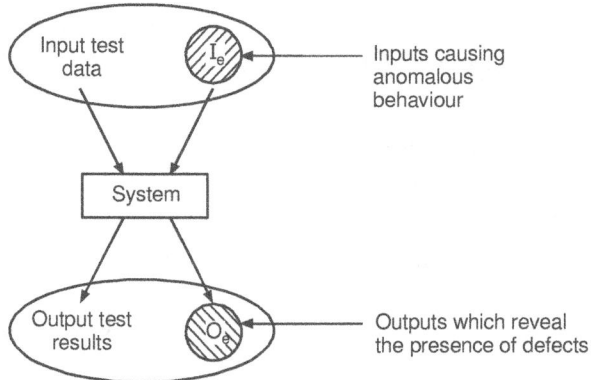

Fig. 7.12: Black-box testing model

- **Objectives of black-box testing are to find out:**
  - Incorrect or missing functions.
  - Interface errors.
  - Errors in data structures and external database access.
  - Performance errors.
  - Initialization and termination errors.
- **Techniques used for black-box testing are:**
  - Equivalent partitioning and
  - Boundary value analysis.
- Black-box testing approaches concentrate on the fundamental requirements of the software.
- Black-box testing allows the software engineer to produce groups of input situations that will fully exercise all functional requirements for a program.
- Black-box testing is not an alternative to white-box techniques. It is a complementary approach that is likely to uncover a different type of errors that the white-box approaches.
- Black-box testing tries to find errors in the following categories:
  1. Incorrect or missing functions,
  2. Interface errors,
  3. Errors in data structures or external database access,
  4. Performance errors and
  5. Initialization and termination errors.
- By applying black-box approaches, we produce a set of test cases that fulfil requirements:
  1. Test cases that reduce the number of test cases to achieve reasonable testing,
  2. Test cases that tell use something about the presence or absence of classes of errors.

7.2.1.1 Equivalent Partitioning

- Equivalence partitioning is a black-box testing approach that splits the input domain of a program into classes of data from which test cases can be produced.
- An ideal test case uncovers a class of errors that may otherwise before the error is detected.
- Equivalence partitioning tries to outline a test case that identifies classes of errors.
- Test case design for equivalent partitioning is founded on an evaluation of equivalence classes for an input condition.
- An equivalence class depicts a set of valid or invalid states for the input condition.

- Equivalence classes can be defined based on the following:
  1. If an input condition specifies a range, one valid and two invalid equivalence classes are defined.
  2. If an input condition needs a specific value, one valid and two invalid equivalence classes are defined.
  3. If an input condition specifies a member of a set, one valid and one invalid equivalence class is defined.
  4. If an input condition is Boolean, one valid and invalid class are outlined.

7.2.1.2 Boundary Value Analysis

- A great many errors happen at the boundaries of the input domain and for this reason boundary value analysis was developed.
- Boundary value analysis is test case design approach that complements equivalence partitioning. BVA produces test cases from the output domain also.
- Guidelines for BVA are close to those for equivalence partitioning:
  1. If an input condition specifies a range bounded by values a and b, test cases should be produced with values a and b, just above and just below a and b, respectively.
  2. If an input condition specifies various values, test cases should be produced to exercise the minimum and maximum numbers.
  3. Apply guidelines above to output conditions.
- If internal program data structures have prescribed boundaries, produce test cases to exercise that data structure at its boundary.

Advantages of Black Box Testing:
- Efficient when used on large systems.
- The tester and developer are independent of each other, testing is balanced and neutral.
- Tester can be non-technical.
- There is no need for the tester to have detailed functional knowledge of system.
- Tests will be done from an end user's point of view, because the end user should accept the system.
- Testing helps to identify ambiguity and contradictions in functional specifications.
- Test cases can be designed as soon as the functional specifications are complete.

Disadvantages of Black Box Testing:

- Test cases are challenging to design without having clear functional specifications.
- It is difficult to identify complicated inputs if the test cases are not developed based on specifications.
- It is difficult to identify all possible inputs in limited testing time. As a result, writing test cases may be slow and difficult.
- There are chances of having unidentified paths during the testing process.
- There is a high probability of repeating tests already performed by the programmer.

7.2.2 White-Box Testing   (Oct. 09, 10, 11, 12; April 10, 12, 13, 14)

- A complementary approach to black-box testing is sometimes called structural or glass-box testing shown in Fig. 7.13.

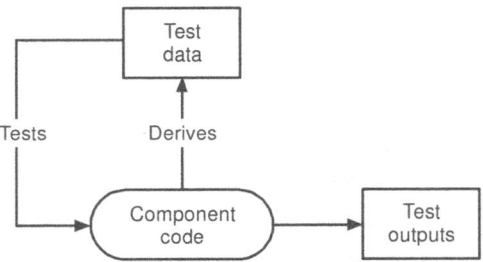

Fig. 7.13: White-box Testing Model

- As the name implies, the tester can analyze the code and use knowledge about the structure of a component to derive test data.
- The advantage of structural testing is that an analysis of the code can be used to find how many test cases are needed to guarantee a given level of test coverage.
- A dynamic analyzer can then be used to measure the extent of this coverage and help with test case design. Techniques of white-box testing are:
    1. **Basic path testing:** This testing allows the test case designer to produce logical complexity measures procedural design and use this measures as an approach for outlining a basic set of execution paths. Path testing designed to execute or all selected paths through a computer system.
    2. **Condition testing:** It is a test case design approach that exercises the logical conditions contained in a program module.
    3. **Data flow testing:** This testing technique chooses test paths of a program based on the locations of definitions and uses of variables in the program.

- White-box testing is a test case design approach that employs the control architecture of the procedural design to produce test cases.
- Using white-box testing approaches, the software engineering can produce test cases that:
  1. Guarantee that all independent paths in a module have been exercised at least once,
  2. Exercise all logical decisions,
  3. Execute all loops at their boundaries and in their operational bounds,
  4. Exercise internal data structures to maintain their validity.

Advantages of white box testing:
- Forces test developer to reason carefully about implementation
- Approximates the partitioning done by execution equivalence
- Reveals errors in "hidden" code:
- Beneficent side-effects
- Optimizations (e.g. chartable that changes reps when size > 100)
- As the knowledge of internal coding structure is requirement, it becomes very easy to find out which type of input/data can help in testing the application effectively.
- The other advantage of white box testing is that it helps in optimizing the code.
- It helps in removing the extra lines of code, which can bring in hidden defects.

Disadvantages of white box testing:
- Expensive
- Miss cases omitted in the code
- As knowledge of code and internal structure is a requirement, a skilled tester is needed to carry out this type of testing, which increases the cost.
- And it is nearly impossible to look into every bit of code to find out hidden errors, which may create problems, resulting in failure of the application.
- Not looking at the code in a runtime environment. That's important for a number of reasons. Development of vulnerability is dependent upon all aspects of the platform being targeted and source code is just of those components. The underlying operating system, the backend database being used, third party security tools, dependent libraries, etc. must all be taken into account when determining exploitability. A source code review is not able to take these factors into account.
- Very few white-box tests can be done without modifying the program, changing values to force different execution paths, or to generate a full range of inputs to test a particular function.

7.2.3 Unit Testing

- Unit testing concentrates verification on the smallest element of the program – the module. Using the detailed design description, important control paths are tested to establish errors within the bounds of the module.

1. Unit Test Considerations:

- The tests that are performed as part of unit testing are shown in Fig. 7.14. The module interface is tested to ensure that information properly flows into and out of the program unit being tested. The local data structure is considered to ensure that data stored temporarily maintains its integrity for all stages in an algorithm's execution.

- Boundary conditions are tested to ensure that the modules perform correctly at boundaries created to limit or restrict processing. All independent paths through the control structure are exercised to ensure that all statements are being executed once. Finally, all error-handling paths are examined.

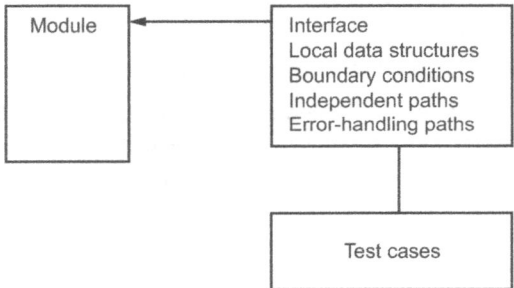

Fig. 7.14 : Unit Test

2. Unit Test Procedures:

- Unit testing is typically seen as an adjunct to the coding step. Once, source code has been produced, reviewed and verified for correct syntax, unit test case design can start. A review of design information offers assistance for determining test cases that should uncover errors.

- Each test case should be linked with a set of anticipated results. As a module is not a stand-alone program, driver and/stub software must be produced for each test units. In most situations, a driver is a "main program" that receives test case data, passes this to the module being tested and prints the results. Stubs act as the sub-modules called by the test modules. Unit testing is made easy if a module has cohesion.

- Unit testing focusses verification effort on the smallest unit of software design i.e. the module.

- The unit test is always white-box-oriented and the step can be conducted in parallel for multiple modules.

- The tests that occur as part of unit testing are illustrated schematically in Fig. 7.15.

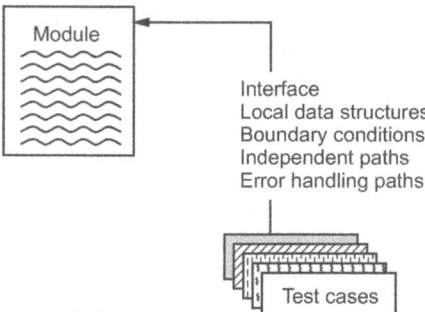

Fig. 7.15: Unit Test

- The unit test environment (or procedure) is illustrated in Fig. 7.16.

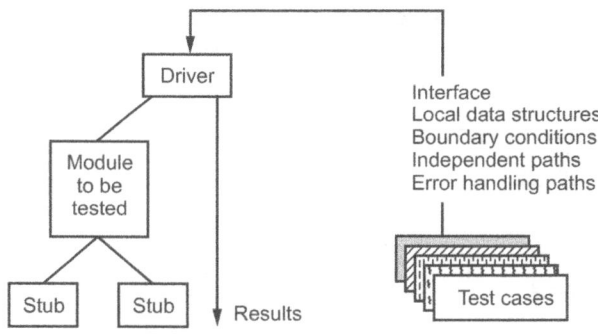

Fig. 7.16: Unit Test Environment

7.2.4 Integration Testing

- Integration testing is a systematic technique for constructing the program structure while at the same time conducting tests to uncover errors associated with interfacing.
- **Non-incremental integration:** The entire program is tested as a whole. A set of errors are encountered. Correction is difficult.
- **Incremental integration:** The program is constructed and tested in small segments, where errors are easier to isolate and correct.
    1. Top-down integration
    3. Bottom-up integration

7.2.4.1 Top-down Integration : (Depth - First Integration)

- Top-down integration is an incremental approach to the production of program structure. Modules are integrated by moving downwards through the control hierarchy, starting with the main control module.

- Modules subordinate to the main control module are included into the structure in either a depth-first or breadth-first manner.

- Relating to Fig. 7.17 depth-first integration would integrate the modules on a major control path of the structure. Selection of a major path is arbitrary and relies on application particular features. For instance, selecting the left-hand path, modules M1, M2, M5 would be integrated first. Next M8 or M6 would be integrated. Then the central and right-hand control paths are produced. Breath-first integration includes all modules directly subordinate at each level, moving across the structure horizontally. From the figure, modules M2, M3 and M4 would be integrated first.

- The next control level, M5, M6 etc. follows.

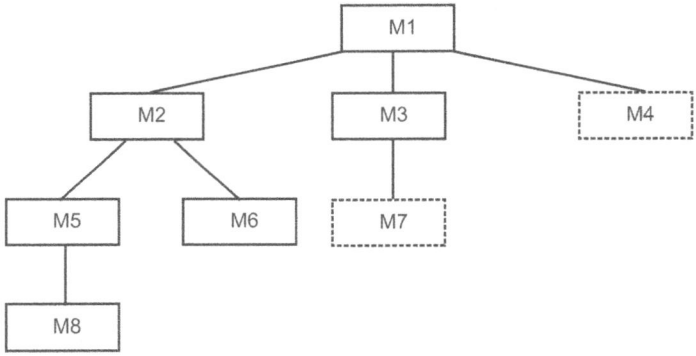

Fig. 7.17: Depth-first Integration

- **Steps:**
   - The main control module is used as a test driver and stubs are substituted for all modules directly subordinate to the main control module.
   - Depending on the integration approach selected (i.e. depth-or-breadth first), subordinate stubs are replaced one at a time with actual modules.
   - Tests are conducted as each module is integrated.
   - On the completion of each set of tests, another stub is replaced with the real module.
   - Regression testing (i.e. conducting all or some of the previous tests) may be conducted to ensure that new errors have not been introduced.

- Fig. 7.18 illustrates the process.

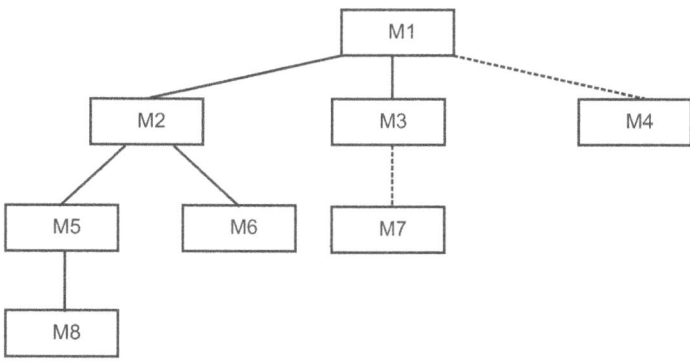

Fig. 7.18 : Top-down Integration Approach

7.2.4.2 Bottom-up Integration

- Bottom-up integration testing begins testing with the modules at the lowest level (atomic modules).
- As modules are integrated bottom up, processing required for modules subordinates to a given level is always available and the need for stubs is eliminated.
- **Steps:**
    - Low-level modules are combined into clusters (called builds) that perform a specific software sub function.
    - A driver (a control program for testing) is written to coordinate test case input and output.
    - The cluster is tested.
    - Drivers are removed and clusters are combined moving upward in the program structure.
- Integration follows the pattern illustrated in Fig. 7.19.
- There has been much discussion on the advantages and disadvantages of bottom-up and top-down integration testing. Typically, a disadvantage is one is an advantage of the other approach.
- The major disadvantage of top-down approaches is the need for stubs and the difficulties that are linked with them. Problems linked with stubs may be offset by the advantage of testing major control functions early.
- The major drawback of bottom-up integration is that the program does not exist until the last module is included.

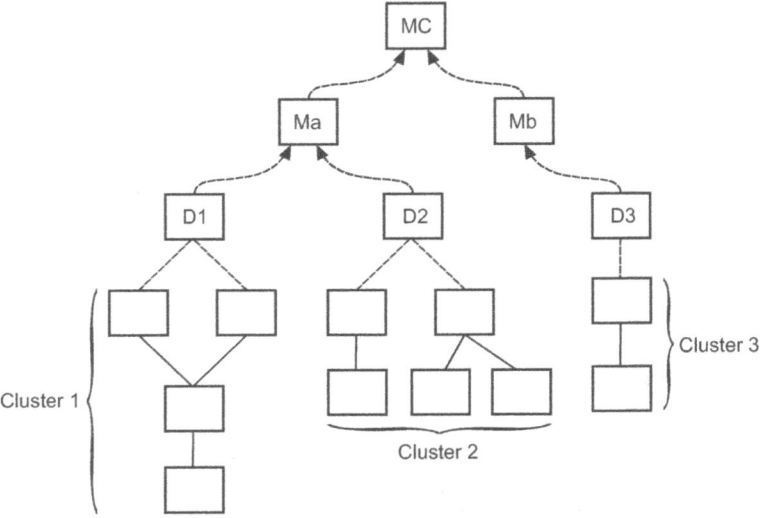

Fig. 7.19: Bottom-up Integration Approach

7.2.4.3 Regression Testing

- Any time you modify an implementation within a program, you should also do regression testing. You can do so by rerunning existing tests against the modified code to determine whether, the changes break anything that worked prior to the change and by writing new tests where necessary. Adequate coverage without wasting time should be a primary consideration when conducting regression tests. Try to spend as little time as possible doing regression testing without reducing the probability that you will detect new failures in old, already tested code.
- Some strategies and factors to consider during this process include:
  1. Test fixed bugs promptly. The programmer might have handled the symptoms but not have gotten to the underlying cause.
  2. Watch for side effects of fixes. The bug itself might be fixed but the fix might create other bugs.
  3. Write a regression test for each bug fixed.
  4. If two or more tests are similar, determine which is less effective and get rid of it.
  5. Identify tests that the program consistently passes and archive them.
  6. Focus on functional issues, not those related to design.
  7. Make changes, (small and large) to data and find any resulting corruption.
  8. Trace the effects of the changes on program memory.

- Regression testing is any type of software testing which seeks to uncover software regression. Such regressions occur whenever, software functionality that was previously working correctly, stops working as intended. Typically, regressions occur as an unintended consequence of program changes. Common methods of regression testing include re-running previously run tests and checking whether previously fixed faults have re-emerged.
- Regression testing can be used not only for testing the correctness of a program, but often also for tracking the quality of its output. For instance, in the design of a complier, regression testing should track the code size, simulation time and time of the test suite cases.

7.2.4.4 Smoke Testing

- Smoke testing is a term used in plumbing, woodwind repair, electronics, computer software development and the entertainment industry. It refers to the first test made after repairs or first assembly to provide some assurance that the system under test will not catastrophically fail. After a smoke test proves that "the pipes will not leak, the keys seal properly, the circuit will not burn or the software will not crash outright", the assembly is ready for more stressful testing.

    1. In plumbing, a smoke test forces actual smoke through newly plumbed pipes to find leaks, before water is allowed to flow through the pipes.
    2. In woodwind instrument repair, a smoke test involves plugging one end of an instrument and blowing smoke into the other to test for leaks, (This test is no longer in common use).
    3. In electronics, a smoke test is the first time a circuit is attached to power, which will sometimes produce actual smoke if a design or wiring mistake has been made.
    4. In computer programming and software testing, smoke testing is a preliminary to further testing, which should reveal simple failures severe enough to reject a prospective software release. In this case, the smoke is metaphorical.
    5. In the entertainment industry a smoke test is done to ensure that theoretical smoke and fog used during a like event will not set of the smoke detectors in a venue.

- Smoke testing is done by developers before the build is released to the testers, or by testers before accepting a build for further testing. Microsoft claims that after code reviews, smoke testing is the most cost effective method for identifying and fixing defects in software.
- In software engineering, a smoke test generally consists of a collection of tests that can be applied to a newly created or repaired computer program. Sometimes, the tests are

performed by the automated system that builds the final software. In this sense a smoke test is the process of validating code changes before the changes are checked into the larger product's official source code collection or the main branch of source code.

- In software, a smoke test is a collection of written tests that are performed on a system prior to being accepted for further testing. This is also known as a build verification test. This is a "shallow and wide" approach to the application. The tester "touches" all areas of the application without getting too deep, looking for answers to basic questions like, "Can I launch the test item at all ?", "Does it open to a window ?, "Do the buttons on the window do things ?".

- The purpose is to determine whether, or not the application is so badly broken that testing functionality in a more detailed way is unnecessary. These written tests can either be performed manually or using an automated tool. When automated tools are used, the tests are often initiated by the same process that generates the build itself. This is sometimes referred to as "rattle" resting – as in "if I shake it does it rattle ?"

7.2.4.5 Alpha and Beta Testing

1. If software is developed as a product to be used by many customers, it is impractical to perform formal acceptance tests with each one. Most software product builders use a process called **alpha** and **beta** testing to uncover errors that only the end user seems able to find.

2. The 'alpha' test is conducted at the developer's site by a customer. The software is used in a natural setting with the developer "looking over the shoulder" of the user and recording errors and usage problems. Alpha tests are conducted in a controlled environment.

3. The 'beta' test is conducted at one or more customer sites by the end user of the software. Unlike alpha testing, the developer generally is not present. Therefore, the beta test is a "Live" application of the software in an environment that cannot be controlled by the developer.

4. Alpha testing is simulated or actual operational testing by potential users/customers or an independent test team at the developers site. Alpha testing is often employed for off-the-shelf software as a form of intenal acceptance testing, before the software goes to beta testing.

5. Beta testing comes after alpha testing and can be considered a form of external user acceptance testing. Versions of the software, known as beta versions, are released to a limited audience outside of the programming team. The software is released to groups of people so that further testing can ensure the product has few faults or

bugs. Sometimes, beta versions are made available to the open public to increase the feedback field to a maximal number of future uses.

- The customer records all the problems that are encountered during beta testing and reports these to the developer at regular intervals. As a result of problems reported during beta test, the software developer makes modifications and then prepares for release of the software product to the entire customer base.

7.3 VALIDATION

- Reasonable expectations are defined in the "software requirements specification" - a document that describes all user-visible attributes of the software. The specification contains a section called **'validation criteria'**. Information contained in that section forms the basis for a validation testing approach.
- Software validation is achieved through a series of black-box tests that demonstrate conformity with requirements.
- After each validation test case has been conducted, one of two possible conditions exist :
    1. The function or performance characteristics confirm to specification and are accepted.
    2. A derivation from specification is uncovered and a deficiency list is created.
- An important element of the validation process is a *configuration review*, (as illustrated in Fig. 7.20) also called as **'Audit'**.

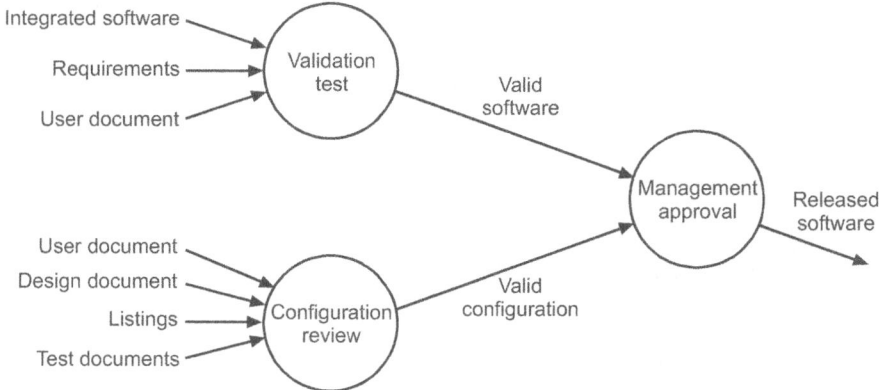

Fig. 7.20 : Audit/Configuration Review

- The intent of the review, is to ensure that all the elements of the software configuration have been properly developed, cataloged and have the necessary detail to support the maintenance phase of the software life cycle.

7.4 VERIFICATION

Verification is the process of evaluating products of a development phase to find out whether they meet the specified requirements. **Are we building the system right?** The objective of Verification is to make sure that the product being develop is as per the requirements and design specifications. To ensure that the product is being built according to the requirements and design specifications. In other words, to ensure that work products meet their specified requirements.

Following activities are involved in **Verification**:
a. Reviews.
b. Meetings.
c. Inspections.

- **Verification** is carried out by QA team to check whether implementation software is as per specification document or not.
- **Verification** process explains whether the outputs are according to inputs or not.
- **Verification** is carried out before the Validation.
- Following items are evaluated during **Verification**: Plans, Requirement Specifications, Design Specifications, Code, Test Cases etc.
- It is basically manually checking the of documents and files like requirement specifications etc.

Practice Questions

1. What is software testing?
2. Why software testing is important?
3. Why quality assurance is important?
4. What are the activities involved in quality assurance?
5. Define testing and debugging?
6. Explain the objectives of testing.
7. Explain the principles of testing.
8. What is testing process? What are testing levels?

9. Write a short note on:
   (a) Unit testing
   (b) Module testing
   (c) Integration testing
   (d) Acceptance testing
10. Explain various stages of system testing.
11. Explain testing process in detail.
12. Explain any two types of testing strategies.
13. Write a short note on white-box testing.
14. Write a short note on black-box testing.
15. What is performance testing?
16. Explain user acceptance testing in detail.
17. Explain the term stress testing.

University Questions & Answers

October 2009

1. List advantages and disadvantages of white box testing. [2 M]
Ans. Please refer to Section 7.2.2.

2. Define Beta testing. [2 M]
Ans. Please refer to Section 7.2.4.5.

3. What is black box testing? Explain methods used in BBT. [4 M]
Ans. Please refer to Section 7.2.1.

April 2010

1. What is black box testing? [2 M]
Ans. Please refer to Section 7.2.1.

2. Explain testing principles and objectives. [4 M]
Ans. Please refer to Section 7.1.2.

3. Write short note on: White box testing. [4 M]
Ans. Please refer to Section 7.2.2.

October 2010

1. What is software testing? [2 M]
Ans. Please refer to Section 7.1.

2. With suitable diagram describe black box testing. [4 M]
Ans. Please refer to Section 7.2.1.

3. Differentiate between white box testing and black box testing. [4 M]
Ans. Please refer to Sections 7.2.2 and 7.2.1.

April 2011

1. Define Beta testing. [2 M]
Ans. Please refer to Section 7.2.4.5.

2. State advantages and disadvantages of BBT. [2 M]
Ans. Please refer to Section 7.2.1.

3. Write short note on: Black box testing. [4 M]
Ans. Please refer to Section 7.2.1.

October 2011

1. Differentiate between white box testing and black box testing. [2 M]
Ans. Please refer to Sections 7.2.2 and 7.2.1.

2. Explain testing principles and objectives. [4 M]
Ans. Please refer to Section 7.1.2.

April 2012

1. Explain testing principles and objectives. [4 M]
Ans. Please refer to Section 7.1.2.

2. Discuss differences between white box and black box testing. [4 M]
Ans. Please refer to Section 7.2.2 and 7.2.1.

3. Write short note on: Software verification and validation. [4 M]
Ans. Please refer to Section 7.3 and 7.4.

October 2012

1. Explain white box testing. [2 M]

Ans. Please refer to Section 7.2.2.

April 2014

1. What is glass box testing. [4 M]

Ans. Please refer to Section 7.2.2.

2. Explain testing principles. [4 M]

Ans. Please refer to Section 7.1.2.

❖❖❖

Case Studies

1. LIFE INSURANCE SYSTEM

- The term is much familiar now-a-days. It assures the Economic stability after sudden death of person having the policy. This is the general and well known view of LIC, but is not so limited.
- System for LIC can be organised in following steps:

(A) Abstract Approach:

1. Purpose:

The area has came to boost with full potential towards the goal due to rapid development and industrialization. This impelled the persons to work restlessly and face many hazardous situations. In these situations, in case of unfortunate expiry or retirement of a person or even after completion of policy period, the only system (i.e. LIC) that can provide you strong economical backbone is LIC.

For this, prespecified amount should be given to the representative of the corporation in installments after fixed durations.

2. Definition:

(i) **LIC (Life Insurance Corporation):** Corporation that assures the economic status of a person after death or successful completion of policy period.

(ii) **LIC Agent:** Authorised person of the corporation acting as an active link between the customers and corporation.

(iii) **LIC Policy:** Specific idea or scheme launched by the corporation in service of customers and attracting to the 'one'.

(iv) **LIC Centre (Called Head branch]:** The wing that handles and manages the records of all customers under the centre.

(v) **Data Entry and Display Subsystems:** Representation of data entry and display subsystems and also the descriptive substructures with KIOS's finishing touch.

(vi) **Validity of Policy:** Life of specifitial beneficial scheme or cut-off-date.

(B) Scope:

Determination for the scope of software is the first software project management activity. The scope identifies primary data fed to system (i.e. LIC), functions and attitude of corporation and the constraints to bound the attitude of the corporation in quantitative manner.

In this phase, to be a part of LIC (customer) the applicant is bounded to provide his descriptive information, clearly mentioning the name of policy and it's duration. The most important aspect or say constraint is 'reception of proved birth-date (i.e. age)' of the applicant. Depending upon the age and profession, policies are changing the area of benefits dynamically (i.e. policies for senior citizens or for freedom fighters). The phase also incorporates the system performance, taking into account the output of a function to which ample of constraints are attached.

The scope also assures the reliability of the system. Hence, depending upon the policy and its associated interest rate, period of validation and profession (status) of the customer in society, the records of customer are manipulated precisely.

The most commonly used technique to bridge the communication gap between customer and the representatives of the corporation and get the communication process started is to conduct a preliminary meeting. The context-free questions are asked to the customer for getting his incentives and ideas and to the corporation to clear understand its policies, constraints. The request behind the work is obviously of the corporation and both the customer and corporation use the system simultaneously.

Area of Economic Benefit:

1. Acquire the greater operating and processing speed.
2. Able to fulfill more and more demands of customers in comparatively less time with higher accuracy. This will attract the mob willing to be a policy-holder.
3. The customer and normal public are introduced with the real scenario and present status of the corporation might be of the social or economical level.

   This will enhance faith of public for the work done by corporation.
4. Easy to manage individual person's finance, biodata and dues.
5. System bounded by the constraints and requirements gives the better hopeful outcome and thus, reduces the expense on manual work.

Criteria for 'good' output:

1. Handles extreme conditions about the age, late installment, dues, validity and give the desired output.
2. Satisfy the corporation (i.e. matching with required output) and the customer (i.e. matching with his prior estimation).

Problems that might be faced in future:

1. There may not be the lower limit of age specified by the corporation, programmer to open the policy. If the age is zero or non-positive, it will contrast the reality i.e. policy for non-existing person.

2. Check on manipulation and not let the interest on the amount of policy-holder to increase in geometric progression but by prespecified percentage of current amount at that time.

Product Functions:

The final functionality of the product have to be estimated in advance and it should be achieved successfully. The Life Insurance Corporation system provides comparative analysis of different policies bounded to different limitations. The customer is recognized by the system and his/her data is displayed on the console output unit, whenever he enter his 'Personal Security Number'.

The LIC system software maintains following data:

(i) Encoding/Decoding the security-code.

(ii) Policy type for each customer, validity in terms of policy duration and regular receipt of installment (cash).

Assumptions:

1. The system itself is much descriptive, the operator should be familiar with some of the basic operations.

2. Without a security code, any account cannot be opened.

3. The person can view only its own financial and data records and of the corporation also to limited extent (i.e. Access rights).

4. Interest rate is constant till completion of validation though changes occurred meanwhile.

Constraints:

1. Different policies are restricted for reserved only (For example, FF and SC).

2. Minimum and maximum age limit for each policy.

3. Evidence for the income source of the customer should be presented.

4. Different interest rates for employee and agents of corporation and ordinary customers.

5. Minimum installation amount and the time duration within which it must be payed.

The LIC centre (Head branch) manages the data bases of all its branches which in turn manages the customer databases.

Design Constraints:

Design should be sufficiently valid and self-explanatory. It is subjected to following types:

1. **Reliability:** The meantime to failure must be beyond 1,00,000 days.

2. **Security:** Preventive measures built into LIC system, to prevent accidental data loss and corruption of data.

3. **Maintainability:** Design should be as an open source, thus new methods can be added easily.

   Software will have complete commented documentation.

(C) Stackholders:

The stackholders are the persons who will have interest in the software to be built. In this case, the stackholder is clearly the corporation and to some extent the 'Agents'. The people are not functionally active and participating in corporations' finance prior to be the customer. So they are not concerned for the stackholders.

(D) Features:

1. **Benefits of different policies:** The system gives descriptive information about the policy in terms of validity for policy (i.e. consider a policy say 'Jeevan Veema' is made to be valid for the duration of 12 years from it's start). System also gives the brief information about the reserved identity of the policies and how it is distinct from other polices.

   System also supports the functional and non-functional components of the corporation. This direct or indirect involvement of the customer makes him feel safety about his policy-investment and increase market status (trusted one).

2. **Conditional extension for selective policies:** Few policies like 'Gruha-Rachna' or 'Jeevan-Veema Insurance Policy' can be extended after successful completion of the policy period provided that extension should not be above 6 months in any case. System also clearly underlines the decreased rate of interest that the policy offers to it's holders (about 5-7% of previous rate) due to policy-extension.

3. The system gives information about the various policies run by the corporation and the community/people which are able for it.

For example, Jeevan-Sanchar Neegam-Veema Policy allows only the persons with annual income about 1.5 lakh and age above 21 years.

4. General software and design-oriented features: As the headbranch controls the wings of corporation, the control is centralised.

Outputs: Current saving, balance, day and amount of next payment, remaining and completed validated period.

Security: Based on the access right, security should be provided to upon the individual record. For this security-codes are given. When entered security-code mismatches with system-stored one, the access for that record is denied.

(E) Performance Requirements:

1. Process speed: The speed for processing of the data record must be superfast, specifically 3-5 seconds after the entry of proper security code.

2. Response time: After the specific commands given to the system software, it should respond more quickly so that it can process more records per unit time.

Context Level Data Flow Diagram

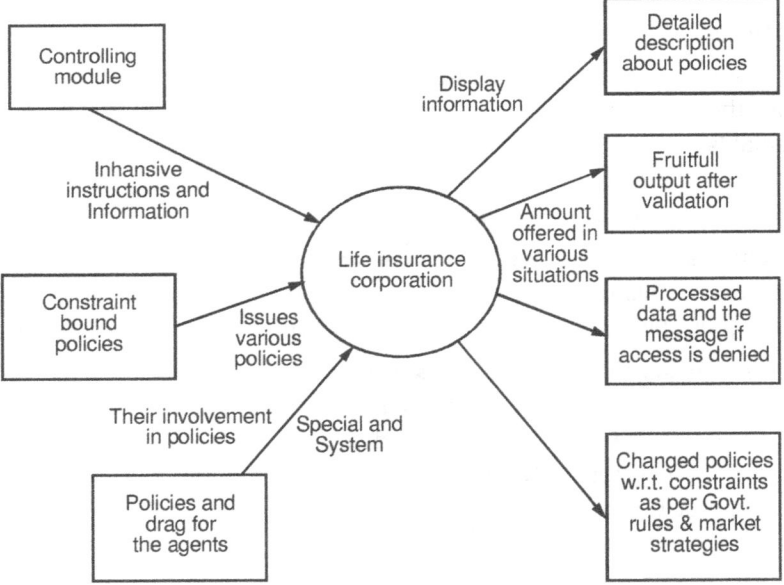

DFD level 0

Level 1 Data Flow Diagram:

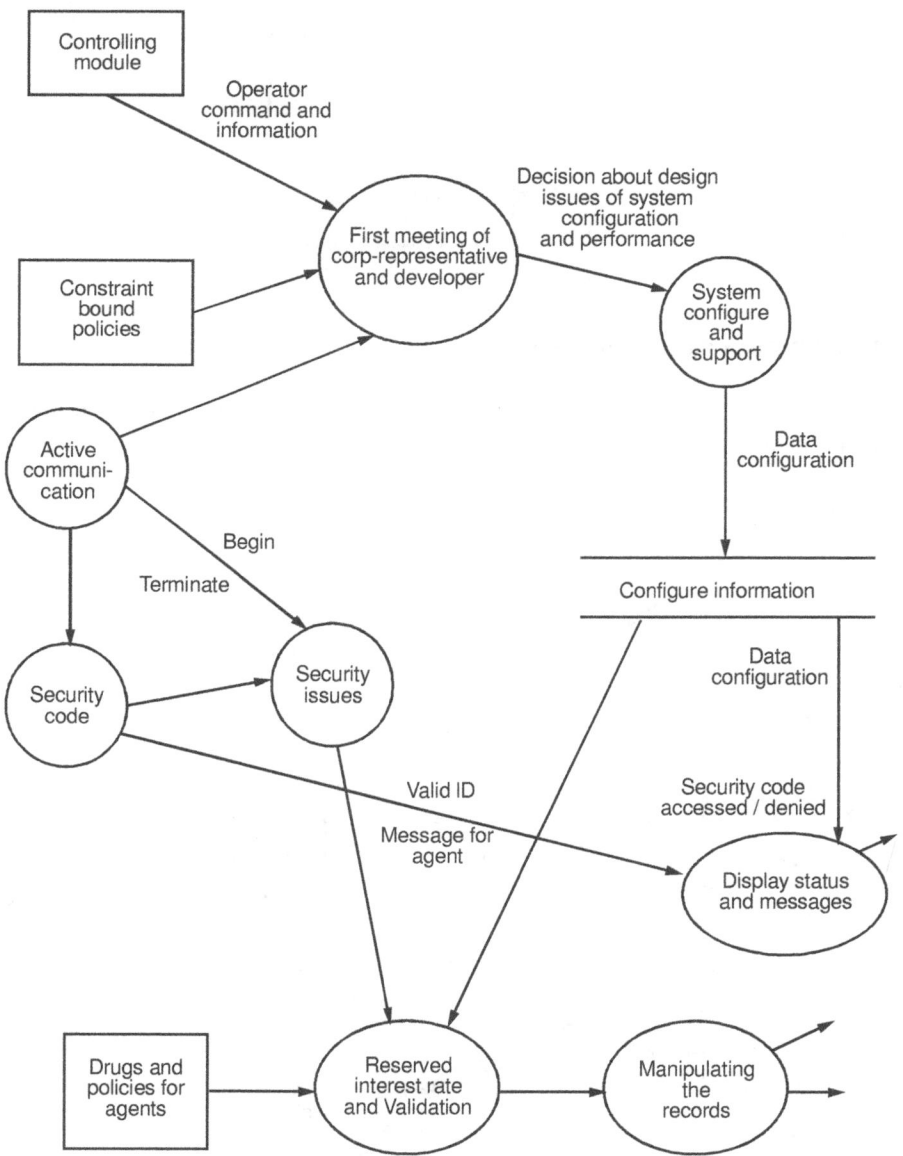

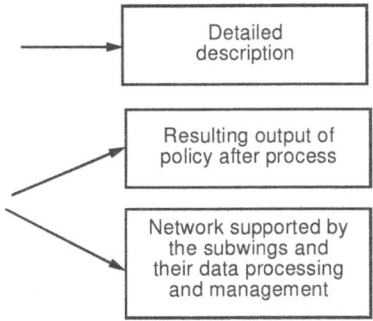

Level 2 Data Flow Diagram:

About manipulation and processes for the records that encompass the boundary conditions.

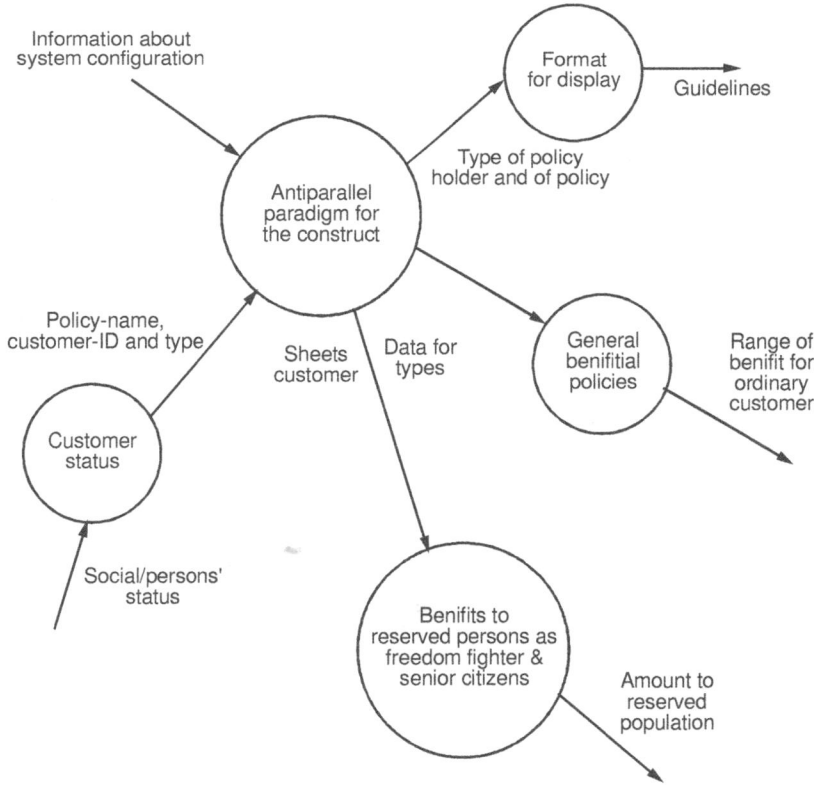

1. **Scope:**

   The scope of this project is limited to the analysis of traffic at one of the major squares in the city. It gives the total number of vehicles moving through the square at any instant of time. It also keeps the level of Air and Sound pollution. It gives the traffic department the trend of traffic at a particular time which helps them to monitor the traffic. The project also displays the temperature and humidity readings. The project is also capable of transmitting information to the next squares regarding the traffic diverting towards that square, when demanded. The system is not automatic and does not have remote controlled capability. It is not concerned with the roadside parking.

   It provides stable, mature and operational traffic control system.

2. **Stake holders:**

   (a) Administrator.

   (b) Programmers.

   (c) Traffic Policemen.

   (d) Town Planning officers.

   (e) DSP and other officers.

3. **Features:**

   (a) Vehicle classification.

   (b) Count of vehicles (2-wheelers, 3-wheelers, 4-wheelers) and count of pedestrians through.

   (c) Turning movements of vehicles and flow monitoring.

   (d) Pollution level air/sound.

   (e) Weather monitoring.

   (f) Transmitting information to next squares.

   (g) Easy to use.

   (h) Relatively low-cost system.

   (i) Allows multiple users to concurrently access and interact with the system.

   (j) Operate 24 Hrs. a day without operator supervision or interaction.

   (k) Generate reports.

   (l) Speed.

4. **Requirements:**

   (a) Software requirements: This software will run on any windows platform (win9x, NT, XP, 2000) operating system. Oracle and Microsoft Visual basic should be preferably installed on the machine to facilitate further software enhancements and to incorporate further changes when put to use.

   (b) Hardware requirements: Hardware required are:
   1. Workstation connected to high speed internet.
   2. Sensors.
   3. Speed guns.
   4. Transducers.
   5. 7-segment display.
   6. FOC.
   7. Frequency meter.
   8. Lasers.
   9. Audio transducer.
   10. Min 20GB harddisk.
   11. 128MB DRAM.
   12. Speed gun.
   13. Interfaces to processor.
   14. The server should be a fast machine such as a Intel Pentium 4 processor with 256 MB DRAM.
   15. It should have power back up supply facility to stay on-line for 24 * 7.
   16. Daily back-up facility should be there to protect the data in case of system crash.
   17. Display screen preferably 17 inches and more.

   (c) Functional requirements: System should interact with number plate of vehicles in the circumference of 1.5 kms to report the culprits breaking the signals and entering into wrong way. System cannot punish the culprit. The information regarding culprits can be passed on to next squares. Stray animals cannot be detected. Speed gun will give the maximum speed of vehicles near a square. System is not concerned with Vehicular Parking. The system also displays the minimum and maximum temperatures along with percentage of humidity.

   (d) Performance requirements: Response time 100 milliseconds/ operation. Reports generation after every 3 hrs. Number of simultaneous users is 20 with 20 workstations connected to internet. Each controller workstation has a high-resolution 2408 × 2048 pixel sony 20-inch colour monitor. Database module should be secure as it contains confidential information. Back-up facility should be there to protect data in case of system crash. The system should be protected from unauthorised access and Hackers.

It should provide a deadlock resolution manager. The user interface should be friendly. Error handling should be layered and a detailed description of errors should be provided and provision for system saving is there.

5. **Feasibility study:**

   Once, the scope is defined and requirements are gathered, the software team and others must work to determine if it can be done within the dimensions just noted.

   Software feasibility has four solid margins.

   (i) **Technology:** Is a project technically feasible ? Is it within the state of art.

   (ii) **Finance:** Is a project financially feasible ? Can development be completed at a cost the software organization, its client or the market can afford.

   (iii) **Time:** Will the project's time-to-market the beat the competition ?

   (iv) **Resources:** Does the organization have the resources needed to succeed ?

   For some projects in established areas, the answers are easy. You have done projects like this one before. After a few hours or sometimes a few weeks of investigation, you are sure, you can do it again.

   Projects on the margin of your experience are not so easy. A team may have to spend some time discovering what the central, difficult-to-implement requirements of a new project are. Do some of these requirements pose risks that would make the project infeasible ? Can these risks be overcomed ? The feasibility team thought to carry initial architecture and design of high risk requirements to the point at which it can answer these questions. In some cases, when the team gets negative answers, a reduction in requirements may be negotiated.

6. **Data Dictionary:**
   1. Signal locations
   2. Vehicle numbers
   3. Reports
   4. Duty officers
   5. Speed
   6. Vehicles
   7. Display
   8. Time.
   9. Distance

7. DFD:

Level 0 DFD:

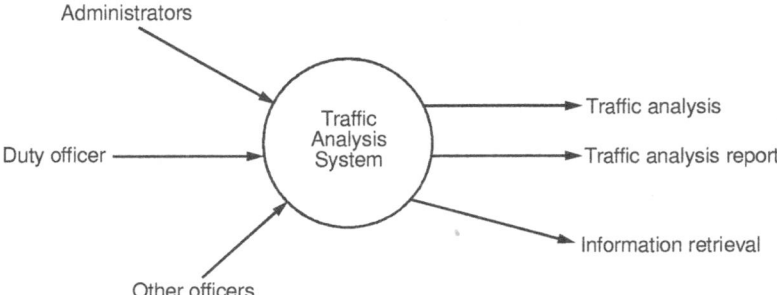

Level 1 DFD:

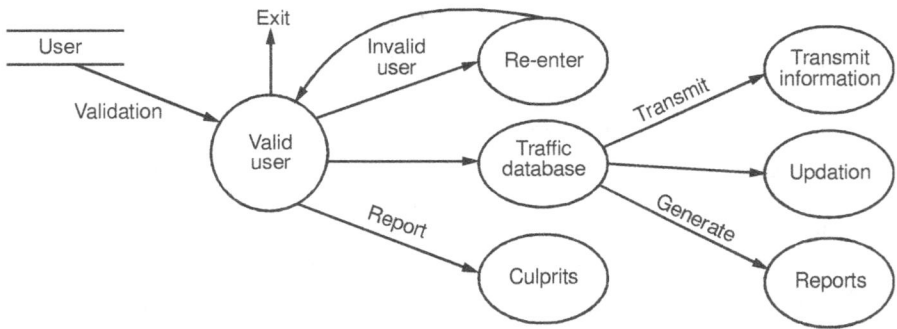

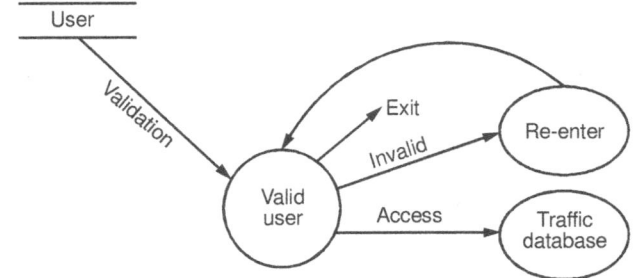

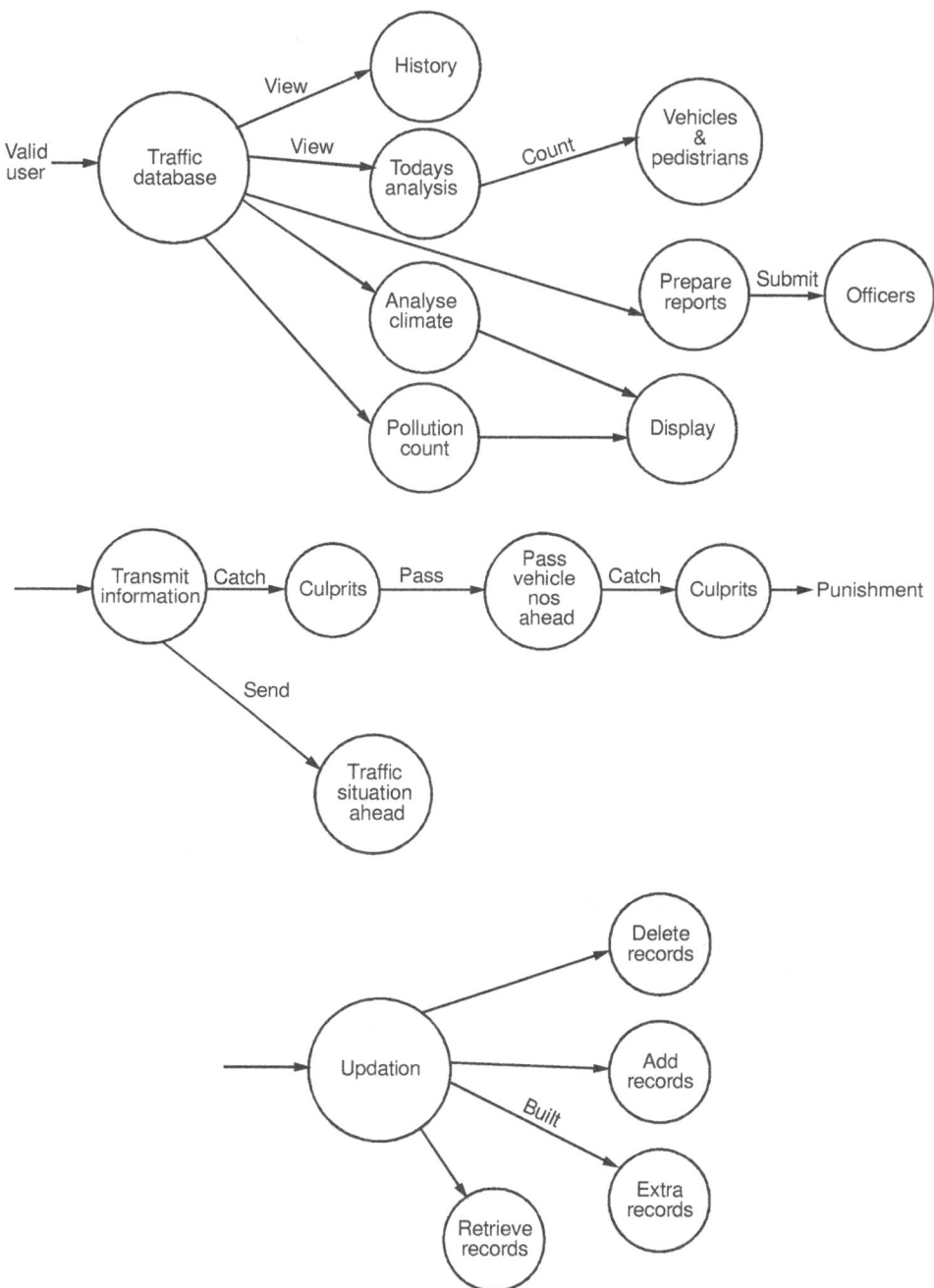

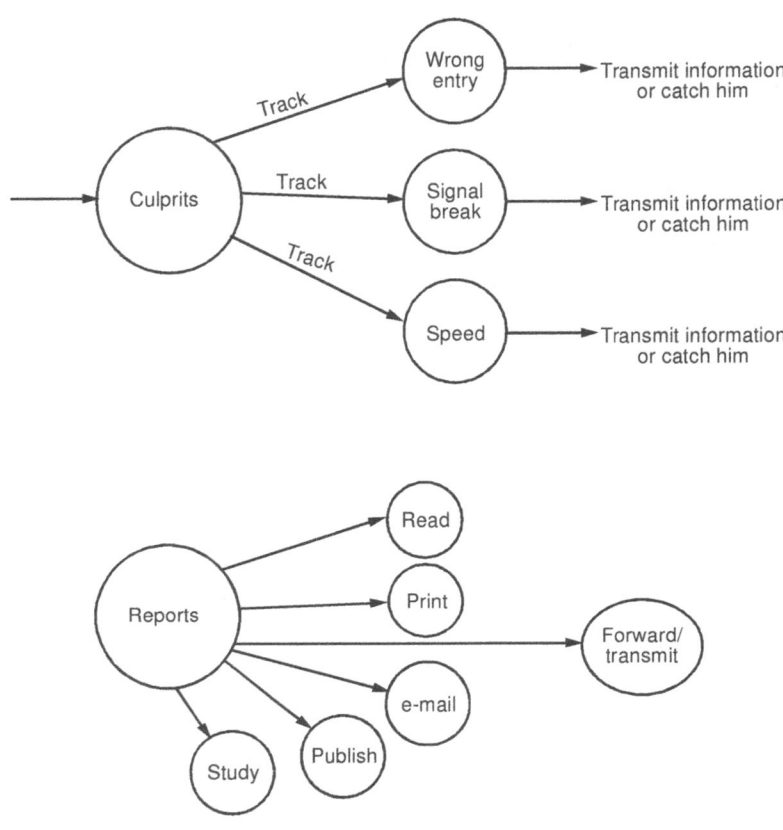

---

3. AIRLINE RESERVATION SYSTEM

1. **Abstract Approach:**

   This software is developed to make tedious job of airline reservation easy for its users. It will provide the information for flight root, necessary requirements to reserve a seat, flight capacity, facilities being provided.

   The site allows you to search for round-trip, one-way or multiple stop itineraries. Your search can include preferences for certain airlines, direct flights only or for tickets with the least restrictions. Customer service is available 24 hours via e-mail and an 800 number. This report guides you through various steps and features of our project to get a clear idea of the system.

2. **Scope:**

   This airline reservation system is used for on-line reservation of airline ticket. Being on-line, this system reduces the precious time of the users in today's busy world.

   In our system, one module will provide all the information about flights. This contains the arrival time, departure time, the halts during the journey. It also contains passenger capacity and the rates according to classes. Another module will provide the information about the seats available and will also ask the user to enter his information. The payment can be made by cash, cheque, draft, credit card, etc. It provides fast updating facility.

3. **Stakeholders:**
   1. The software team:
      - project manager
      - programmer
   2. Administrator
   3. Employee
   4. User.

4. **Features:**
   1. Easy to use.
   2. High accuracy.
   3. User-friendly interface.
   4. Fast updating facility.
   5. Quick information regarding flights.
   6. Facilities provided during journey.
   7. On-line reservation.

5. **Requirements:**
   1. **Software requirement:** This software is windows based developed using 'Java', 'Database software (oracle)', Turbo C.
   2. **Hardware requirement:**

      Machine – Intel Pentium IV

      RAM – 256 MB

      Hard Disk – 80 GB.

      Operating system – MS – DOS.

3. **Functional requirement:**
   - (i) **Details about flight:** Other flights available for same route.
   - (ii) **Cancellation facility.**
   - (iii) **Immediate updation:** It should immediately reflect the changes in the seats available.
4. **Performance requirement: Static:** Care of error handling is taken into account so that system should give good performance.

Dynamic:
   - Record updation.
   - Search algorithm.
   - List of passwords if user forgets the password system will give the clue.

Safety requirements: If data entry goes wrong, then the passenger and flight database will be affected.

6. **Feasibility Study:**

   Time: The team may have to spend a particular time slot for deciding what are the requirements, central idea and overall structure of the system. Near about one month will be required for organizing team, designing the system and some more days for coding and testing the system. The team member should follow a proper plan and take efforts so that, they don't have to face any risk in the middle of developing the system or in future. There should also be proper understanding among the team members.

   Cost: The cost required will depend upon the hardware or software required for developing the system and money which get spend on people working on that system. The total cost will be in the form of human expenditure, hardware and software expenditure. The cost can also increase if some change in the system is demanded by the customer.

Data Flow Diagrams:

Level 0:

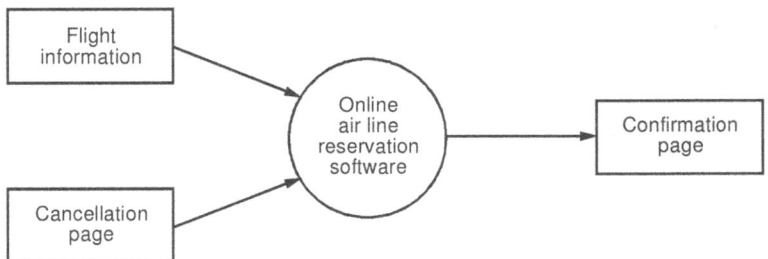

Level 1:

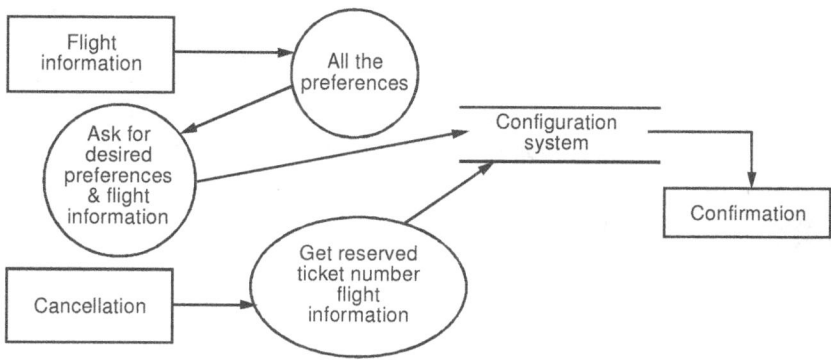

Level 2:

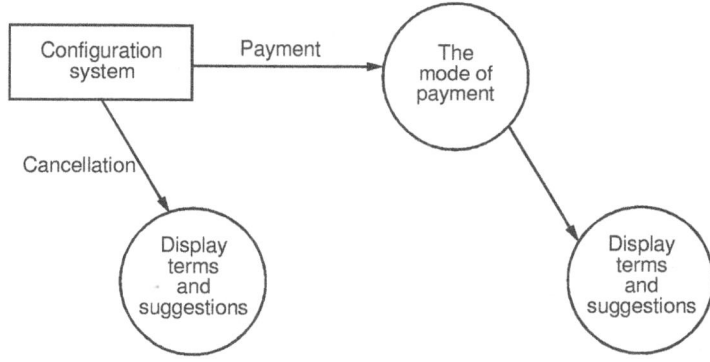

4. RAILWAY RESERVATION SYSTEM

- Customers get the form from the railway station and they fill the form with proper information such as destination, type of class, tickets required etc. After filling the form customers submits it to the reservation counter. Clerk at the window validates the information and if proper, accepts it. System also supports the cancellation of the booked tickets depending upon following conditions:
  1. If cancelled before 48 hours from train departure, 80% of money returned.
  2. If cancelled before 24 hours from train departure, 40% returned.
  3. If cancelled before 4 hours from train departure 10% returned.

- While reservation, customer will get detailed information about how many seats are available and train status. This information is displayed at railway station on LCD, which is commonly visible to all. If user doesn't get the ticket then he will be made waiting and is put on waiting list. The complete timely detailed information regarding the number of tickets available at a particular instant, passenger information, arrival and departure information etc. should be provided by the system.

Objectives of the system:

- Proper ticket booking of user with user satisfaction.
- Providing finely detailed information regarding tickets booked.
- Maintaining waiting list.
- Generating adhoc reports depending upon Manager's requirement.
- Evolve high computing strategies.
- Finding out performance of tickets booked at station.

Functional Decomposition Diagram:

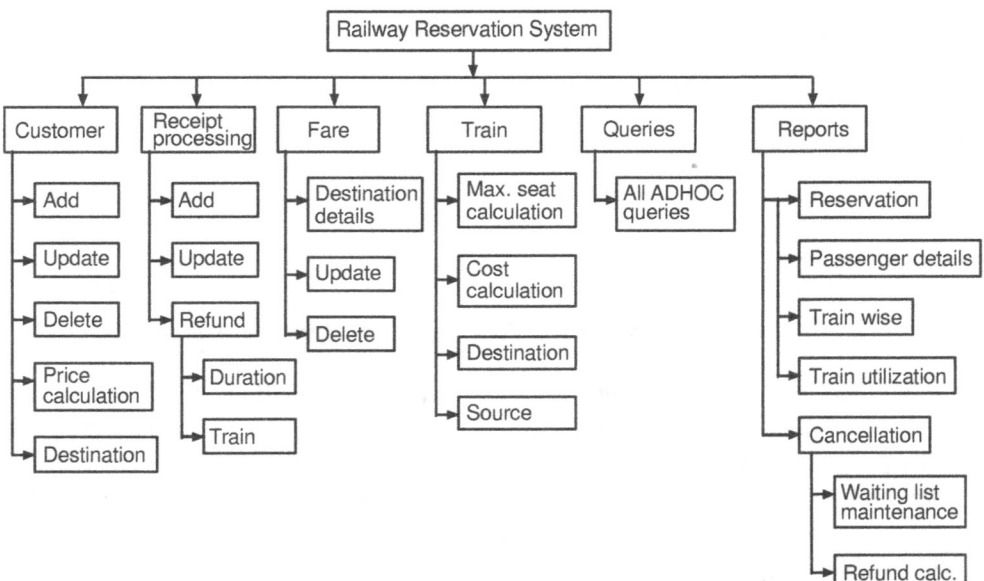

Entity-Relationship Diagram

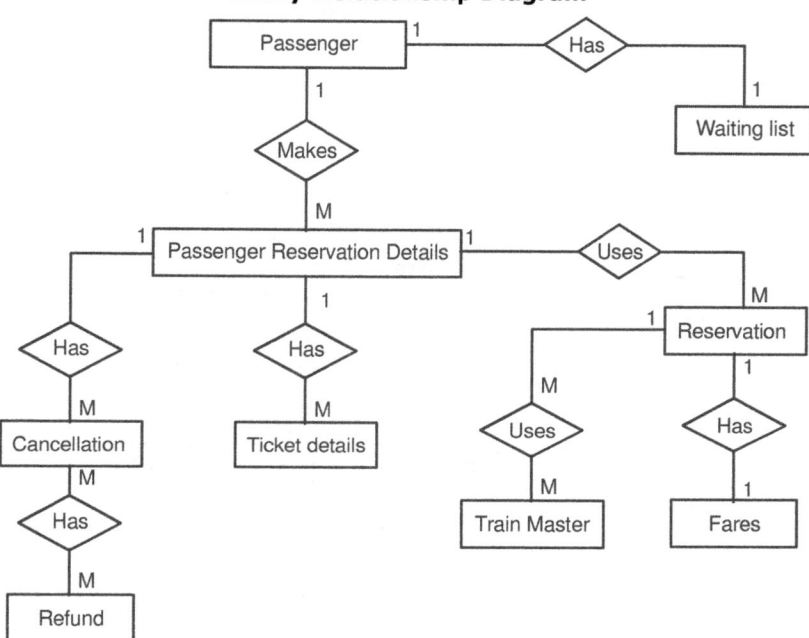

Context Level DFD

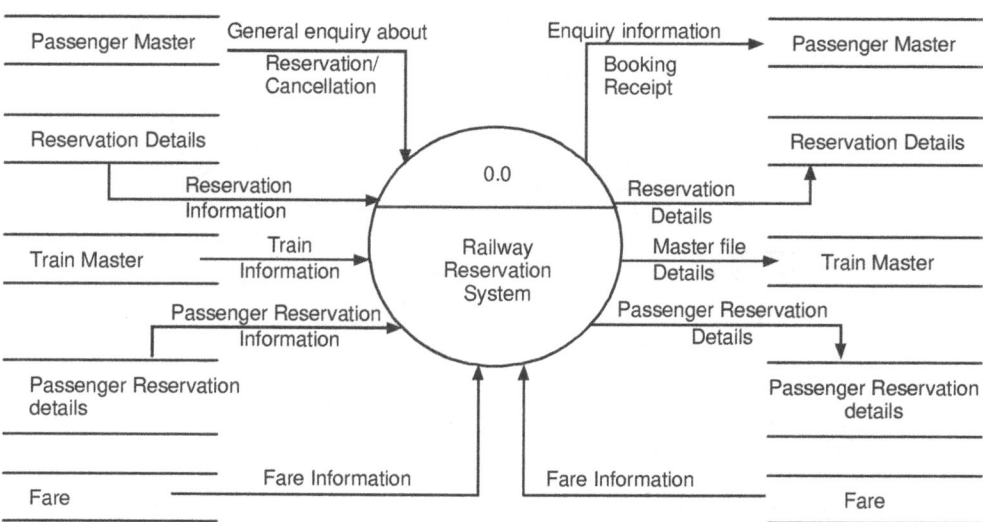

First Level DFD

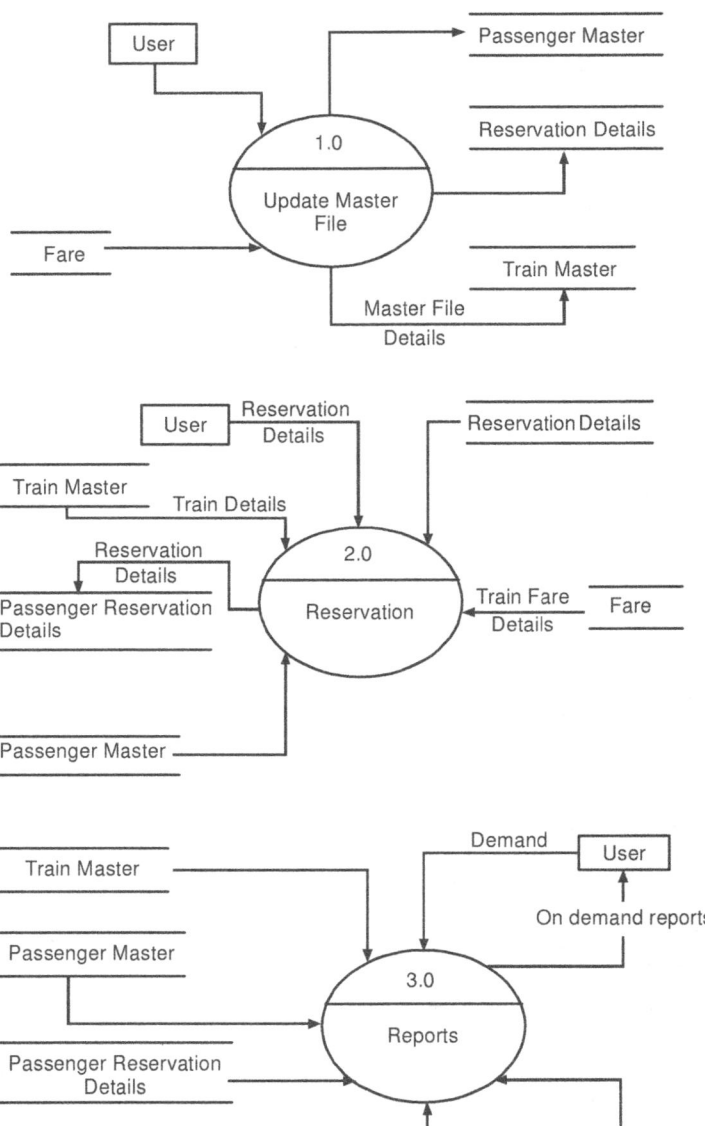

Second Level DFD

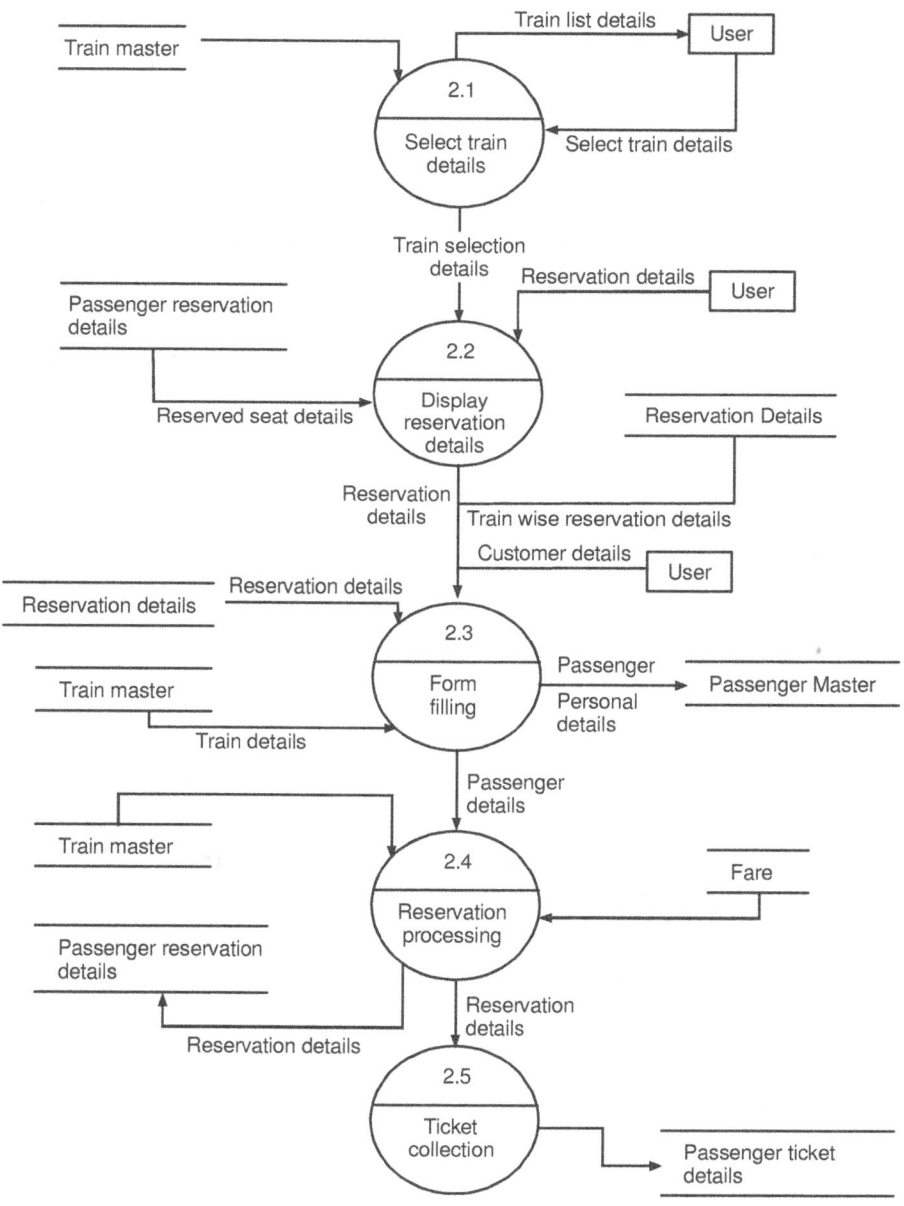

Third Level DFD

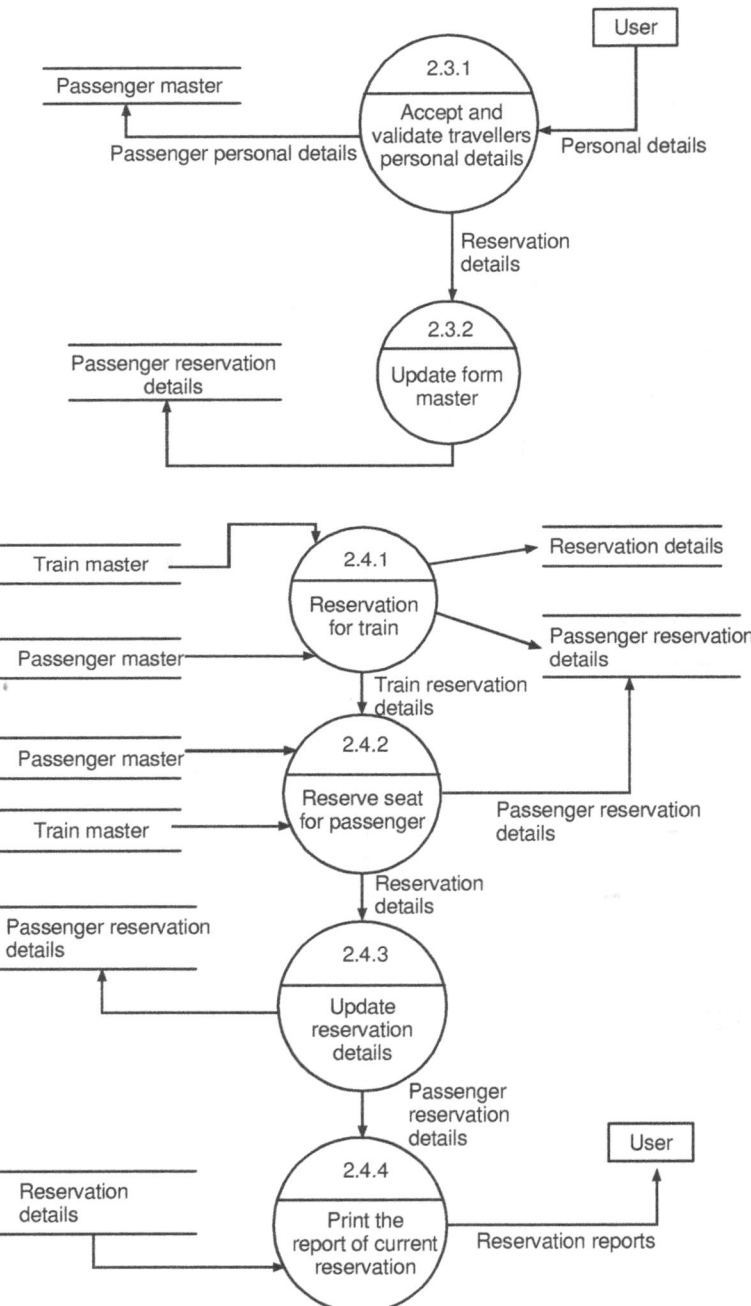

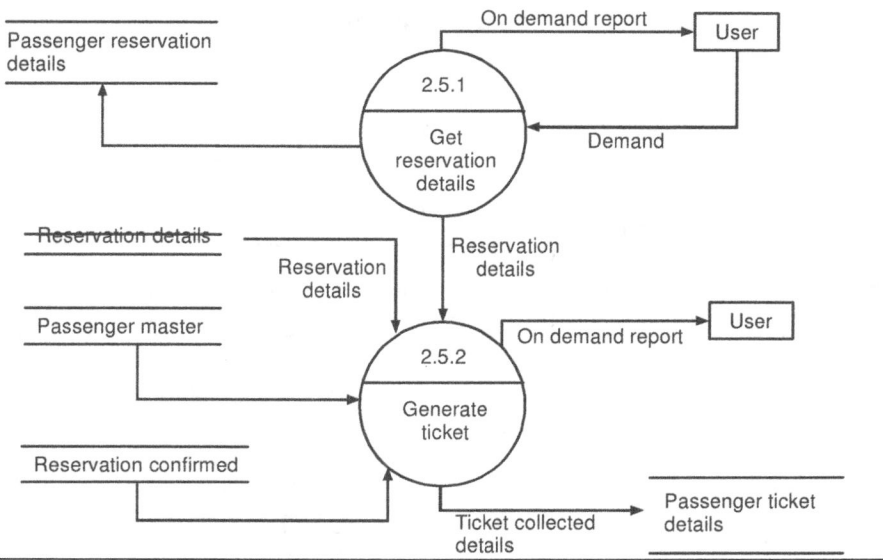

5. HOSPITAL MANAGEMENT SYSTEM

- Patient get admitted in the hospital. The system is used to maintain. In-Patient Department (IPD), Out-Patient Department (OPD), patient record and bill of patient. It also manages important information about various words in the hospital like ICU, General, Private, Semi-Private and Delux.

Functional Decomposition Diagram

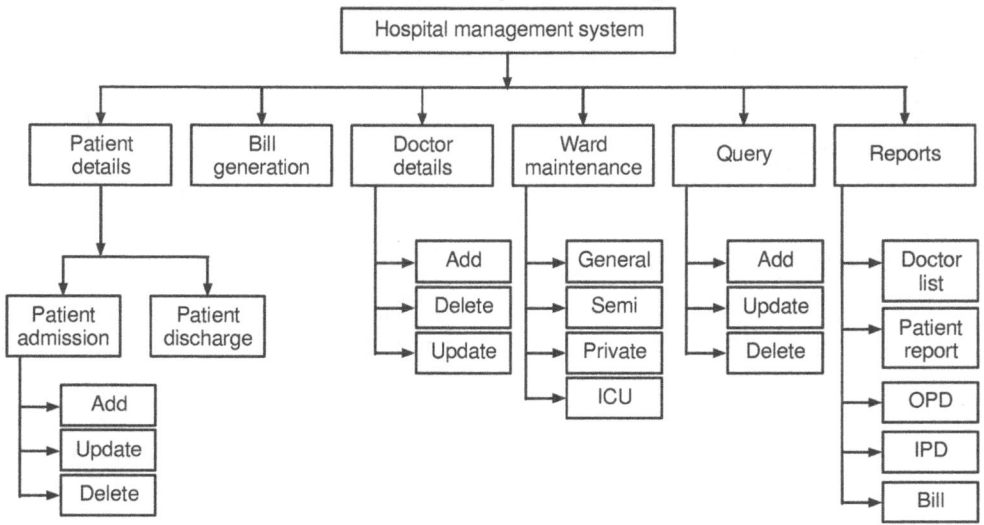

Structured Chart

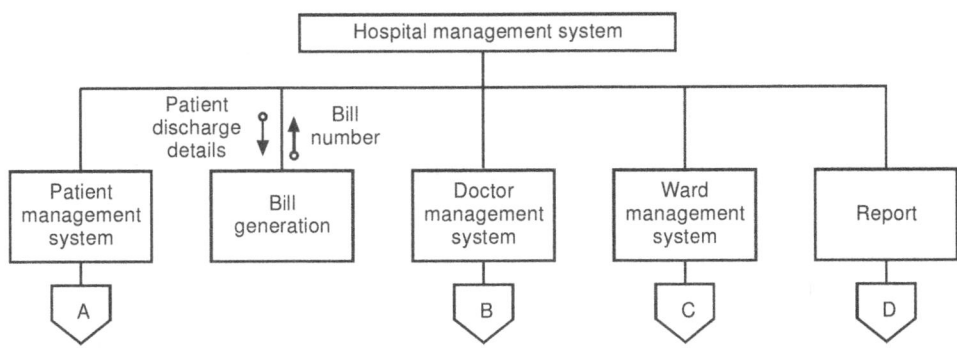
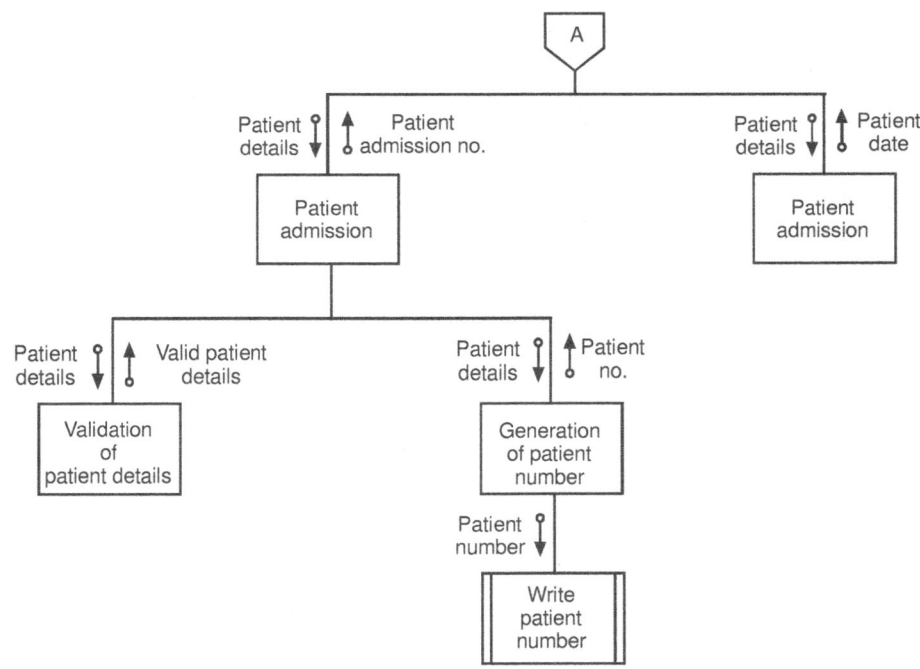

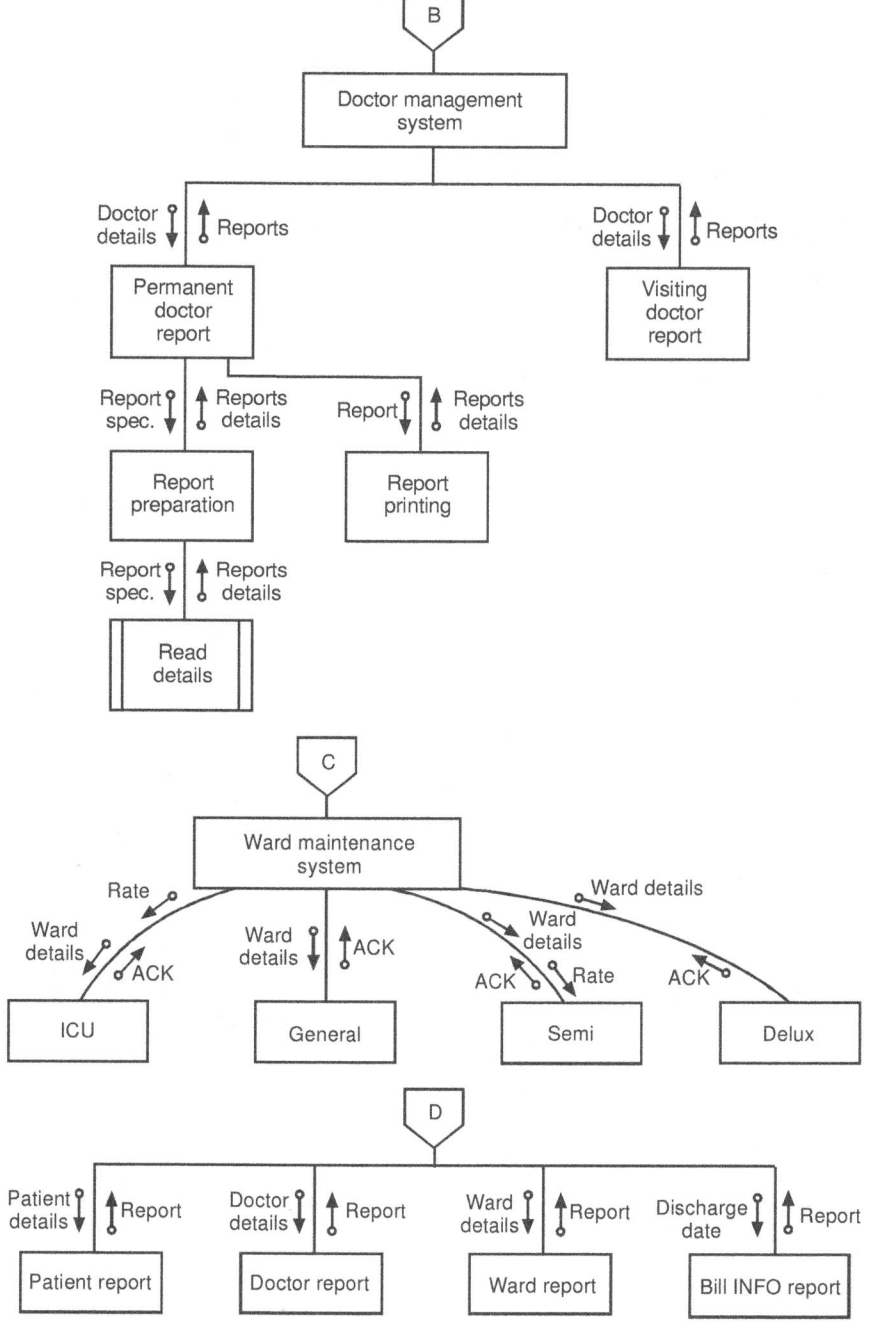

Context Level Diagram

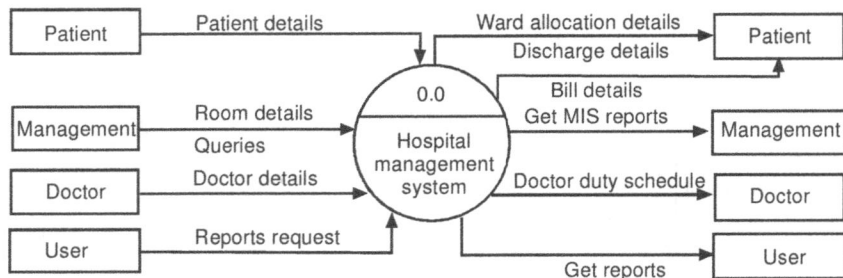

First Level DFD

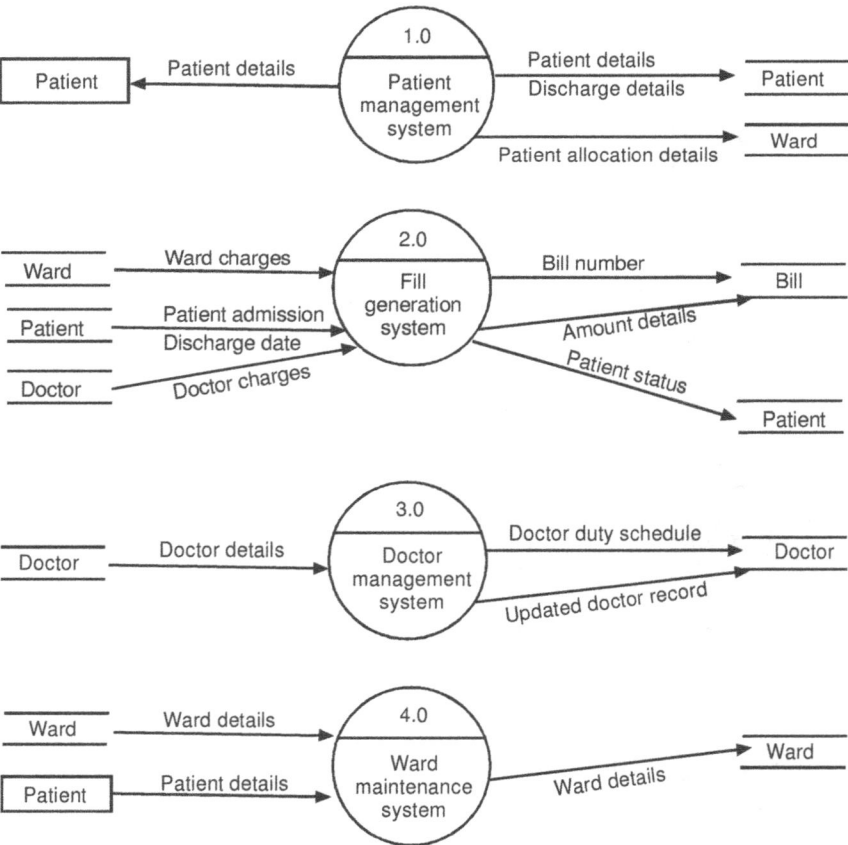

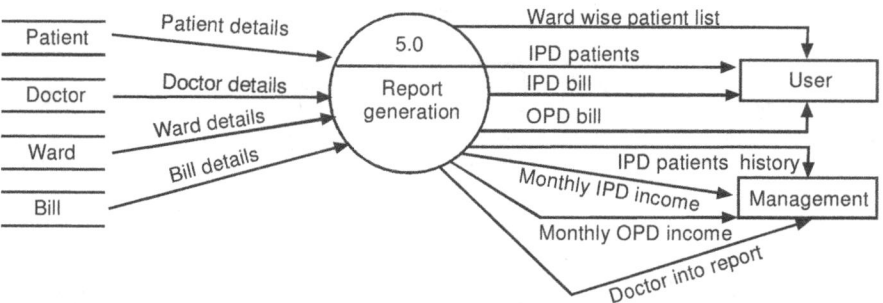

Second Level DFD

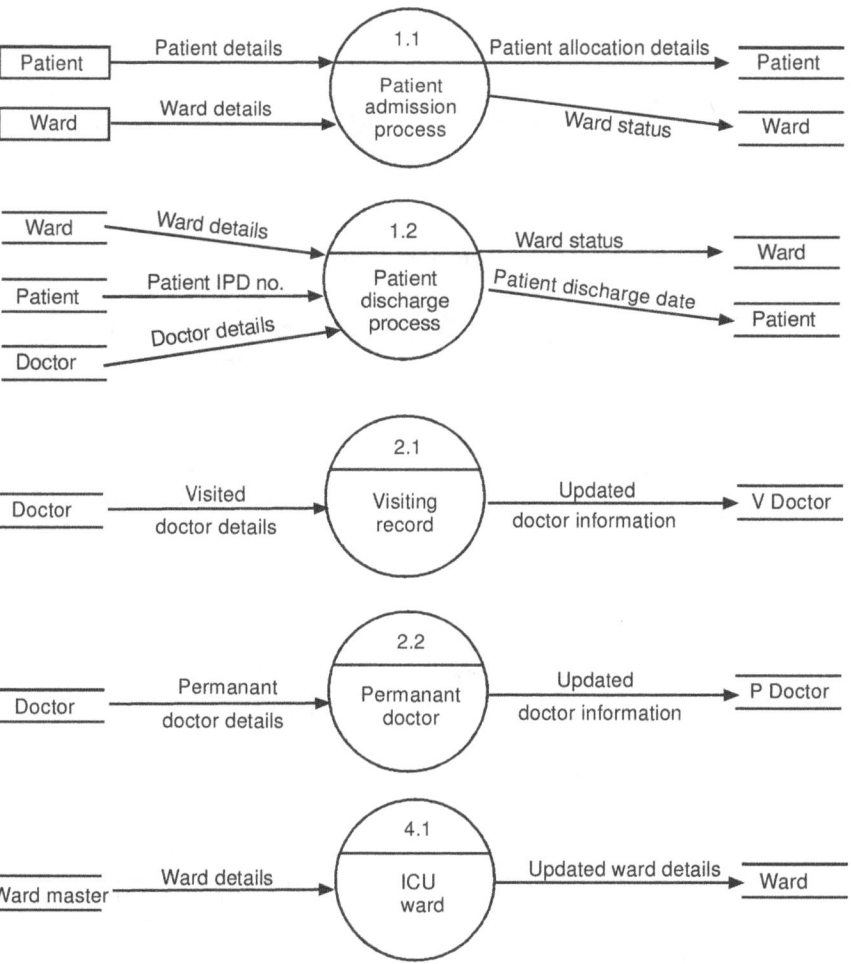

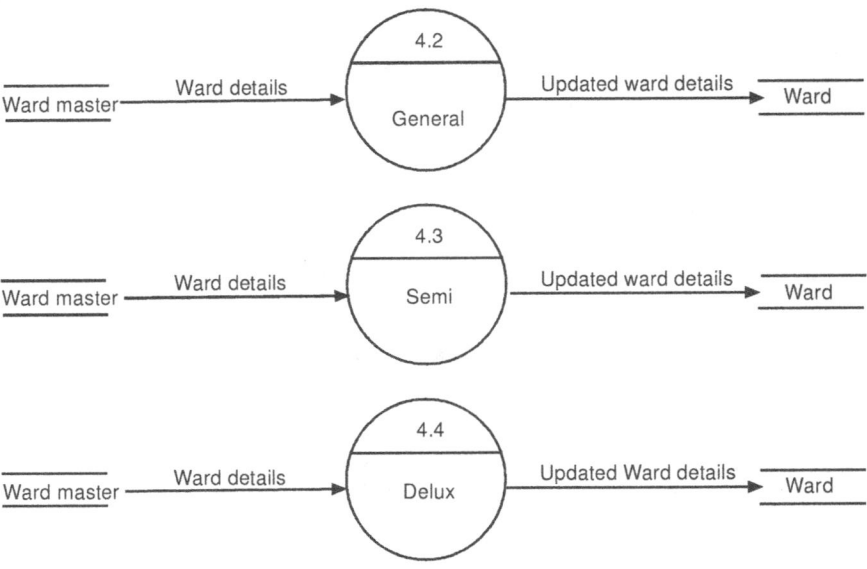

E-R diagram

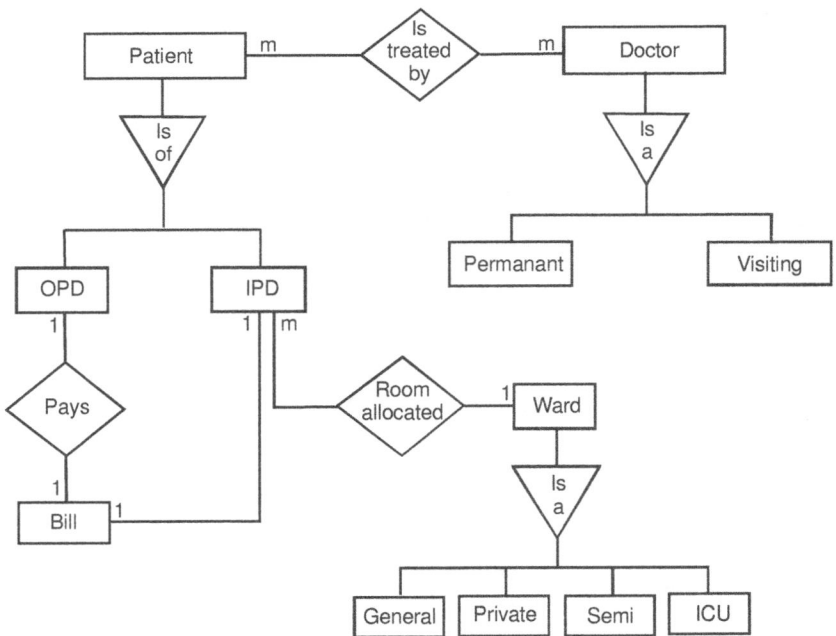

Data Dictionary:

Table: Doctor

Field	Data type	Description
d_no	Number	Doctor ID no.
d_name	Text	Doctor name
d_addr	Text	Doctor address
d_spec	Text	Speciality of doctor
d_type	Text	Doctor is permanent or visiting
d_phone	Number	Doctor phone
d_charge	Number	Visiting doctor charges

Table: IPD Bill

Field	Data type	Description
bill_no	Number	Bill number
P_no	Text	Patient ID no.
P_name	Number	Patient name
room_charge	Number	Room charges of different types
medicine_charge	Number	Medicine charges
other_charge	Number	Other service charges
total	Number	Total amount to be paid

Table: DOC Patient

Field	Data type	Description
P_no	number	Patient ID no.
d_no	number	doctor_no.
P-date	date	checking data

Table: IPD Patient

Field	Data type	Description
P_no	Number	Patient ID number
refd_name	Number	Reference doctor name
P_name	Text	Patient_name
P_addr	Text	Paitent_addr
P_reason	Text	Reason to admit
P_phone	Number	Patient phone
P_blood group	Text	Patient blood group
P_sex	Text	Patient sex
P_cont_person	Text	Contact person
admission_date	Date/Time	Admission date
dicharge_date	Date/Time	Discharge date
ward_type	Text	Ward type
room_no	Number	Room number of ward
bed_no	Number	Bed number for room

Table: OPD-patient

Field	Data type	Description
P_no	Number	Patient ID number
P_name	Text	Patient name
P_addr	Text	Patient address
P_phone	Number	Patient phone
P_reason	Text	Reason to admit
P_sex	Text	Patient sex
P_date	Date/Time	Visited date
O status	Number	Specifies whether patient has paid the bill or not.

Table: OPD-bill

Field	Data type	Description
bill_no	Number	Bill number
P_no	Number	Patient ID number
d_no	Number	Doctor number
charges	Number	Charges to be paid

Table: Ward

Field	Data type	Description
ward_type	Text	Ward type
Room_no	Number	Room number
Bed_no	Number	Bed number for patient
Allocated	Number	Allocated bed or not

Table: Ward Master

Field	Data type	Description
Ward_type	Text	Ward type
no_of_room	Number	Number of rooms in hospital
no_of_beds	Number	Number of beds in each room
charge	Number	Charges per day for each room in different ward.

Output Reports:

1. List of patient admitted in hospital.
2. List of doctors visited in hospital.
3. List of permanent doctors.
4. Patient admitted between the given date.
5. Free bed allocation report.
6. IPD bill for patient report.
7. IPD bill report.
8. IPD patient history report.
9. Total bill collected per month.

6. FIXED DEPOSIT SYSTEM

- Fixed deposit (also called "time deposit") in a banking scheme in which some amount of money is kept in a bank for a specified amount of time. To have a fixed deposit, the customer must have a bank account. He also has to fill up a form indicating the amount, maturity period, nominee name … etc.

- There are two ways of fixed deposit schemes-cumulative and non-cumulative. In cumulative type, user withdraws the money on completion of the specified time. On the other hand, in non-cumulative type, user can withdraw it after one month, quarterly, sixth monthly. Alternatively, the user can save his interest in his saving bank account.

- User can obtain a loan of 85% of the amount deposited. Bank keeps the remaining 15% with it for security purposes. He has to pay an interest rate of 2% extra. He can even withdraw the entire amount before the completion of period (i.e. prematurely), but he gets amount with less interest rate.

- If user does not withdraw the amount even after completion of period, bank pays him with the regular interest rate for the additional period.

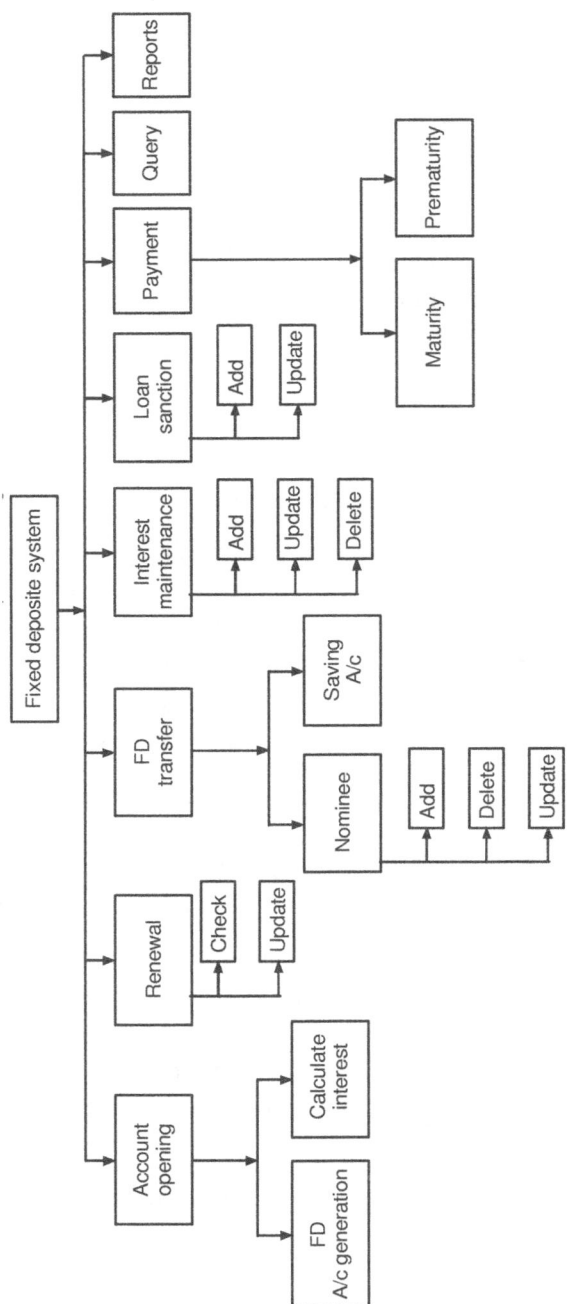

Functional Decomposition Diagram

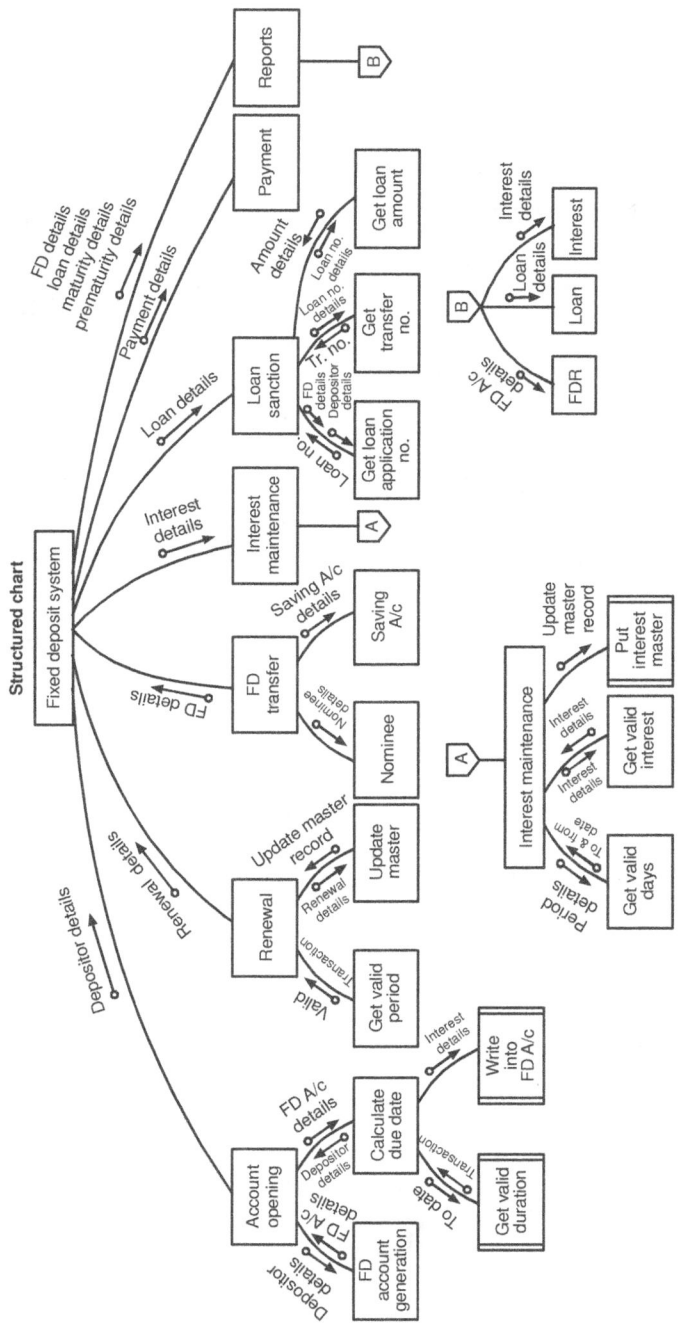

Context Level DFD

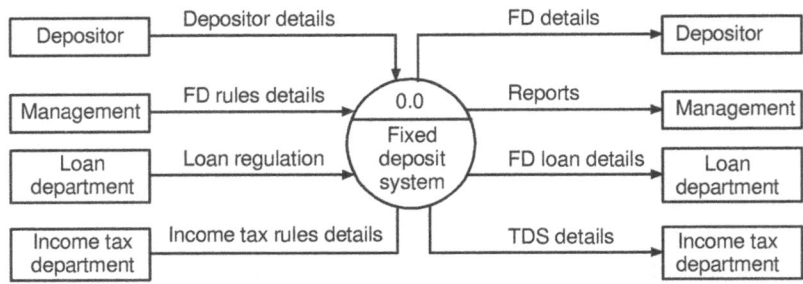

First Level DFD

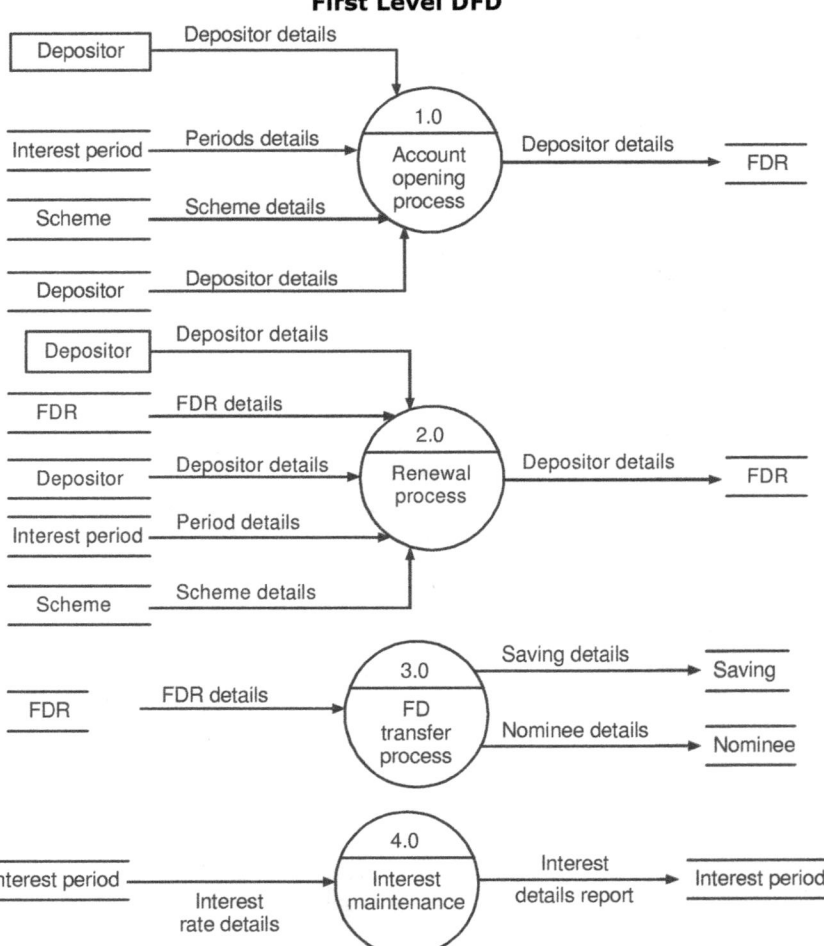

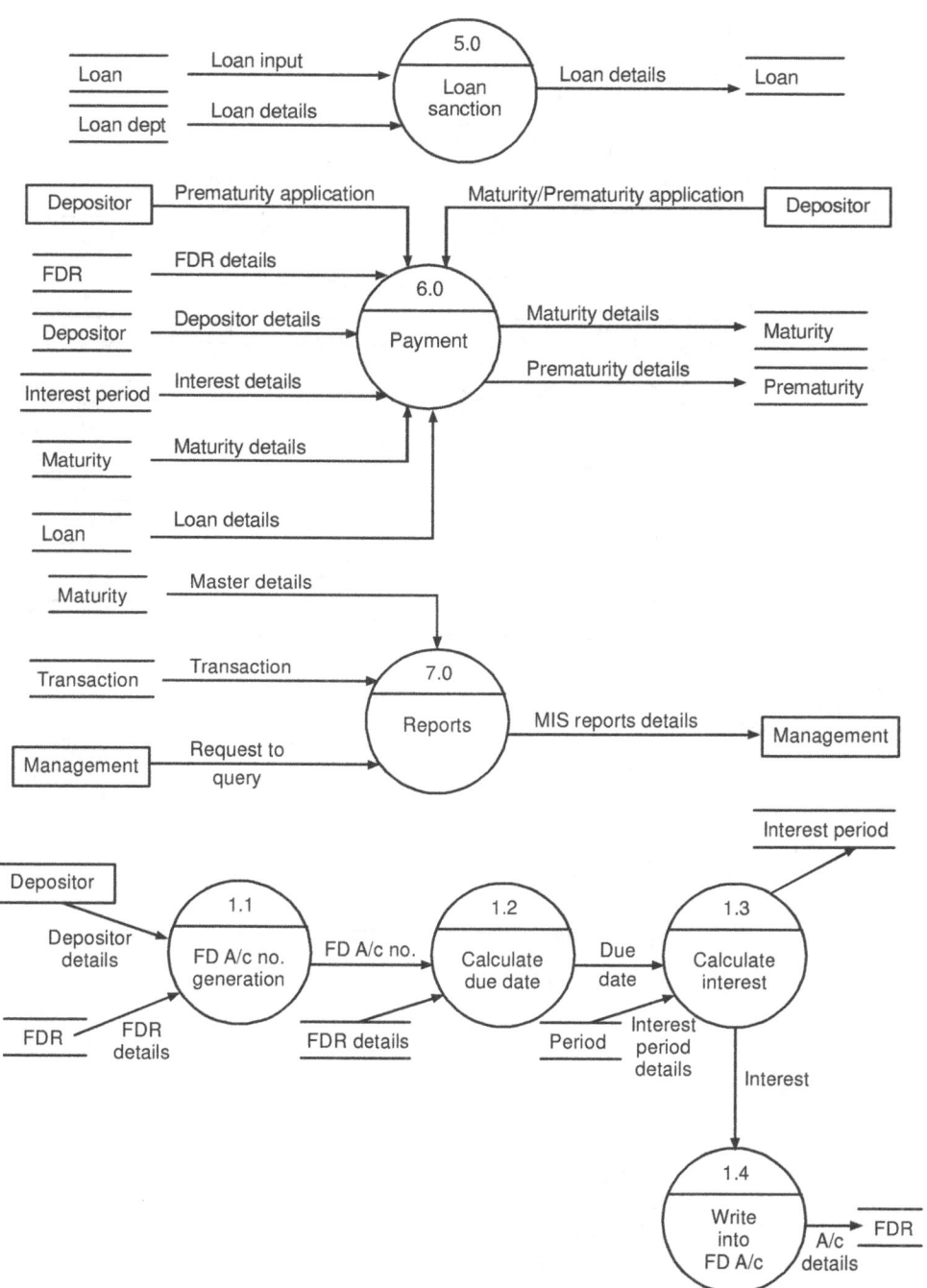

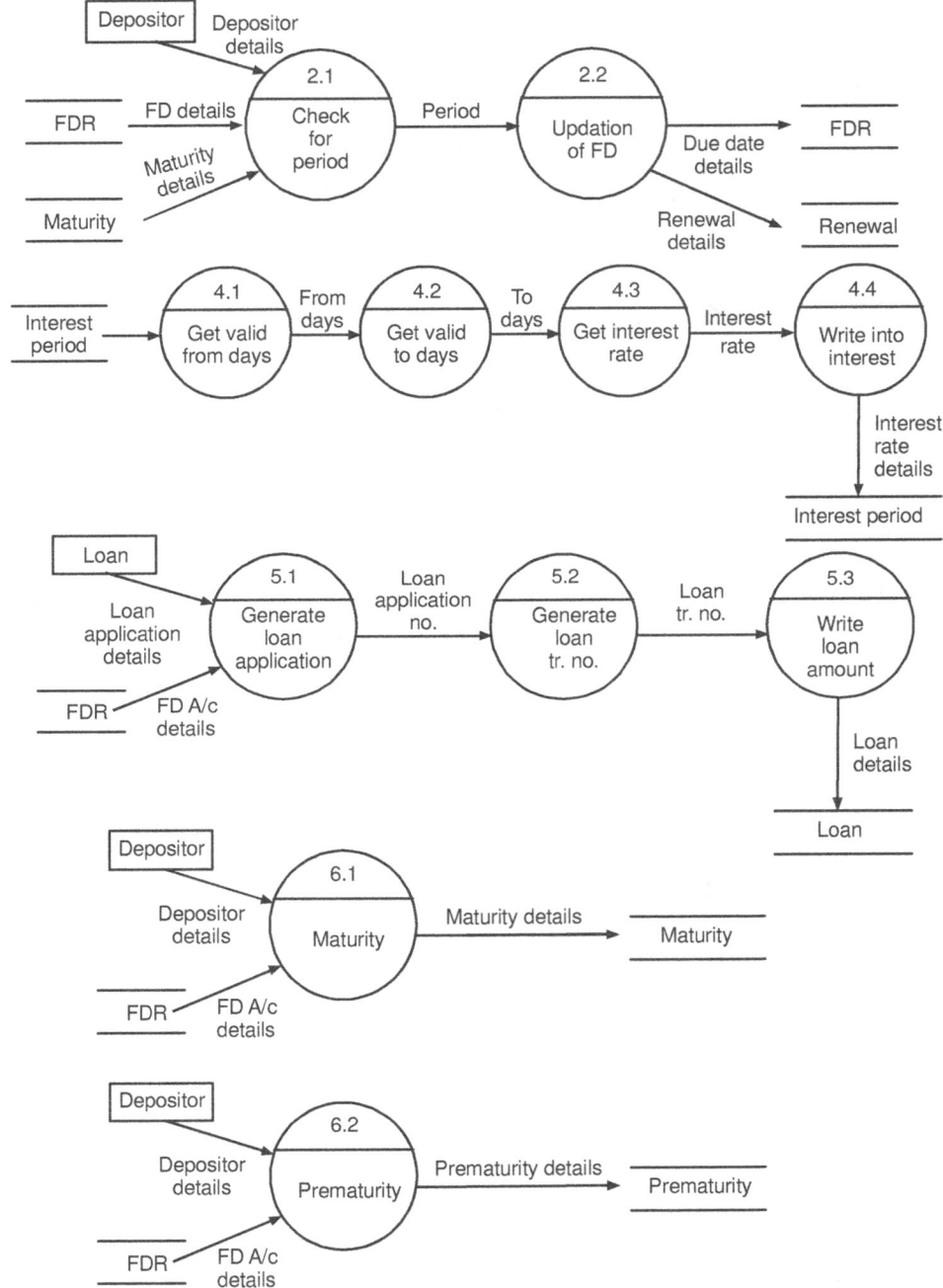

Data Dictionary:

Table: Account open

Field_name	Data type	Description
Saving Acc_no	Number	Account number
Date	Date	Date of opening
Name	Char	Name of person
Birth_date	Date	Date of birth
Sex	Char	Sex of person
Per_addr	Char	Permanent address
Cur_addr	Char	Current address
Phone_number	Number	Phone number
Annual_number	Number	Annual income
Amount	Number	Deposit amount
Days	Number	For how many days

Table: Interest-period

Field_name	Data type	Description
From_days	Number	Starting date of interest
To_days	Number	Upto date
FD_interest_rate	Number	Interest rate

Table: Permaturity

Field_name	Data type	Description
FD acc_number	Number	Acc number
Saving Acc_no	Number	Saving account
Name	Char	Name of person
Open_date	Date	Date of opening
Date_today	Date	Date today
Principle_amount	Number	FD amount
Total_days	Principle amount	Total days
Loan_amount	Number	Loan amount
Loan_paid	Number	Loan paid
TDS_amount	Number	TDS amount

Table: Maturity

Field_name	Data type	Description
FD acc_number	Number	Acc number
Saving Acc_no	Number	Saving account
Name	Char	Name of person
Open_date	Date	Date of opening
Maturity_date	Date	Date of maturity
Principle_amount	Number	FD amount
Total_days	Principle amount	Total days
Loan_amount	Number	Loan amount
Loan_paid	Number	Loan paid
TDS_concession	Number	TDS concenssion
Receipt_number	Number	Receipt number

Table: Loan pay

Field_name	Data type	Description
FD acc_number	Number	Acc number
Saving Acc_no	Number	Saving account
Name	Char	Name of person
Loan_date	Date	Date of getting loan
Today_date	Date	Today date
Principle_amount	Number	FD amount
T_loan-amount	Number	Total loan amount
Am_paid	Number	Amount paid

Table: FD-nominee

Field_name	Data type	Description
FD Acc_number	Number	FD account number
Nominee_name	Char	Name of nominee
Relation	Char	Relation of nominee
Address	Char	Address of nominee
Age	Number	Age of nominee
Sex	Char	Sex of nominee

Output Reports:
1. Fixed deposit certificate/Receipt (FDR).
2. Account closing maturity wise report.
3. Account prematurity report.
4. Lost of depositors.
5. Daywise account opening report.
6. Interest report monthly on FD's.
7. Loan payment report (yearly/monthly).

7. PURCHASE AND INVENTORY CONTROL SYSTEM

Goals:
1. To run the stores effectively.
2. To hold the technical responsibility for the condition of material.
3. To create a buffer input and output so that inflow characteristics of the material may affect the outflow as little as possible.

Overview of the system:

"Gitai" is large supper market.

Its sale is approaching towards 10,000 lacks.

There has several branches throughout Maharashtra. It has several departments containing items like stationary, grossary etc. These inventory should be maintain properly so that customers need fulfill immediately on demand.

Objectives:
1. Customer satisfaction by providing better service.
2. Effective use of working capital.
3. Reduction in loss of wastage.
4. Decreasing inventory carrying cost.

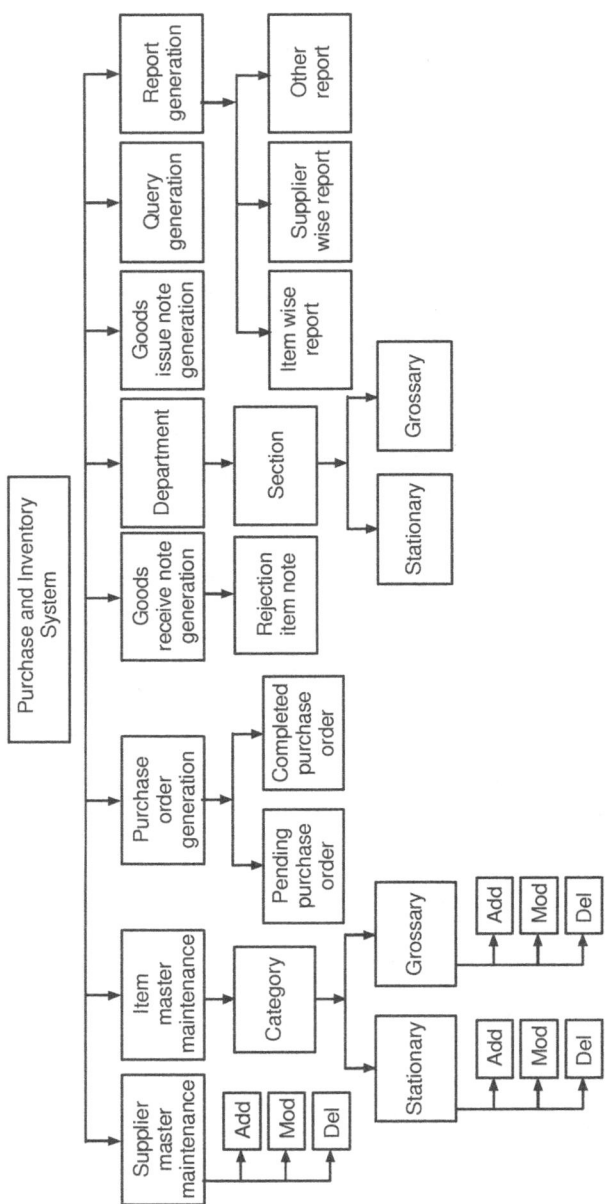

Functional decomposition diagram

Context Level DFD

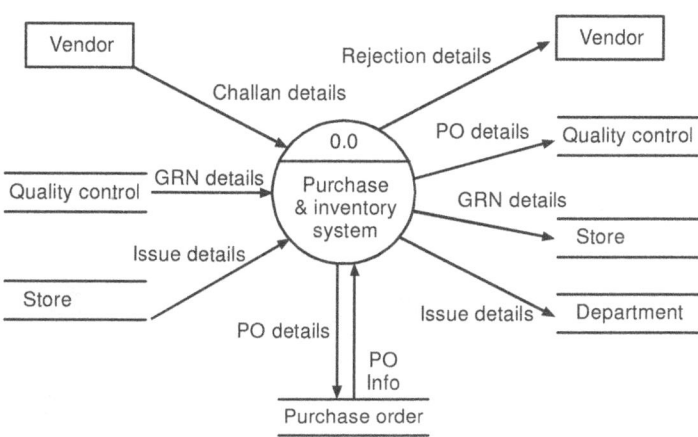

First Level DFD

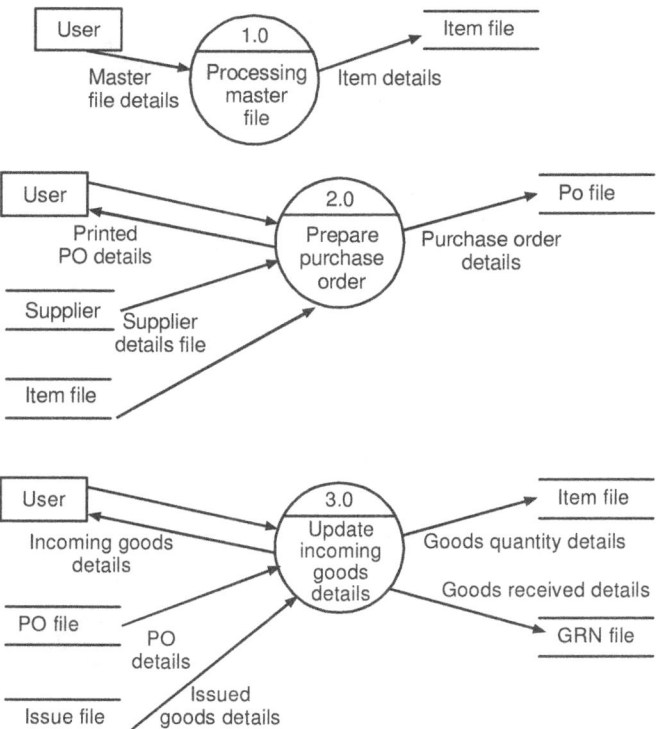

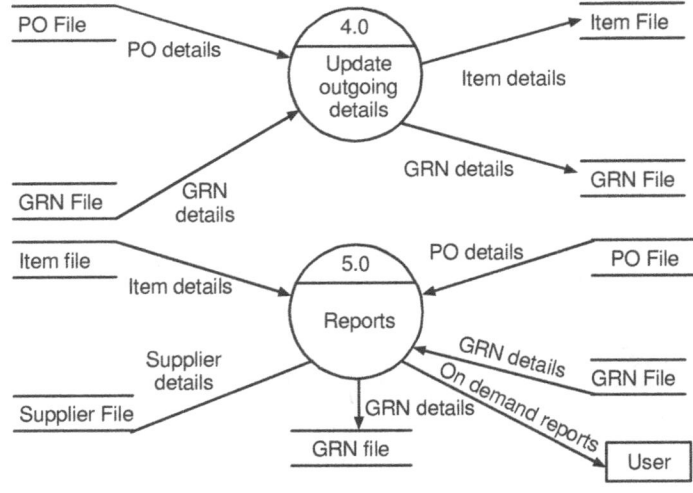

Second Level DFD

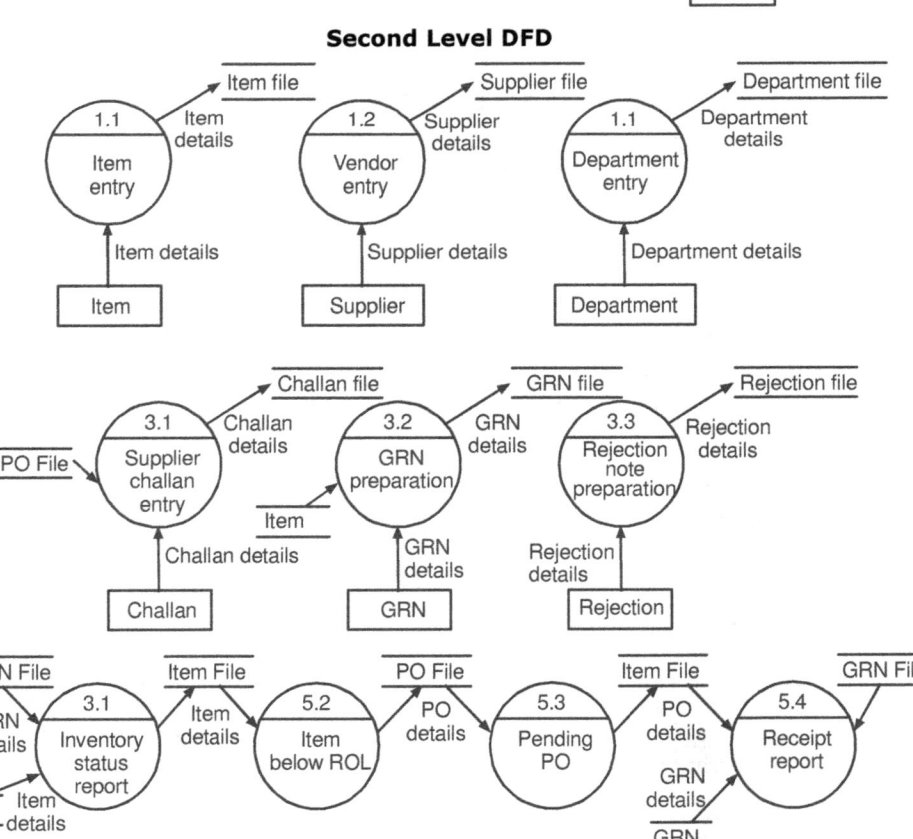

Data Dictionary:

Table: Supplier

This is supplier table to store the information about supplier.

Fields	Description
Supp_code	Contain supplier code (**Primary key**)
Supp_Name	Contain supplier name
Comment	Contain other information of supplier
Pincode	Contain pincode of address
Phone_no	Contain contact number of supplier
Fax_no	Contain contact number of supplier (if any)
Contact_person	Contain name of person to contact
Supp_address	Contain address of the supplier
Email_id	Contain Email_ID of supplier

Table: Item

This is the table to store the information about item.

Fields	Description
Item_code	Contains code of item (**Primary key**)
Item_name	Contains name of the item
Category	Contains type of item namely stationary grossary
Supp_code	Contains supplier code (**Foreign key**)
Quantity	Contains quantity of items
Unit_of_measure	Contains unit of item
Max_level	Contains the maximum number of item should be present
Reorder_level	Contains minimum number of items should be present

Table: Purchase Order Master (PO Master table)

This is purchase order table to store the information about purchase order.

Fields	Description
PO_number	Contains purchase order number (**Primary key**)
Supp_code	Contains supplier code
Date	Contains date of purchase order
Completion_date	Contains the completion date of purchase order
Category	Contains category of items
Status	Contains status of the purchase order whether complete or incomplete
Contains	Contains terms and conditions for purchase order

Table: Purchase order detail (PO Details Table)

This is the purchase order detail table to store the information about purchase order

Fields	Description
Po_no	Contains purchase order number (**Foreign key**)
Item_code	Contains code of item
Quantity	Contains the quantity of items

Table: Goods receive note master (GRN Master Table)

This is the good receive note table to store the information about good receive

Fields	Description
GRN_no	Contains goods receive note number (**Primary_key**)
GRN_date	Contains date of the goods receive note
PO_no	Contains purchase order number for goods receive note
Supp_code	Contains supplier number who has delivered the purchase order
Category	Contains the category of goods received
Comment	Contains the comment on received goods.

Table: Goods receive note detail (GRN Details Table)

This is the goods receive note detail table to store the information about goods receive.

Fields	Description
Grn_no	Contains goods receive note number (**Foreign key**)
Po_no	Contains purchase order number
Item_code	Contains the item code
Accepted_qty	Contains the accepted quantity of the items

Table: Goods issue note master (GIN Master Table)

This is the goods issue note table to store the information about goods issued

Fields	Description
Issue_no	Contains issue note number (**Primary key**)
Dept_no	Contains department number to which user issuing goods
Category	Contains the category of the goods for issue
Issue_date	Contains date of the goods issue

Table: Goods issue note detail (GNI Details Table)

Fields	Description
Issue_no	Contains issue note number (**Foreign key**)
Item_code	Contains item code of the item
Available_stock	Contains the number of items available
Issue_qty	Contains number of items issued

Table: Department

This is department table to store the information about department

Fields	Description
Dept_no	Contains number of the department (**Primary key**)
Dept_name	Contains name of the department

Challan Table

Fields	Description
Challan_no	Contains number of challan
Challan_date	Contains date when challan is issue
PO_no	Contains purchase order number
Supp_code	Contains code of supplier
Total_amt	Total amount on challan.

Output Reports:

1. Item code wide report.
2. Item name wise report.
3. Report for item below reorder level.
4. Supplier wise rejection of item report.
5. Category wise report.
6. Department wise report.
7. Most demanded item wise report.
8. Less demanded item wise report.
9. Purchase order wise report.
10. Pending purchase order wise report.
11. Completed purchase order wise report.
12. Goods receive date wise report.

University Questions

April 2013

1. Case Study [16 M]

   Consider Nationalized Banking System which providing following facilities :

   Opening New Account, Withdrawal, Deposit along with this it should calculate Interest for balanced amount on account. Accountant should provided different Reports to Bank Manager

   (a) Identify all Entity
   (b) Draw E-R Diagram
   (c) Draw Context Level DFD Draw First Level DFD

April 2014

1. Solve the following: [16 M]

   Draw context level DFD, first level DFD and identify all entities for "Railway reservation system".

❖❖❖

UNIVERSITY QUESTION PAPER
APRIL 2015

Time : 3 Hrs. Marks : 80

Instructions :
1. All questions are compulsory.
3. All questions carry equal marks.

Q.1 Attempt the following : (Any Eight) (16)

(a) Define Interfaces.

(b) Explain any 2 skills of System Analyst.

(c) Define software.

(d) State the qualities of good design.

(e) Define the term Data Dictionary.

(f) What is an Entity?

(g) State any two advantages of RAD model.

(h) Define the term Module.

(i) State all the symbols of DFD.

(j) Define S/W Testing.

Q.2 Answer the following : (Any Four) (16)

(a) Explain Prototyping model in detail.

(b) State difference between verification and validation testing.

(c) Explain system. concepts in detail.

(d) Explain Role of System Analyst as an architect and as a salesperson.

(e) Explain Mc Call's Quality factors in detail.

(f) Explain structure chart in detail.

Q.3 (a) Design a Prototype Report for Electric Bill generation for Electric company. (08)

(b) Sales tax is to paid by customers based on following conditions.

  (i) If customer is from Maharashtra and has sales tax exemption certificate the no sales tax is to be paid by customer.

  (ii) If customer is from Maharashtra but does not have sales tax exemption certificate the 8% sales tax is to be paid.

  (iii) If customer is out of Maharashtra 4% central sales tax is to be paid. Draw decision tree and decision table for above case. (08)

Q.4 Short Notes : (Any Four) (16)
    (a) Integration testing.
    (b) Software characteristics.
    (c) SRS documentation.
    (d) Types of Module.
    (e) Feasibility study.

Q.5 Consider a "Employee Payroll System". (16)
    (a) Identity all the Entities.
    (b) Draw a context level DFD.
    (c) Draw a 1st level DFD for the above case.

www.ingramcontent.com/pod-product-compliance
Lightning Source LLC
Chambersburg PA
CBHW081713180426
43192CB00054B/2707